THE ONE AND THE MANY

The Joanna Jackson Goldman Memorial Lecture on American Civilization and Government

The One and the Many

 America's Struggle for
the Common Good

MARTIN E. MARTY

Harvard University Press
Cambridge, Massachusetts
London, England

First Harvard University Press paperback edition, 1998

Library of Congress Cataloging-in-Publication Data

Marty, Martin E., 1928–
    The one and the many : America's struggle for the common good /
Martin E. Marty.
        p. cm. — (The Joanna Jackson Goldman memorial lecture on
American civilization and government)
    Includes bibliographical references and index.
    ISBN 0-674-63827-1 (cloth)
    ISBN 0-674-63828-X (pbk.)
    1. Political participation—United States. 2. Associations,
institutions, etc.—United States. 3. Community life—United
States. 4. Public interest—United States. 5. Common good.
I. Title. II. Series.
JK1764.M37 1997
322.4'0973—dc21
96-48411

TO W. CLARK GILPIN

Co-teacher, critic, exemplar, friend

My fourth and last dean at Chicago

Acknowledgments

My thanks to my thoughtful hosts James H. Billington, Prosser Gifford, and Lester Vogel of the Library of Congress, where the Joanna Jackson Goldman Memorial Lecture was delivered; to my mentoring editor Aida Donald at Harvard University Press; to Jonathan Moore, who carries research assistance beyond the call of duty; to Myron Marty, my most helpful critic through six decades; to my imaginative literary partner Micah Marty; to my unfailingly helpful editor in Chicago, Barbara Hofmaier; to Elizabeth Gretz, who has been similarly valuable for this book at Harvard; to Ann Rehfeldt, who helps produce my publications and solves the problems I create along the way; to my editing and proofreading and critically conversing spouse, Harriet Marty; and to my faculty colleagues Catherine Brekus, Jean Bethke Elshtain, Don Browning, and Dean W. Clark Gilpin, who read the manuscript and made many useful suggestions. Finally, I acknowledge the influence through the decades of my late colleague Arthur Mann, a social historian who reported on his half of our dialogue regarding the meanings of the national motto *E Pluribus Unum* in *The One and the Many: Reflections on the American Identity* (1979). Now I contribute my half in this updated report that shares Mann's title but whose subtitle reflects certain changes in the culture since he wrote almost two decades ago.

Gustave Flaubert once said that "Criticism is the tenth Muse and Beauty the fourth Grace." These muses brought helpful criticism through the seasons of writing this book just as through all seasons they bring grace to my life.

Contents

The One

The world is full of partial purposes, of partial stories . . .
To sum up, the world is "one" in some respects,
and "many" in others.

William James

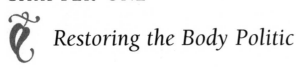

CHAPTER ONE

Restoring the Body Politic

The body politic in America was intended to be or to become one. The Latin motto on the Great Seal of the United States has suggested this since 1776: *E pluribus unum*, "one from many." Then the phrase alluded to the many colonies, now states, becoming one. Today the idea refers to much more than the mere relation of states to nation. Exactly what has to be included in the "many" is a subject of almost shattering controversy.

The result is a trauma in American society that stems from a decades-long conflict over the way "the one and the many" relate in national life. The resultant shock to the body politic has been severe. During the final quarter of the twentieth century many groups of citizens have come to accuse others of having wounded them by attempting to impose a single national identity and culture on all. The other set, in turn, has accused its newly militant adversaries of tearing the republic apart. They do this, it is said, by insisting on their separate identities and by promoting their own mutually exclusive subcultures at the expense of the common weal. Taken together, these contrasting motions produce a shock to the civil body, a trauma in the cultural system, and a paralysis in the neural web of social interactions.

The "body politic," says the dictionary, is "the people of a politically organized nation or state considered as a group." One could also refer to it in the plural, "bodies politic," because the tremors and jolts to the system and the people in it often occurs in its groups or subcommunities—the very ones that provide, or are advertised as providing, identities for many of their members. The "politically organized nation" serves less well than do these groups, according to the claims of many within them. It may even work against their best interests. And I speak of "restoring the bodies politic" because today's traumatic trends have left many citizens alienated from or unaware of resources that might bring healing both in the nation as a whole and in the identity groups.

A national trauma at the century's end could have any number of causes. Political differences over international affairs, economic policies, and social upheavals connected with crime, drugs, or corruption increasingly disturb and disrupt the civil order. Yet it is even more important to note that not one of these differences, serious as they are, can be creatively addressed if the republic itself is dominated by those who press conflicting accusations and opposing claims to their ultimate ends. If the partisans' goals came to be fully realized in developed political forms or should issue in chaos, the very idea of the republic would be shattered and its practical workings would be aborted. For this reason the current version of the conflict over the one and the many is appropriately called *the* American trauma.

Can we speak of a *post*-trauma America? To do so might suggest two interpretations. First, to talk about the trauma in the past tense could mean that the worst of the conflict is over and that a new circumstance is emerging. Although I may point to a few signs of this kind of change, such a conclusion overall would be premature and misleading. Second, the use of such wording could suggest that responsible citizens, of whatever inclination and commitment, must begin to envision approaches that will restore civil conversation. And it would help them find fresh ways to tell their common and separate stories alike as a step in recovery. They have already lived long enough with this trauma and its effects.

In making my argument, I will not be using various conventional terms and others like them: culture wars, multiculturalism, radical left, radical right, political correctness, tenured radicals, deconstruction, fascist, hegemony, patriarchal oppressors, postmodern, or radical feminists. These words, though they have on occasion enhanced and enlivened political debate, signal elements of the trauma that has done violence to the American body politic for a third of a century.

Such terms belong to the vocabulary of those parties that have been in conflict over how "the one" and "the many" relate to each other in

American life. I do not for a moment mean to dismiss the issues to which they are connected. Many of these concerns remain alive, although they are being transformed with the passage of time. For reasons soon to be made clear, however, such terms and concepts are too identified with earlier phases of the traumatic situation to be of much use for approaching the future. They now promise only diminishing returns. It is time to conceive new modes of national existence for "after the trauma," if such a day comes.

The issues of the one and the many in American life will never go away—nor should they, in a vital society that includes many peoples. They have been with us since at least 1492, or 1607, or 1619, or 1787, or 1924. Those dates are markers to help citizens recall how the mixture of peoples and interests in the Americas has kept changing with the arrivals of first continental Europeans, followed by English-speakers, and then Africans, and then those who founded this republic, followed by many more who flocked to it, and finally those who restricted immigration, all of whom jostled one another, even as many of them displaced peoples who were here before 1492. Every generation finds itself facing the issues of the one and the many. Each generation seems to find that the problems it faces are more intense and urgent than the ones before it.

In her presidential address at a meeting of the Organization of American Historians in 1982, Gerda Lerner spoke on this situation. She spoke as a historian must, and she was, in many ways, preaching to the converted. She was telling her colleagues that "story" and "stories" are determinative in a civil society. But every congregation has its backsliders, weak members, and heretics. So among those who were listening there were no doubt many who needed to be converted or reconverted.

Some of them had been brought up fashionably to say that history no longer had anything to do with narrative. Modern-day historians, they were schooled to think, could never be storytellers. Others may have been wavering in their continuing faith in story. Many had grown up in the 1970s and 1980s, when articulate leaders of divisive groups instructed citizens to believe that they had no stories to share: to each her own. Still others had never reflected on the import of Lerner's main topic: "history as memory and as a source of personal identity." And beyond the convention hall where she spoke, there was, of course, a larger public that needed to be alerted or convinced by her words:

> By tracing one's personal roots and grounding one's identity in some collectivity with a shared past—be that collectivity defined by race, sex, class, ethnicity, religion, or nationality—one acquires stability and the basis for community . . . Without history, no nation can enjoy legitimacy or command patriotic allegiance.

Lerner went on to say that, "deeply rooted in personal psychic need and in the human striving for community," stories about life in a shared past are vital. She maintained that some people or peoples understood this need better than others. "None can testify better" to the need for stories, she noted, "than members of groups who have been denied a usable past." She pointed to some of these:

> Slaves, serfs, and members of subordinate racial or national groups have all, for longer or shorter periods of time, been denied their history. No group has longer existed in this condition than have women. [Such groups have been uncovering their stories and] in the process, inevitably, the established version of history has been revised. In the American setting, this has been the case in regard to Afro-American history and Native-American history, both fields that have moved from marginality to the mainstream and have, in the process, transformed and enriched knowledge of the nation's past.

Gerda Lerner used the term *group* as she referred to women. She also mentioned racial and national *groups*. Throughout this book I shall also use this neutral term. She contended that these groups and their stories have helped enrich knowledge of the American national past. The converse of this claim is that if the stories of any substantial groups are untold or if and when the groups turn exclusive about their histories and talk only among themselves, the nation will be impoverished. It is such impoverishment that has helped induce the shock that I am calling the American trauma.

Citizens in all groups, including those that Lerner did not single out as sufferers, today have problems with their corporate memory and therefore with their personal identity. Some of them, because they were once members of privileged and powerful groups, used to have a virtual monopoly when it came to the act of telling the national story. Today such citizens increasingly share privilege and power with others who, in Lerner's terms, have "moved from marginality to the mainstream." Now along with people who were once regarded as marginal, this elite or former elite has to wrestle with the problem of its own identity. W. E. B. Du Bois, quoted by Lerner, gave this problem a name, calling it this "peculiar sensation, this double-consciousness, this sense of always looking at one's self through the eyes of others."

Lerner cited Du Bois as he was discussing the acute situation of African Americans. They perpetually experienced what he called "two-ness." For them, identity meant being "an American, a Negro," with "two souls, two thoughts, two unreconciled strivings" and "two warring ideals in one dark body."

The president of the Organization of American Historians recognized a special mission in her year in office to speak as a woman to and for women. She admitted that "in many decisive respects the condition of women cannot be compared with that of Afro-Americans." Yet women, too, made up a group that experienced a double-consciousness. Lerner pointed to this as a "sense of being central and yet defined as marginal, essential and yet defined as 'the Other.' " If they would learn and tell their story, women could help alter this sense. Because they are the largest of all the groups, representing slightly more than half the population, they could certainly help to transform and enrich knowledge of the national past.

The new situation of groups in America has unsettled many and stirred others. People who were never conscious of their story, who would even have said that they despised history, have become curious about their own. They are eager to have it represented in the public forum. Many fight for a place in college curricula and in university study programs. Politicians have to reckon with groups and their stories, for these have altered the way the public understands power. Church bodies increasingly and not always creatively must deal with caucuses and voting blocs. Executives in the worlds of radio, television, film, commerce, and libraries take drastic measures not to tell stories that offend any groups. They try to uncover histories that will please virtually all elements of the public.

Lerner wanted her audience to do its part. She concentrated on education and goaded the teachers who heard her and who would read her printed address:

> Above all, we seek to tell a story and tell it well—to hold the audience's attention and to seduce it, by one means or another, into suspending disbelief and inattention. We seek to focus concentrated attention upon ourselves and to hold it long enough to allow the students' minds to be directed into unexpected pathways and to perceive new patterns.

Lerner recognized how hard it is to find such pathways and patterns in a nation characterized by trauma, as ours is today. Once upon a time those who told stories might have been able to assume some continuity in the life of the groups and the nation. But discontinuity now rules. Therefore "now as never before," she said, we citizens "need to have a sense of meaning in our lives and assurance of a collective continuity." Both of these are hard to find because, as she put it, "the problem of discontinuities has never loomed larger than in this generation." Speaking of this problem as it affected the whole nation, she stressed that when people in particular groups get along, "shared values, be they based on consensus or on the recognition and acceptance of many ways of form-giving," will "link the individual to the collective immortality of the human enterprise."[1]

Historians, of course, have not been alone in pointing to the need for story and stories in contemporary life. Immigrant peoples almost by instinct vie to have their ways of life depicted to those who do not yet know them. In a way, parades of ethnic groups in cities are themselves instruments to make identities known.

Other professions also have a stake in the issues. Anthropologists, in particular, had recognized stories' crucial importance. Many philosophers, too, care very much about the human story. Among them, Alasdair MacIntyre has earned a name for the way he worries about the public, its character and virtue, and the identity of persons and groups within it. Concerned as he is about the difficulty, even the near impossibility, of people in various groups understanding one another when they are in competition, he has clung to a central thesis. He argues that the human

> is in his actions and practice, as well as in his fictions, essentially a story-telling animal. He is not essentially, but becomes through his

history, a teller of stories that aspire to truth. But the key question for men is not about their own authorship; I can only answer the question "What am I to do?" if I can answer the prior question "Of what story or stories do I find myself a part?"

That last question is an eloquent summary of what is on the minds of many who seem confused or lost because they have no clear identity. It points to what is on the agenda of people in groups that have been bristling about earlier insults or suffering from past assaults by other citizens. The question evokes the concerns of groups and peoples who have become militant about being heard and about realizing their rights and entitlements today.

In sympathy with all of them, MacIntyre has had more to say about himself and about those who share life in our society. He has argued that "there is no way to give us an understanding of any society, including our own, except through the stock of stories that constitute its essential dramatic resources."[2]

Storytelling between the Totalists and the Tribalists

"Our own" society, which for MacIntyre means the United States, has for some time been shrouded in dust kicked up in conflict over how to deal with the clashes of groups and their stories. The confusions of those who have lost their way in this dust contribute to the national trauma. Those who know the longer national history as it has conventionally been told can see that the conflicts represent new variations of old struggles over how to deal with the problem of the one and the many, of how the nation as a whole relates to the groups within it and how the groups relate to one another. For those who truly know the record, cherish guiding principles, or love Latin, the current round comes down to issues condensed long ago in the national motto, E pluribus unum.

All kinds of people can get into the act over these concerns. Politicians debate it in their ways; philosophers and bartenders and school boards in others. As a historian, I join the company of those who accent the role of story and stories. As a historian of religion in American culture, I pay special attention to myth and symbol, rite and ceremony, in these matters.

If story is so important, it is evident that the narratives and myths of each group and of the nation in a larger sense must be allowed to be told and heard across boundaries and in all sectors. Only then can the virtues and values that people claim for these stories be tested. Only thus can they flow in various directions within the separate groups and between any of them and society at large.

These have not always been able to flow, and there are new barriers against interaction among them today. I propose to frame the situation in the following way.

Two specters, movements made up of leaders whom I shall call *totalists* and *tribalists,* contend today. Both insist on their separate and exclusive stories. Both have had a part in inducing the trauma of polarization in the United States

Totalism is the name assigned to the idea that a nation-state can and should be organized around a single and easily definable ideology or creed. In such a case, the state can and should give priority to a set of doctrines and then somehow enforce conformity to the ways of life that go with them. Totalism appeals to those who are weary of complex and fragmented experience. They are the strangers lost in the modern city, assaulted by mass media, jostled by impersonal forces. The totalist appeal is especially alluring to those in our century who have demonstrated what Peter Gay called a "hunger for wholeness."[3]

Such hungerers often contend that the public and political orders should minister to their craving for wholeness. Totalists profess to abhor what they see as a spiritual, intellectual, and moral vacuum on the world scene and seek to fill the vacuum with their alternative ideology. In our time millions have championed forms of nationalism that they expected would provide a framework for their lives. Nationalism itself, they thought—and many still believe—would establish sets of boundaries for all people who live within a particular society.

The totalists, in the nature of the case, do not much care what happens to minorities and dissenters. Or one could say that they do care. They care that those who are not in step with the powers that be and who are not in harmony with nationalist demands should not have rights. This century has seen extreme forms of totalism in the scowling and scourging totalitarian governments. This book is not about them. But totalism has also taken somewhat milder forms in republics. It has had advocates who wear smiling faces in the United States in every generation, not least of all our own. These milder forms should not be ignored, either for what they portend or for what they call attention to. Left to themselves, they would only perpetuate the effects of the trauma.

Tribalism, a more familiar word, on the other hand, challenges totalism in many nations. Its movements often cross the sometimes artificial boundaries of nation-states. Tribalism is the name I give to the reality that begins with the idea that most nations as a whole cannot or should not help provide ideologies or patterns of life for the varied peoples within them. Therefore only the peoples and groups to which one naturally belongs, or chooses to belong, or even invents as new constructs, can provide coherence. Only these can give people an identity and then empower them. Only the group, it is said, can produce the ethos and the programs for those who resent the encroaching impositions of nationhood. Only thus can people resist the intrusions of government and the power of those who wish to dominate.

The tribalists claim that the central governmental authority or patterns of dominance that neglect the groups cannot provide proper entitlements to those who belong to them. So they tell stories that will enhance their own tribal claims. The temptation is strong for them in the process to turn their backs on others and become exclusivistic about these myths and their meanings.

The tribalist impulse beyond the boundaries of the United States can assume the shape of military and terrorist extremisms. This book is not about such extremisms. Tribalism also characterizes milder counterparts to these. They prosper sufficiently today in the United States. They are proper subjects for any inquiry about the one and the many in America.

The word *totalism* is not yet in the dictionaries, though *totalist,* as applied to the person, is now there. Much of the definition is positive. But a negative shadow hovers over it, for the totalist, according to the *Oxford English Dictionary,* is "one who inclines to treat or regard things as a whole; one concerned with the whole social environment, esp. as a means of thought-control." And totalist can now also refer to something impersonal. *A Supplement to the Oxford English Dictio-*

nary furnishes this instance from 1964: "A 'totalist ideology' refers to any doctrine which attempts a complete, unified explanation of world and society."

The positive colorings suggest that behind the *ist* and hence behind the *ism* there can be genuine and healthy interests. These may include concern for the whole globe, the whole environment, or the whole person beyond what the groups in isolation can promise. Students of the human scene, for example, understand that the religious quest and the search for better health alike are devoted to the experience of wholeness. As a catholic Christian I am aware that the word *catholic* comes from the Greek *kata* (through) + *holos* (whole): *katholikos* = "through-the-whole." It can refer to the way faith penetrates the whole of being.[4] Given all these positives, one must say that the problems implied by this term do not derive from "total" but are associated with the suffix *ism*.

The word *tribalism,* in contrast, is securely in the dictionaries. It refers to "the condition of existing as a separate tribe or tribes; tribal system, organization, or relations." To this definition *A Supplement to the Oxford English Dictionary* now adds that tribalism is "loyalty to a particular tribe or group of which one is a member." That which is "tribal," it continues, is "characterized by the tendency to form groups or by strong group loyalty." The dictionary illustrates this with a negative reference by a prominent theologian: "According to Reinhold Niebuhr, 'the chief source of man's inhumanity to man seems to be the tribal limits of his sense of obligation to the other man.' ".

In *tribalism* Niebuhr included "race, language, religion, class and culture as important traits." In a subsequent generation some might by instinct put a *"sic"* after Niebuhr's generic use of the word *man*. But given that theologian's alertness to cultural change and nuance and his sensitivity to people and situations, Niebuhr no doubt would later have spoken of humans, not only men. And he would thereupon have shown awareness of the need to add *gender* as an agent in the forming of tribes, as Gerda Lerner did. Niebuhr also did not include *ethnicity* and *nationality* as her list did. But he did note *language* and *culture* as tribal traits, as she certainly would. So the catalog of actual and potential tribes grows. Tribes as such do not *have* to contribute to trauma.

To balance Niebuhr's pejorative reference, let us consider the positive side of the tribe. Thus philosopher Eugen Rosenstock-Huessy, in his 1970 essay "Tribalism," somewhat romantically related tribe to family:

> The tribe is the *couche,* or the source, of families. The families them-selves are transient; the tribe is eternal, the lasting form . . . Tribalism, therefore, is not biological, and belief that it is leads inevitably to mother-worship and ancestor-worship in the most primitive sense . . .
>
> The word "path" we should make the foundation of our political understanding of tribalism. The tribes tried to find paths in the jungle, paths in time, paths in the thicket.[5]

Despite such words about tribal pathbreaking, today the negative side of tribalism ordinarily dominates, so the term needs to be han-dled with care. Thus a pioneering modern use of the term appeared in Harold R. Isaacs's *Idols of the Tribe: Group Identity and Political Change.* The first lines of his book presented a chilling global vision:

> We are experiencing on a massively universal scale a convulsive in-gathering of people in their numberless grouping of kinds—tribal, ra-cial, linguistic, religious, national. It is a great clustering into separate-nesses that will, it is thought, improve, assure, or extend each group's power or place, or keep it safe or safer from the power, threat, or hostility of others. This is obviously no new condition, only the latest and by far the most inclusive chapter of the old story in which after failing again to find how they can co-exist in sight of each other with-out tearing each other limb from limb, Isaac and Ishmael clash and part in panic and retreat once more into their caves.

Isaacs already saw in 1975 that tribalism persists and increases in our own time as part of an ironic, painful, and dangerous paradox: the more global our science and technology, the more tribal our politics; the more universal our system of communications, the less we know what to communicate; the closer we get to other planets, the less able we become to lead a tolerable existence on our own; the more it becomes apparent that human beings cannot decently survive with their separatenesses, the more separate they become. In the face of an ever more urgent need to pool the world's resources and its pow-ers, human society is splitting itself into smaller and smaller frag-ments.

Tribal life, one may presume, could have been benign or relatively unthreatening in some bygone times and distant places. But the invention of modern weapons and the efficiency of communications now render tribalism potentially lethal. Groups need only a few dollars for supplies and a few recipes for how to mix them to produce devastating explosives to advance their threats.

Tribalism on the world scene in its extremist forms takes a monstrous human toll. Isaacs estimated that in the first three decades after World War II, "by conservative reckoning," surely more than ten million people had been killed in "mutual massacring" as a result of tribalism. That was a generation ago, when such destruction had only begun. Isaacs, of course, did not find many dead bodies in the United States. But he did notice the "refragmenting and retribalizing" already going on in America as elsewhere, though it was not yet traumatic here at that time.[6]

International Contexts for National Issues

Why bring up the extremes of totalism and tribalism, one might ask, if they represent poles beyond the tendencies ordinarily seen in the United States? My own inquiries on this domestic subject have been inspired by several comparative global projects. In all three instances the University of Chicago, through the divinity, humanities, and social science faculties of which I am a part, provided sustained conversation and motives for my research.

First, the American Academy of Arts and Sciences in 1987 asked me (with R. Scott Appleby) to direct a six-year, five-volume study of modern religious fundamentalisms around the world. Some of these movements, we found, expressed totalist temptations. These were evident in Sudan, Iran, Algeria, and wherever revolutionaries saw an opportunity to impose a single religious vision and polity on a nation.

Other extreme fundamentalisms, however, succumbed to tribalist lures. They strove to produce stories and activities that would provide identity, power, and boundaries for their special groups of believers within various national polities. If they could not take over a whole polity, they could form tightly defined groups, draw clear boundaries, keep outsiders at a distance and insiders together. Such fundamentalists could read their choice of scriptures in isolation from others and interpret them to one another, far removed from a world they saw as antagonistic—which it normally was.

Second, my assignments as senior scholar in residence at the Park Ridge Center for the Study of Health, Faith, and Ethics have led to similarly comparative work on global issues devoted to the role of religions in pursuing wholeness and healing. In connection with these assignments—related to controversies over birth control, population planning, sexual expression, forms of the family, and abortion—it has been easy to see both totalist and tribalist movements making their claims.

Third, I have been working on a Park Ridge Center study on "civil discourse" and am following it with a multiyear project sponsored by the Pew Charitable Trusts. In these endeavors we address a set of questions about how people tell stories, argue, and converse in a world where totalisms and tribalisms, especially when these are heated by religion, encounter each other.

This book reflects the preoccupations that stand behind some of the questions that arise in these three international contexts. Domestically, these preoccupations suggest why it is important to come up with new and creative ways of looking at the one and the many.

Horror Stories from Global Scenes

Comparisons and analogies can be helpful, but they can also be misleading. Experience gained from studies of other times and places around the world where totalists have been active can lead one to be fearful of conflict over issues in America. After all, the imposing of creeds by authoritarians has produced rivers of blood in Europe and Asia. Because of the efficiencies and follies of the totalitarians of this century, millions of victims are in their graves. As a consequence of efforts by leaders to mesh all beliefs into state religions, a legacy of mistrust and cynicism concerning most religious belief that is not under the control of the state or privileged by it resides among those inclined toward totalism. Spiritual devastation has resulted, and more is pending.

In using the word *total* (as in *totalitarian*) I am not insinuating that those in the United States who want to insist on something like a universal "religion of democracy" are thought-police. Nor am I implying simply that those who would impose a privileged "Judeo-Christian framework" on the United States are storm troops of the spirit. These envisionings sound an overstatement of the "it can happen here" variety.

At the opposite pole, experience gained from studies of tribalist movements around the globe today can distort our vision of what goes on in ordinary life in America. The revolutionaries and terrorists who in the name of God or of tribal deities assassinate rulers are stark examples of what can go wrong when people are sufficiently moved to exclude and then to hate others. It is dangerous business to draw simple analogies between the tragic efforts at such "ethnic cleansing" on the other side of the globe and the complex situation closer to home.

I mention these extremes to illustrate how in our own century, most of the globe is torn over exaggerated versions of conflicts that have totalist and tribalist casts. If these extreme movements have written the script for the tragic events of our century, it is wise to pay attention to what in them might be contagious. Pointing to milder apings here of the forces and furies elsewhere can be instructive. Only cultural chauvinism would lead one to think that the United States is wholly exempt from the spirit of the times that crosses other latitudes and touches all the longitudes on a small globe.

Yet movements in the United States deserve to be considered on their own terms and seen on their own scale. The stories that inevitably will be retold in our decades, stories of the death of millions who were living in the Americas when Europeans came five centuries ago, in some ways match those of genocide elsewhere in our time. The narrative of the enslavement of the African millions who were brought here, an account still not sufficiently familiar or appreciated among unheeding publics, matches that of the worst of human cruelty anywhere, in any time.

Similarly, the forced removal of Native Americans over the trails of tears to reservations wrought terrors that are too easily forgotten by those whose ancestors inflicted them. Epics of barbarism are found within United States borders as well as beyond. All these sagas taken together provide a backdrop against which citizens can and must view their current activities. They provide measures of what, in the name of God, self-centered and aggressive people have produced over long periods of time and as formal policy on these shores, leaving various minorities in demoralized or traumatized circumstances.

Whoever listens to the guns in Bosnia, views the devastations wrought by tribes in Rwanda and Burundi, or reviews accounts of decades of hostility between two religious tribes in Northern Ireland knows how murderous tribalisms can be. They make the battles over the one and the many in the United States today look mild by contrast. These domestic versions occur in school board elections and actions, as citizens fight over the choice of books in the library or the responsibilities of schoolteachers, not over who shall be marched off in violent waves of "ethnic cleansing." The conflicts among tenured university professors over curriculum or between groups of students who want their own ethnic studies programs and centers also look petty by contrast, though up close they can be bruising. The teapot tempests over the imagery of mass media in America are simmerings compared with the boiling furies where tribes elsewhere use explosives. Why bother then with American adjustments to new times, some may ask.

What motivates this inquiry into the story and stories of peoples and groups in America is the belief that citizens, wherever they are, have a responsibility for the public climate and the fragile social order. That belief in turn derives from my sense that the American experiment itself is a delicate venture, a gossamer fabric, and that it is threatened today. One need not believe with Abraham Lincoln that the United States is the "last, best hope of earth" to feel called to invest energies in it. Without turning nostalgic or defending primitivist theories about the golden past, I shall be arguing both that the United States is paralyzed and that its moral, spiritual, and intellectual capital are in need of restoring. In truth, we are all in need of "restoring." This chapter's title captures something of my thesis, but "re-storying the bodies politic" says even more.

Intentions

This book does not belong in the "How To" category. It is not a medical text, as it were, for dealing with post-traumatic national existence. Let me give examples. Whenever a community is torn between those who would censor library books perceived to offend "Judeo-

Christians" and those who insist on free speech, conflict resolution squads may be called in. This is not a manual for them. Nor is it addressed to members of an aggrieved ethnic, racial, or gender caucus planning a sit-in or to university administrators faced with demands by interest groups for separate study programs or housing units.

Nor do I wish to address the conflicts of recent decades in over-familiar terms. That is why I avoid the words mentioned earlier. As a historian and journalist, I receive many magazines each periodical cycle. Most of those that issue from left and right, from supporters of a national "one" and from the subcommunities' "many," regularly refer to and further inflame issues and accounts of events with chronicles of offenses by partisans on their other side. These get answered tit for tat, in both content and tone. An extensive literature of this sort also appears in the form of books.

But citing such literature is neither necessary nor helpful for present purposes. Every incendiary illustration I could reproduce here would distract from the goal of informing possible conversations across the boundaries of groups and communities. Opportunities abound elsewhere for reading who is making which claim or demand, who is being besieged, or who has won new rights. If conversation across boundaries and gulfs and over the walls of exclusivism is to prosper in the United States, citizens need places where they can talk about what we should address. In this book I want to envision some ways to create places and spaces for such conversation.

Unconventional Partners

In order to help alter conventional ways of entering the argument, I will carry on extended conversation with some partners who are not often included. Some may find it strange to think of books as being part of a conversation. Conversation is usually oral, undertaken with people who are living and near at hand. We are not limited to them, however. Machiavelli says that when he entered his library at the end of day, he put on garments "regal and courtly," because he was about to begin conversation there with great and generous people—all of them long dead. He would address questions to them, and they would generously impart something of their wisdom.[7] Books should not be considered finished products. As long as they challenge and judge us, evoking our response along the way, they remain unfinished and open to conversation—some of it, as here, extended.

Many times we cannot predict where a conversation will take us, where it will go. One person speaks, and another takes the new themes in unforeseen directions. So it will be here. I will be keeping certain writers on the platform for pages at a time, teasing out of their writings meanings they may not have originally intended, though I hope in every case to represent them accurately and be faithful to what they said.

I will draw, for example, on the conservative British philosopher Michael Oakeshott's distinction between a "civil association" and an ideological community, as well as on his theme of "modes of being" and discourse. I will also draw on the thought of a Calvinist political scientist, Johannes Althusius. His concept of a republic as a *communitas communitatum,* a "community of communities" made up of "symbiotes," will here be translated into the concept of a republic as an "association of associations," also in symbiotic relations to one another.

The conversation will continue in dialogue with U.S. Supreme Court Justice Felix Frankfurter, who near mid-century discussed the role of symbols in forming the "binding tie of cohesive sentiment" in a free society. He was ready to have them imposed by law, although I shall argue for the greater effectiveness of relying on persuasion, on voluntary access.

Alasdair MacIntyre pointed to the problem of publics whose groups live with "incommensurable universes of discourse," worlds that cannot provide a common basis for discussion or mutual evaluation. But he also has been friendly to history and implied that there could be some commensurability in stories. MacIntyre thus states part of the problem and part of the solution in the issues of the one and the many.

Those who look for more familiar checkpoints will find them, I hope, in the work of James Madison, the dominant influence on my thinking about the republic, and especially about religions and a republic. And I will refer as well to the observations made by Alexis de Tocqueville on associational life in this republic.

Unconventional Terms

If several of these figures are not the usual conversation partners at tables today, neither are all of my terms the most conventional. Again, this is so because I hope to find in them instruments for fresh conceptions and proposals. My historian's instinct leads me to resurrect terms like "the one and the many." At the same time, I will be importing other terms, like *symbiotes,* to be explained later. And some will be used in special senses.

Community, for example, is a word that implies deep and intimate communion. Many use it to refer to the dream that the whole nation or a large and complex group within it must be united under a single set of symbols and must privilege a particular ideology. As I use the word or a version of it, *subcommunity,* it will instead be connected more realistically with life in some (though not all) of the groups that share space in America.

Community of many sorts is realized in extended families, local communities, neighborhoods, clubs, caucuses, congregations, and some smaller and focused elements in the groups marked by race, sex, class, ethnicity, religion, nationality, language, and culture, at least as we have tallied so far. Many of these groups as a whole, however, cannot be a true and deep community any more than can a nation. They are instead associations.

Association, then, implies a broader commitment to common purposes on the part of those who associate with one another. The term refers to the alliances of those who make up the citizenry. The nation-state itself is a "civil association." An association implies commitment but demands less of a creedal bond or less personal intimacy than does a community. People associate with one another to promote enterprises, as they do in business or in the voluntary sector. There can be more "spiritual space" between those who have a looser association than between those in tight community.

In some nostalgic stories, the United States *was* a community "in the good old days," when citizens seemed to be more or less like one another. Many complain with good cause that the absence of community today threatens the common good in a time when so many peoples and interest groups speak up. Others, however, believe that the United States was a community only in the bad old days. Back then, in their eyes, a dominant set of people conspired to kill, conquer, remove to reservations, enslave, and abuse everyone else, whose descendants now have their turn to counter them by speaking up for true community—their own.

These chapters challenge the assumptions of even the mildest totalists that a nation cannot survive or prosper unless its citizens gravitate toward and accept or have imposed on them a single ideological framework, creed, and ethos.

Similarly this book challenges the assumptions of even the most genteel tribalists. They argue that unless each of the groups acquires autonomy and forms an exclusive subcommunity, each will only be oppressed and abused by an elite that claims to speak in support of the common good for all.

The third challenge is to those whose realism I share but whose utter pessimism I do not. They say that it is impossible or too late to foster any communication or generate meaningful association among those who tend toward totalism, those who tend toward tribalism, and those half-committed between these tendencies.

Of course, some leaders and some populists are utterly confirmed and entrenched in their positions. They have much at stake, personally and professionally, in the status quo. All societies include people like this. But there is evidence that the majority of the population can be drawn into a search for the common good while enjoying the particularity of their own groups, so long as they are not forced to accept the terms of the existing partisan leaders.

It could well happen that, where there are only two sides, representatives of antagonistic groups would read a book like this as a tract supporting the other side. But I believe strongly that there are other and better ways than the current ones to frame the issue.

In the United States today, on almost all of the themes that provoke visceral reactions and bristling responses, the polls find that 10 or 15 percent of the people are hard-liners, absolutists, militants on each side. (Those imprecise percentages may fall short of satisfying survey researchers, but they are close enough for present purposes.) These 10 or 15 percent I picture metaphorically atop two mesas, cannonading each other across a valley that separates them.

That leaves 70 or 80 percent of the population in the valley. Much of the time most people here can go about their business undisturbed, aware only of distant rumbles or whizzing sounds far above their heads. But at other times verbal grenades lobbed across the valley fall short and drop where they may later explode on the uncommitted. At still other times most people must take cover and hope that the battle will quiet down. Their changing locations and position in the valley are often determined by their reaction to the current belligerencies. Whoever has spoken loudest most recently will have done the most alienating. Finally, on occasion some will find the aggression of one or another of the parties to be appealing and will climb a metaphoric mesa to join one party of belligerents.

If such an image has any ties to reality, then this book can be seen as an address to any of the people or groups in that valley who are trying to relate to their larger social environment. What seem to be lacking in recent years are conceptions and counsels for those who are not yet committed and are never to be committed to the extremes.

A final and I hope also helpful entrée into the topic is an examination of the special use of the terms *sentiment* and *affection,* with their eighteenth-century contexts in mind. This society, this civil association, to the extent that it does cohere, is held together not simply by law and certainly not by ideology or creed. Instead, as Justice Felix Frankfurter wrote in 1940, "the ultimate foundation of a free society is the binding tie of cohesive sentiment," and some of that sentiment remains available. So I shall make much of sentiment in its classic sense, in which the emotional is combined with the intellectual or the reasoned life.

Meanwhile, the affectionate or affective side will be seen to be richer and more complex than current notions of affection (implying soft love) would suggest. This approach stressing "cohesive sentiment" and "affection" can be realistic, reasoned, hard, expressive, and devoted to rights and justice. I hope it will be so here. I belive that this understanding should help move us beyond current impasses and the kinds of shouting that have begun to weary many citizens.

The approach put forward in this book rests also on the distinction between argument and conversation. Although these chapters will concentrate on story and stories, they will also include argument, without which a society cannot pursue justice and welfare. But argument, as defined later, will not dominate. In argument one contender knows the answer, turns it into a proposition, and debates it with the intent to convince or defeat an opponent. The preferred model here instead is conversation. In conversation one does not know the answer. Instead, conversationalists are guided only by the questions.

Conversation partners do not know everything about what is best for the society and how to attain it. They relish the presence of others, of those who are different; they enjoy the contributions of the many in a pluralistic society. Together, they converse, about both the particular and the common good; about the American *plures* and the American *unum*, as in *E pluribus unum*—toward some end, but not always a well-defined one.

Stories and Traditions Possess the Citizens

These conversation partners converse, but about what? About their identities, their memories, their histories, their stories in the context of other stories. Before they even try to theorize about narrative, to determine why particular stories make up the traditions of their nation, or of their groups within the nation, and of their own selves, they busy themselves choosing the stories. A reading of the record of controversy in recent decades shows that they are asking the same question, in one form or another, that MacIntyre asked: "Of what story or stories do I find myself a part?"

Eugene Goodheart, a professor of literature and an anti-utopian, spoke some years ago to a radical generation whose members were united, he said, in their apocalyptic disaffection from the institutional life of the country. He also noted that "deeper than the disaffection is a shared Manichean sense of their own innocence." While not dismissing the radical critiques, Goodheart argued that "the implicit paradigm for the mind behind the current demand for relevance is *tabula rasa*, purged even of the vestiges of Christian, Judaic, or classical traditions." To his list I will add "American" traditions. Times and contexts have changed, but much of what Goodheart said is still relevant.

Amnesia and the rejection of history remain powerful forces, but since the time Goodheart wrote, a new factor has appeared. Remarkably, story and stories have begun to come back in favor and currency. Today citizen groups fight over who has the right to tell them and interpret them: who gets to pick the library books, the stories for schools, the canon for university classrooms? Goodheart's comment on the way traditions possess generations therefore remains relevant:

> The *tabula rasa* is a presumption of innocence. It is not the result of genuine discovery, for instance, that the Christian and classical traditions are no longer part of us. The enactments of our personality and character are involuntary, often compulsive. We are not free to choose what we are or even what we will do. We cannot simply wish away traditions that we have grown to dislike. The very dislike may be conditioned by the fact that they still possess us, if we do not possess them. If Judeo-Christian and classical traditions are still alive in all of us (as I suspect they are), despite attempts to deny them, then an education that fails to address itself to these traditions (I do not speak of arguing for or against them) would fail according to the ideal of relevance.

More recently the argument of many groups is that dislikable European, Judeo-Christian, and classical sets of traditions are *too* alive. Those who claim these accounts traumatize others, it is charged. These stories are possessed by and told by the wrong people, who manipulate others so that they also become possessed. Arguments over whether the presumed tradition should be enhanced with texts and perspectives from other traditions, including Asian and African, are not at issue here; I for one argue enthusiastically for such enhancements. Nor was Goodheart celebrating the traditions as having nothing but the positive to offer. "To keep the traditional culture alive in us is not necessarily to affirm or celebrate it," nor "is it necessarily an act of pious pedantry." Rather, "if the tradition contains within itself permanent human possibilities, then it is necessary to keep it alive as a kind of repository of options."[8]

So it is with the traditions we do like, the stories we claim: they possess us. But who possesses them? Telling and examining stories that acquire an almost mythical character reveal much about how the one and the many can connect in our time. In the following pages we will hear and reflect on one of them.

CHAPTER TWO

 Possessing Our Common Stories

America has no common stories, say partisans of the idea that the nation has become nothing but a collection of many exclusive groups. America has to have common stories, say advocates of the contrary notion, who argue that if exclusivistic groups tell their own stories only to themselves there can be no meaningful national life. A third set contends that certain of the same stories promote the vitality of the separate groups and the common good alike. In all three cases, story matters.

"Story" here stands for all the narrative and explanatory elements that illumine the background and portray the markers of identity for a subcommunity. People tell and hear stories whenever they make efforts to find out and say who they are and whenever they listen for the signals that help them make sense of others.

American citizens, however, who today try to make sense of their life together as "one" *in* a nation and *as* a nation run into plaguing questions. Who runs the show? Who writes the songs and tells the stories? Who owns those stories? Should all the people, especially in their groups, possess one set of stories and interpret them all in one way? Are these narratives all part of what some have called a grand story, a metanarrative? Or do citizens in their various groups possess only separate stories that isolate people from one another? Must they only compete with and contradict each other? Will the acts of telling and explicating the stories always have to produce conflict between instead of harmony among groups?

Almost every American story, it is true, can be told either from the viewpoint of those who search for the "one" nation or from the viewpoint of the "many" groups and subcommunities that make it up. As in every society, the narratives that possess the citizens, the stories that have to be told, are accounts that begin at the beginning. Call them creation myths.

In the United States, these myths deal with the Native Americans as they were encountered by Europeans and then, in more limited ways, by Africans. Soon the myths instead tend to become stories of the Europeans who did the encountering. The storied traditions routinely continue with the high points, the great turnings in the lives of peoples. They tell of how the several colonies became one nation and how that nation was divided over slavery and became embroiled in a civil war. The disputed stories continue to be developed down to the present, through a century of immigrations, depressions, and wars won and lost. Any of them retold could illustrate the main points at issue as citizens debate who possesses these stories.

Older citizens, for instance, measure their years with one mental landmark. They can all recall exactly what they were doing when the radio brought them news on Sunday, December 7, 1941, of the Japanese attack on Pearl Harbor, the attack that signaled the beginning of the Second World War for the United States.

Middle-aged citizens rehearse their place in time by a second incident. They tell each other what they were doing when radio, television, or the neighbors alerted them to an event that disrupted the national sense of order and mental security. They remember when President John F. Kennedy was shot on November 22, 1963. Just as World War II was the aftermath of Pearl Harbor, so the grief and turmoil associated with the Kennedy assassination carried over to those of Robert F. Kennedy and Martin Luther King, Jr., as well as the murder of numbers of others who worked for change. In the middle generation's minds, these incidents signaled an era of instability and insecurity. People became aware that chaos, irrationality, and randomness could threaten the open society at its foundation.

As older generations make games of answering the questions "What were you doing when you heard about Pearl Harbor?" or "Where were you when Kennedy got shot?" the younger one has added a third: "What were you doing when the space shuttle *Challenger* exploded?" According to many reports, the congealing event for younger people (thanks to television) was the destruction of that technological marvel and patriotic symbol in January 1986.

Such an event and the stories about it are usefully examined by anyone who believes—or wonders whether—a common narrative can be a credible subject of debate and conversation in a diverse nation. It turns out that this single incident illustrates many of the ways differing groups cherish their part in stories. Ten years later, those who as elementary and high school students observed the *Challenger's* fall into the Atlantic Ocean have become young adults, a stage when, it is said, they are most prone to being alienated from grand narratives, national histories, group stories. Yet this one is theirs. Like all mythlike stories, this one is open to numberless interpretations, though they tend to fall into several families.

"What were you doing when the *Challenger* exploded?" Those who are now members of the college-age group and those just older, unless they were living beyond U.S. borders or truants who roamed off the school premises on January 28, 1986, at 11:38 A.M. EST, will say that they were in the classroom or assembly hall at school. Together, with their teachers' support and interpretation, they were watching the lift-off of the spacecraft via television. There were many reasons for teachers to use a major media event for instruction and entertainment, but they had special grounds for valuing this one. In 1986, "The Year of the Teacher," a schoolteacher had been chosen to be aboard.

The Ambiguous Case of the Space Shuttle Challenger

The production of the *Challenger* and the preparation for the launching matched the mood and the priorities of the American majority in the 1980s. True, some pacifists grumbled that the whole space program was misconceived. Less a scientific venture than an extremely expensive adventure in Cold War politics, it represented to them and may well have been a foolish misuse of funds. It is not hard to find in the record editorial murmurings by social activists: why spend so much money sending objects and people into space when a new underclass was forming in urban ghettos and impoverished rural areas? Some scientists could even be heard complaining that space science was being favored. Why not put money into microbi-ological research, for example, into attempts to find cures for cancers? All such gripes and moanings could easily be dismissed. The government, most media, and a majority of citizens generally found good reason to back the program.

The *Challenger* represented the boldest and most expensive chapter in the National Aeronautics and Space Administration's manned space program. Those who had to secure funds for it knew how to appeal to the public. Americans were also completing their third decade of a space race with their Cold War enemy, the Soviet Union. NASA and its congressional backers, in search of continued and increased funding, extravagantly promoted the flight. They conspired with television producers and commentators to use the launching to boost patriotism, to advance national pride.

Many scientists and industrialists also celebrated the *Challenger* and its potential achievements. The space program had been sold as the most advanced example of technological triumph to date. It was designed to evoke the most profound devotion to the very idea of exploring and discovery. Americans had always needed frontiers, and the physical frontier in the American West had disappeared a century before. But with the new frontier in space, humans pushed further on the horizons of scientific venture and personal heroism. Citizens could endure many frustrations and postponements along the way, but they did not lose interest in the promise of the space shuttle.

The Cast of Characters

Was the costly flight an example of American innocents in action, as many were taught to think? The astute promoters and programmers, highly aware of the way groups of Americans by 1986 felt about being represented in national causes, took great pains in selecting a crew. To send into space seven white male scientists would have been its own disaster. In earlier decades, the corps of astronauts had indeed been all male, all white, all of European descent, all scientific or military people by profession. The first break in such ranks, this one on gender lines, had occurred three years earlier when Sally Ride became the first woman in space. In order to meet public demands and to counter political pressures, NASA knew that henceforth it had to fill its crews with members attractive to the press and the public.

Within a year after the event at least two sets of interpreters were already debating about the choice of the crew members and the reasons for the choice. One school held a jaundiced view, typified by Malcolm McConnell, author of *Challenger: A Major Malfunction*. He groused that by 1986 the corps of riders, or scheduled riders, into space had already included "bizarre junketeers: the Teacher-in-Space, a senator and a congressman, a Saudi prince." McConnell reported that "people even spoke seriously of singer John Denver being offered a ride."[1]

Not long before the flight, NASA staged the ritual display of the elect personnel for a photograph opportunity and press conference in Florida. As they lined up, McConnell overheard a photographer say of the *Challenger* crew, "Looks like a war-movie propaganda platoon. Got one of everything." She was basing her reaction on a reality that McConnell recalled: back in World War II films, "every bomber crew seemed to embody America's ethnic melting pot." Now at Cape Kennedy he could update the observation: "This was about as heterogeneous a group of Americans as could be assembled aboard the space shuttle."[2]

By virtue of their flight experience, at least three of the cast clearly belonged aboard: Mike Smith, who led the crew, Dick Scobee, and Ellison Onizuka. Onizuka almost incidentally brought the advantage of adding to the perceived heterogeneity of the group. A Buddhist from the Kona Coast of Hawaii, he was an Eagle Scout whose image as a super-American would have helped any of those with long memories of anti-Japanese sentiment to forget about his racial heritage.

Equally at home in such a diverse company was Ron McNair, a physicist with a doctoral degree. McNair was from a small southern town; as a Baptist deacon and an African American, he also added to the ethnic mix and made it possible for millions more to identify with the *Challenger*. Three years after Sally Ride's pioneering, the nation could begin to take for granted the presence of a woman. Judy Resnik, also a Ph.D. and an electrical engineer with an expert scientific mind, was Jewish. She might have been quite private about her religious expression, but faith was a plus in the casting of this

crew. Private enterprise also had to be personally represented. Crew
member and engineer for Hughes Aircraft Greg Jarvis, "Mr. Normal,"
embodied the corporate world of space mission customers-to-be, a
fact that irritated critic McConnell.

Finally, there was Christa McAuliffe, the best-known addition to
the cast. She was being publicized for the teacher-in-space role she
was to fill. Teacher, yes, plus woman, mother, wife, New Englander,
and Catholic, she was a natural for the 1986 flight. The Ronald Reagan presidential campaign of 1984, wanting to show its support for
education, had chosen to promote the idea of a teacher in space. On
August 27, 1984, Reagan announced that he had directed NASA to
"choose as the first citizen passenger in the history of our space program one of America's finest—a teacher." McAuliffe was the one.[3]

Her biographer represented the enthusiastic school of reporters
and interpreters to counter the more jaded sort represented by
McConnell. R. T. Hohler, in *"I Touch the Future . . .": The Story of
Christa McAuliffe,* rhapsodized about the crew and the groups of
Americans it exemplified. Here is his introduction of the cast of *Chal-
lenger:*

> Its passengers would include Francis Scobee, Judith Resnik, Ellison
> Onizuka and Ronald McNair, four of the thirty-five astronauts who
> were selected from a crush of more than eight thousand applicants in
> January 1978. They were a military pilot, a Jewish woman, an Asian
> American and a black—symbols of NASA's commitment to carry Amer-
> ica's cultural rainbow toward the stars.

Hohler confirmed the rainbow vision in the case of McAuliffe:

> On cue, she talked about looking down from the shuttle on Spaceship
> Earth—a Disney concept—imagining a planet where no differences
> divide blacks and whites, Arabs and Jews, Russians and Americans.
> "It's going to be wonderful to see us as one people, a world with no
> boundaries," she said. "I can't wait to bring back that humanistic
> spirit."[4]

After the disaster that befell *Challenger,* the nation heard reports
that long before takeoff tensions had developed among the crew, in
part over the press notice being given to some crew members on the

basis of their ethnicity or gender. Citizens began to take apart the space age mythology. Critics grumbled that the credentials of some crew members seemed a bit thin to professionals and space flight veterans aboard. Still, after the crew members had presented themselves as a group and then individually to the press before takeoff, one "young woman education writer who was covering her first space shuttle mission"—here we keep relying on the eyes and ears of Malcolm McConnell—beamed, "They were beautiful. They're just like, well, the *best* America can offer."[5]

After many delays, with the nation, not least of all its schoolchildren, watching, an immediately smooth and dramatic liftoff finally occurred. America's odyssey, its epic voyaging, was continuing. Voices communicating back to earth confirmed the true trajectory of the story. Before seventy seconds had passed Pilot Mike Smith exulted for his crew: "Feel that mother go ... Wooo ... hooo!" Earth was already 50,000 feet below. Judith Resnik, that very private-minded and often reserved scientist, forgot both her reserve and conventional word order in her enthusiastic outcry: "Shit hot!"

Six-tenths of a second before the shuttle sent its last telemetry data at 11:39:13.628, Mike Smith was heard to utter his last words: "Uh-oh." On the ground, mission control spokesperson Steve Nesbitt in horror watched monitor screens go dead: "Flight controllers here looking very carefully at the situation. Obviously a major malfunction." The ground communications officer reported, "We have negative contact. Loss of downlink."[6] Tens of millions of citizens, and many more around the globe, watched *Challenger* explode, sending its crew to the ocean depths, symbolically as low as hopes for further manned space flight in the immediate future were ever to sink.

The Clash of Interpretations

The failure of *Challenger* is susceptible to many interpretations, some of which match the tropes of epic literature. As such, it will be debated for decades to come. Already we have seen that McConnell, critic of the propaganda about the space mission and a questioner of what was then called manned space flight, offered a very different version of the story than did Hohler, who focused on the drama of an individual life. Beyond these two, various tragic, pathetic, and ironic interpretations developed within the next decade, with doubtless more to come. They show how difficult it is for people to accept the idea that one set of stories could serve all citizens or could easily prevail.

First, there was tragedy of the sort familiar to readers of epics. The crew of seven had walked confidently into the shuttle on Launch Pad 39B at the Kennedy Space Center, waving for the cameras and a national viewership. They could not know that the masters of their fate, leaders at NASA and Morton Thiokol's Wasatch Division in Utah, had been minimizing a design flaw that was soon to kill them. They were walking not into the space technology triumph of the age but into a preventable death trap.

Also, of course, the plot has pathos. The presence of the civilian schoolteacher Christa McAuliffe was designed to be instructive about positive values. She drew sympathy because she came to be seen as an idealistic and innocent victim of the sort good stories should include.

Irony is present as well. The explosion, the result of a chain of errors, exposed the irrationalities in a program that had been advertised as the best example yet of technical rationality. It revealed private intrigues within a public project. With this disaster the United States suffered a terrible reversal of everything that had been intended. Religionlike myths of NASA's prowess had developed, with governmental and NASA encouragement, because the space program was becoming harder and harder to sell politically. A favorite biblical text of Reinhold Niebuhr, the master of irony among theologians, therefore seems appropriate: in the face of human pride, He "that sitteth in the heavens shall laugh" because "the people imagine a vain thing" (Psalm 2:4, 1).[7]

Rituals for the One before the Many

To understand how such interpretations could emerge, one does well to recall with McConnell the romanticism with which most Americans had greeted the space shuttle myth:

> To the public the Orbiter was a magical white bird, a nimble spaceliner
> that provided wholesome diversion on the evening news. The shuttle

made them proud to be Americans; it gave them a warm sense of confidence about the country's high-technology future. In the past five years, press accounts had likened the gleaming Orbiter to a phoenix. The space shuttle had become the symbol of America's technological and political renaissance, a bold, successful gamble, the quintessence of this optimistic decade. The Orbiter rose beyond its own awesome fires, clean, powerful, high above the ashes of military defeat and political turmoil that had scarred the past twenty years. To millions of people, the space shuttle was a patriotic icon, the tangible symbol of what was best in American civilization, a product of daring scientific prowess, free-enterprise innovation, and insightful political leadership. The space shuttle had carried us back to the frontier and made us proud again.

That was the myth that surrounded Challenger.[8]

After the disaster, reports on emotional reactions preceded interpretation. Millions in the nation grieved, mourned, and ritualized their anger, frustration, trauma, and loss. Television and the press brought word of the ways in which the larger national population reckoned ceremonially with its mixture of emotions. The ample *New York Times* coverage replicates accounts of other media and can serve to document some of this dialectic of ritualizations.

Thus on the day after the disaster, January 29, the reporter Sara Rimer recounted stories of still necessarily diffuse individualized responses. They reflected the benumbed and ill-focused reactions that are often portrayed as typical in television coverage of disasters. Rimer found many citizens "mesmerized by the terrible scene of the shuttle exploding," watching "a scene that would be replayed throughout the day and night."

Rimer properly observed: "It seemed to be one of those moments, enlarged and frozen, that people would remember and recount for the rest of their lives—what they were doing and where they were when they heard" the news. One citizen told her that when his sister phoned him at work with the news, "it was like the Kennedy thing." A 38-year-old teacher observed, "I compared today to Nov. 22, 1963 when I was in a high school Latin class. I told them they will remember this day forever."[9] Grief counselors not only at the high school where McAuliffe taught but in many other schools helped the young cope. The students had special difficulty making the story that they had been told about patriotism and technical pride match the story they had watched, one of disaster and defeat.

The New York Times looked up the street to Central Park, where on February 2 the city, like so many other cities, had honored the astronauts. Mayor Ed Koch offered what the reporter Crystal Nix called a "nonsectarian prayer": "O Lord, we pray that you may receive the souls of these your servants. They died in service of their country and in service of all mankind. We shall remember them always." Nix quoted a typical participant: "It was just as sad as when President Kennedy was shot or the wars, any of the happenings." Another passerby complained that she had not been notified of the ceremonies that she chanced to come across too late: "It would have been nice to come here to a service out in the open rather than to just watch it on television."[10]

For the national observance, an attempt to gather all the strands of rite and ceremony into one cord, President Ronald Reagan spoke. It was the finest rhetorical hour for a rhetorically gifted president, an effective priestly and pastoral moment in the career of an experienced master. This speaking belonged in the traditions of chief executives, who have been taught (though they also know it by instinct) that they must act as ministers in such moments of national shock. Often chief executives and commanders-in-chief use Arlington National Cemetery or the White House steps for their ritual. In this case the center of mourning was shifted from Washington to Houston. The choice of the Texas city made sense. There five of the crew members' families lived.[11]

At times of national mourning, foreign leaders contribute to the ritual with condolences. Pope John Paul II sent word to Reagan of "the Holy Father's deep sorrow." The Cold War rival leader Mikhail Gorbachev produced an expected message about the Soviet "feeling of sorrow." Another enemy, Col. Muammar el-Qaddafi of Libya, tried to score points: "In this era, all nations, all peoples, must cooperate together, to develop their lives." He then propagandized: "So we are very sorry to see this crisis and to see a superpower using its power and resources against a small country like Libya."[12]

At the Houston ceremony the congregation sang "God Bless America" and "America the Beautiful" and sobbed when T-38 jets flew over in the "missing man formation." The Presbyterian father-in-law of

Sally Ride, the Reverend Bernard B. Hawley, gave the invocational prayer. Then the black-suited president, intending to speak to and for the whole country, now united in grief, mentioned the national "sorrow for ourselves," all citizens, who would miss the astronauts on earth. But he added that the sorrow "should be tempered by the joy that they are receiving the blessings God reserved for them. We shall all see them together again."

The language he used was more explicit about an afterlife than what many would hear from pulpits in congregations whose members affirm belief in the "resurrection of the dead." Reporters noted how welcome religious language was at the ceremony and how ready to provide it was the president, in words like the ones he addressed to the victims:

> For those who knew you well and loved you, the pain will be deep and enduring. A nation, too, will long feel the loss of her seven sons and daughters, her seven good friends. We can find only consolation in faith, for we know in our hearts that you who flew so high and so proud now make your home beyond the stars, safe in God's promise of eternal life.[13]

Such language about faith that was held in common by "us," the citizens of the United States, would be incomprehensible or even offensive if invoked in most nations of once-Christian Europe. In the United States, however, the speech would have been more remarked upon if the president had *not* resorted to such language at such a time, when the American story was, through it, being extended.

Church religion also took on a uniting character in the week of ritual mourning. Hundreds of Houston-area churches scheduled memorials at which citizens could express themselves. Michelene K. Robertaccio, who directed marketing for the Clear Lake Area Economic Development Foundation, certified the earthliness of the heaven-bound crew: "The astronauts lived here. They were our friends and neighbors. They went to our churches. Their kids went to our schools. They weren't people on television to us."[14]

Nor did Washington, the normal locale for national observances, neglect the occasion. The reporter Robin Toner observed that "there was a churchly air to the ceremony" held at the National Air and Space Museum on the Washington Mall, which became an instant memorial and shrine. Senator John Glenn of Ohio, the first astronaut to orbit the earth for the American program, spoke there: "We are a people who are curious. So we try and we triumph, and we try again and we triumph again." Glenn recognized, as he had to, that tragedies came with the triumphs, but he put a gloss on it all: this setback "doesn't mean that things end at that point." He elaborated on the experience of the seven dead astronauts. They carried, Glenn said, "that questing, those dreams, those hopes that epitomize the very best of our nation."[15]

Meanwhile in the third logical base for national observance, reporter William E. Schmidt resorted to religious language as he watched tourists and townspeople turn the Cape Canaveral Spaceport U.S.A. visitors' center into a place for mourning, another shrine: "Many of those who visit here have come as if on a pilgrimage, not only to bear witness to the site of history's worst space disaster but also to reaffirm their essential faith in the nation's space achievements."[16]

Nationally regarded religious professionals were also called in for their say. The *New York Times* interviewed Billy Graham, who commented:

> We've had so many of these tragedies lately that I think it has sobered the American people and made it much more easy to talk philosophically and religiously to people . . .
> I also think a tragedy like this tends to bring us together almost like the events of Pearl Harbor many years ago. It makes us realize how interdependent we are on each other.

In Chicago, Cardinal Joseph Bernardin, leader of the American Catholic bishops, applied the meaning of the event to individuals who made up the nation and its groups: "I just think that our faith in God makes it possible for us to accept the human tragedies that we face in life. We don't have answers to all of life's mysteries."

In the secular sphere, the Librarian of Congress Daniel J. Boorstin, who had written at length about explorers and discoverers, wept after the explosion. The disaster, he said, "does affect us deeply; something like this brings the nation together. The space program in general has done that; people understand the grandeur even if not the technology, and to share that grandeur is what makes a great nation."[17]

The reporter Daniel Goleman interviewed counselors to learn what was on the minds of the citizens with whom they dealt. He quoted Mardi Horowitz, a psychiatrist at the University of California at San Francisco, who noticed that in the wake of such tragedies one could discover "the sense of a world crumbling. We don't believe our institutions can fail us in such a dramatic fashion. It's a shocking symbol of the fragility of all our hopes, of human technology, and finally of human life." Horowitz related the shock to the therapy of the ceremonies: "The psychological purpose of ritual is not just to honor the dead but to re-establish a common bond and counter the sense of being alone in a hostile universe."

Goleman also quoted Ronnie Janoff-Bulman, a psychologist at the University of Massachusetts at Amherst, who noted: "Such a disaster challenges our basic trust that the world is a predictable place." Anger follows the loss of trust. The disaster "jarred us into an awareness that the world is not always just; we felt betrayed by the universe." Horowitz added, "The shuttle has played a powerful role in our collective fantasy life as a symbol of an American dream. It's an image etched in our minds of American power," power now lost.[18]

Rituals for the Groups

While words like "we," "our," "our people," "our nation," "her seven sons and daughters," "her seven good friends," "our institutions," "American dream," and "common bond" all stress the larger complex, the leaders of mourning and the press were also sensitive to the context of subgroups. Thus it was reported that the family of Judith A. Resnik chose to forgo the common ceremony in Houston and to mourn at Temple Israel in Akron, Ohio.[19]

Some commentators took note of the fact that natural sympathy for what is close to one can block sensitivity to larger common life, including transnational themes. Thus Dr. Willard Gaylin, president of the Hastings Center, mentioned that television made the astronauts seem so real everywhere in the United States. He provided a term that well serves the theme of this book. How does the story of what is most near—the tribe, the group, the subcommunity, the nation— promote the search for an identity?

I connect all this with what I call a theory of proximal identification. It's not pretty, but we tend to identify with things close to us. If your child burns his hand it causes you more pain than if something awful happens to India. You may care what happens in India, but your child causes you more real pain. That's why local news interests people so much.[20]

Gaylin referred to the danger that television could do too well at forming a national convergence of sentiments. But the localization of ceremonies complementing the national mourning and bonding might have given him further evidence of such proximal identification. For those who lost astronauts from their own geographical community or ethnic or gender subgroup, the identification *was* pretty, and it demanded recognition.

In Beaufort, North Carolina, James G. Martin led the memorial service for Michael Smith, who, in the group language of the day, represented European Americans. A county commissioner there, with a profound local sense, said that "for this community, the loss seems overwhelming because Mike Smith was one of us. When Mike died, a little part of us died with him. We all shared his life and we all mourn his death."[21]

In South Carolina Governor Richard W. Riley honored the African American Ronald McNair at the astronaut's home congregation, Wesley United Methodist Church. It was observed that the hero had played the saxophone and taught karate there. Identifying his story with that of the people of his local setting, the physicist's brother, Carl McNair, said that while "Ronald had gotten hundreds of honors around the world, I don't think there was anything that meant more to him than the black and white people working together in South Carolina to honor him, a black man who picked cotton, cucumbers and tobacco."

McNair's old classmate the Reverend Jesse Jackson made his familiar point about diversity and unity. Jackson, as ready as governors and mayors to be close to the event, ritually reminded the congregation of his own political symbol, the rainbow: "On this journey, there were two women, a Jew, a black, an Asian, white males and an A & T graduate from one of the endangered black schools of our country. It was a rainbow in the sky." And Billie Fleming of the local National Association for the Advancement of Colored People chapter said that "Ron McNair knew that as a little black boy . . . God had touched him and given him certain talents and abilities and that he would not let race, creed or color be an obstacle and that he would go on to accomplish what God intended him to do."[22]

From Washington, the Georgetown professor Eleanor Holmes Norton picked up the theme voiced by Jackson:

> I feel the same sense of loss for each one of the seven. But I cannot help but note that for me this flight somehow symbolized America as we are trying to make it, an America with a black, an Asian, a woman, and with white men, perhaps the most fully integrated flight ever made, all joining in a common cause. . . . I believe in America's resilience and that we will use this tragedy to rebuild.[23]

Most attention was focused on the local memorial in Concord, New Hampshire, for Christa McAuliffe. There her cousin, Father James Leary, celebrated the mass while Boston's Cardinal Bernard Law presided in the church where the teacher had tutored confirmation classes. In line with Willard Gaylin's theory of proximal identification, the Reverend Daniel Messier said of her: "She was Concord. When she stepped on that shuttle, Concord stepped on that shuttle."[24]

Then, for Asian Americans, there was Ellison Onizuka, the first astronaut who, as we already noted, was Japanese American, Hawaiian, and Buddhist. Pauline Yoshihashi tracked observances by those of his lineage for the *New York Times*:

> He was quietly and frankly proud of that heritage; in turn, many people who were Hawaiian or Japanese American or Buddhist saluted him as one of their own. He presided over their festivals, spoke at their functions, practiced their religion and continually thanked them for helping him along his way.

Locals also remembered Ellison Onizuka as typically American. His older brother remembered: "Around us, he was just El. When he'd come home, he'd drink beer and talk story, and be just another guy." Noted Yoshihashi of Onizuka: "In high school he became involved in Buddhism, the Boy Scouts, and the 4-H Federation." Also, "Buddhism played an important part in his life." Onizuka had recently presented a medal decorated with a wisteria blossom, the symbol of his Jodo Shinshu faith, to Monshu Koshin Ohtani, the abbot of Jodo Shinshu Buddhism, and to Bishop Seigen Yamaoka, head of the Buddhist Churches of America. The reporter reflected on how Onizuka used his faith to deal with life and death. Many of the rest of his fellow citizens celebrated his technical expertise, his professionalism, his Eagle Scout outlook, and his place in American history.[25]

Subversion of the Stories' Plots

So far I have reported on leaders, reporters, and ordinary citizens who stressed positive patriotism to honor the heroic dead. But healthy storytelling, argument, and conversation in a free society have to include questioning and challenging of all the stories, whether told to support the *unum*, the one nation, or to reinforce the allegiances to the *plures*, the many ethnic, racial, or religious groups.

One set of questioners was suspicious of the use of the "rainbow" symbolism that sentimentalized and rendered superficial the relation of group to group in a time of conflict. Many serious critics since have rigorously questioned the expressions of idealism, the exaggerations of American harmony, and the appropriateness of the ceremonialization of the explosion.

Thus Howard S. Schwartz, an organizational behavior theorist, commented critically on the enthusiasm of McAuliffe's biographer. In Schwartz's more radical vision, the launching of *Challenger* never had to do fundamentally with science. It had all resulted from the deliberate creating of a symbol, an act of American narcissism. The product was an art form that had been designed to replace reality. "Through some of their institutions," Schwartz commented, "societies talk to themselves about themselves." He cited the anthropologist Clifford Geertz's familiar reflection on the Balinese cockfight to illumine the American ceremonies:

> Like any art form—for that, finally, is what we are dealing with—the cockfight renders ordinary, everyday experience comprehensible by presenting it in terms of acts and objects which have had their practical consequences removed and been reduced (or, if you prefer, raised) to the level of sheer appearances, where their meaning can be more powerfully articulated and more exactly perceived.[26]

While trying to make his case that the shuttle venture was a sign of narcissism and of the decay of cultural organization, Schwartz cited J. J. Trento to the effect that

neither the U.S. military nor the CIA had any interest in manned space flight. The meaning of the space flight program was symbolic from the outset and remained so. In the case of the space shuttle *Challenger* . . . the image that I had of the voyage—Americans transcending their differences and their finitude, floating blissfully together in space— was in fact that meaning of the voyage itself.[27]

When the meaning of social institutions is symbolic, Schwartz asked, "does this not raise the possibility of a rift between the meaning of the symbol and the social reality it is presumed to reflect?" Might not society, he went on, grow so enamored of the image it creates of itself "that the fact that it is only a symbol may be forgotten or repressed?" Finally, "if that were to happen, could that not make a problem for the very existence of the symbol itself?"

In the face of all these questions about symbol and reality, Schwartz proposed "that the symbol of manned space flight that NASA intended and was intended to project came to contradict the social and organizational realities that were necessary for its staging." Although he was interested chiefly in illusions of perfection, I pick up on the lesser but here more relevant staging of symbols that suggested that in space Americans could overcome their profound group conflicts and differences. Schwartz quoted the comments of McAuliffe's biographer concerning her vision of looking down on earth and seeing the planet as "one people, a world with no boundaries" between peoples. Schwartz's reflections are thought-provoking:

What is striking to me about these images is not only the denial of social differentiation that they represent, but the way they manifest the denial of difference in their failure to distinguish the symbol from reality. Christa McAuliffe will go into space and "see us as one people" with no differences between blacks and whites, rich and poor, and so forth. But of course there are differences, and flying a hundred miles above them does not reconcile those differences; it only obscures them.
Or consider the idea of sending America's "cultural rainbow" toward the stars. At a time when America's racial groups appear to be becoming

irretrievably divided, when America's sexual relationships have become
. . . problematic . . . , when heavily armed Neo-Nazi sects are trying to
organize the secession of the American Northwest, the idea of America's cultural rainbow as being a unity in diversity is simply absurd and
the idea of bringing it into being by flying people in space is bizarre.
Indeed, from a psychoanalytic point of view it is precisely the tensions
among these groups that makes the symbol of their resolution attractive. What gives this image its clinical cast is the failure to distinguish
between symbol and reality.

Therefore, for him and for many others, the "denial of social differentiation is an aspect of the denial of difference that puts the sense
of reality into a precarious position." On those terms, Schwartz
judged that "the selection of [Christa McAuliffe, despite her lack of
scientific training] expressed the message that the American public
did not have to do anything to experience utopia in space, but that
they could do it just as they were."[28]

It is not likely that most leaders of groups in the cultural rainbow
of Christa McAuliffe would be content with the token symbolism of
that crew. Dominate us, oppress us, victimize us, and then throw us
a little compensation by having one of us aboard a spaceship—and
then expect us to feel satisfied with representation: is that how things
are to be? One pictures such complaining and questioning from the
groups and the subcommunities that were trying to effect change in
1986. But they would have been outnumbered by the members of
each mentioned group and by the public beyond them who *did* see
the *Challenger* casting and disaster as a story about all of us. Not
about all of us homogenized, but all of us in our group particularities
and our coming together as citizens of one nation.

A story like this about a space shuttle raises issues for interpreters
who bring many interests and perspectives. Like legends or epics in
all cultures, this one is ambiguous throughout. Heroism and corruption, science and the politics of exploitation—all meet in such stories, whether they are from the world of Greek myth, the Bible, or
the time of the founding of nations.

Often critics of the notion of stories told and heard in common
argue that those who dominate in a culture win everything through
their choice of stories. If so, they traumatize those forced to live by
their stories. But they have not listened carefully to hear how ambig-

uous and contradictory are all the heroes of all the stories. One thinks, for example, of biblical instances. Suppose Americans are persuaded to pay close attention to the biblical narratives. Will they all be converted to a positive view of what these disclose? It is hard to think of any biblical heroes—Abraham, Jacob, Moses, Deborah, David, or in the New Testament the disciples of Jesus—whose stories are not open to many kinds of interpretations. Most of the saints would be jailed in our time; it would take a highly secretive leadership or some very successful launderers to present and sustain stories and explanations favorable only to the elites who tell them.

My main concern in coming chapters will be to see how such stories are viewed on one hand by those who seek a single American plot and on the other by those who stress subplots of the contending groups. For now, it is clear that even citizens of the younger generation, who may have been ignorant of history or uninterested in events of the remote past, have found in events like the *Challenger* disaster that certain stories possess the citizens in common and that even in their separateness they themselves are among the possessed. If stories are so rich, it is no wonder that some claim to own them while others accuse the claimants of using stories in their efforts to dominate. The best way to approach the controversy is to notice first how contenders for the "one" have stated their case and how they look and sound to everyone else.

CHAPTER THREE

One People, One Story

Few Americans would think they could promote the common good by advocating that one set of storytellers or a single grand storyline could or should dominate over all others. They would also resist the efforts by an elite or establishment, the central government, any corporate network, or a media ethos to be privileged, or to suppress the stories of their many groups and force them into a single mold. Power is at issue. Set the songs for a country, determine its stories, and you will have power. So say students of cultures past who have listened to troubadours and bards, folksingers and writers of epics. Ancient kings often erased the names and legends of predecessors from monuments so subjects in later generations could know only one story. Then the act of ruling became easier, more efficient, less confusing. Moderns in effect sometimes try the same.

In monarchies and tyrannies, it was somehow easier to control the choice of stories, the cast of storytellers, and the interpretation of narratives and myth. In republics, especially those where pluralism is rich and mass media are ample, it is somewhat more difficult to do the controlling. Yet critics of the American republic and modern media have found many reasons to perceive control in effect. Elite and dominant sets of people, in both commercial and governmental sectors, are said to possess privileged access to the instruments of storytelling. They have control, and they use that control. They are in a position to determine what it is that serves people who are seeking to determine the spheres of what Gaylin calls their "proximal identifications."

The totalitarians and authoritarians of the century, for instance, have had complete control in many nations. The terrifying film *The Triumph of the Will* gathered up and propagated the myths of Hitler's Nazi Germany. Mussolini found ways to see that only one kind of signal transmitted the themes of his tyranny in Italy. The Soviet Union made exhaustive efforts to dominate all transmission, to create a single governmental myth, to wipe out all histories that the rulers found uncongenial, and to punish even mild dissenters. Cuba and China kept doing the same, even after the end of the Soviet Union. Anyone in such nations who sought independent outlets of expression would be traumatized, suppressed, or even destroyed.

In the United States it is less easy for the government or particular commercial elites to possess and control the people's stories. With hundreds of television channels, thousands of radio stations, and millions of books available, there are simply too many outlets for the powerful to be able to suppress all that they find uncongenial. With several political parties, scores of racial and ethnic groups, hundreds of church bodies, and thousands of educational institutions, there are too many agencies interested in transmitting their version of the American story or their part of it for anyone to have a monopoly.

Still, the drive for monopoly in America remains strong. Various federal government administrations have put energy into a plot line that favors their work and will. Huge media conglomerates can so overwhelm competition that it is not economically feasible for communicators who go against the stream to seek funds and find outlets. Large elements in the public give evidence that they like to be cowed and that they welcome the notion of conforming to one way of being American, which also means having one set of ideals and ideas projected for them to follow.

In the eyes of some religious conservatives, for example, currently more expressive than their rivals, the storytellers that threaten them are unrepresentative of the whole populace. These alternate messengers are portrayed as members of a conspiracy among secular humanists and liberals to propagate versions of American history and human values that are designed to rule out religious faith. In the eyes of the rightists, the humanist suspicion of religion (particularly the Judeo-Christian versions of it) in the interest of keeping church and state separate leads to the setting forth of an alternative religion. In such a reading, there can be no neutral ground, no pluralist playing field. The stories that shape the nation will be either God's or Satan's, Christ's or the Antichrist's, truly American or alien. "Civil libertarians," in the eyes of their beholding enemies, simply have chosen a neutral sounding code name to disguise their ideological uniformity.

Conversely, those who oppose the religious right, including most other religious citizens, uneasily observe efforts by the right to gain control of a political party and then of a nation. With such control, the critics charge, one minority element would fashion the stories that are told in the public schools, retold in library books, and favored in political life. To these critics, the "Judeo-Christian tradition" as evoked by groups on the right is a modern invention, a disguise for very particular versions of that tradition. Similarly, barely behind the façades of friendly sounding themes like "Christian America" are raw efforts to promote one kind of Christianity as the dominant force in national life. It alone would possess the stories and be able to tell them.

Those who claim that one set of citizens has a right to ownership of the national stories are almost always interested in reclaiming a particular past. Sometimes they are merely nostalgic. They have been told that in earlier times things were simpler. People knew each other. They shared certain values. They knew what absolutes were and what were the absolutes. They did not have to reckon with so much pluralism, so many confusing signals from such diverse peoples and groups. Let us recover those days, they urge. Those who favor the telling of separate stories in order to promote exclusivisms are traumatizing the nation.

One group of Americans, which we have already seen, insists that a single grand narrative belongs to all citizens, however differently they interpret it. They believe their story, be it called Judeo-Christian or secular or democratic humanist or whatever, is ready to serve America after its trauma. In their argument, it matters little from what continent your ancestors came or what your religion, gender, class, or set of interests is. Somehow all the grand stories belong to everybody. And because citizens will use stories to determine how they will live and what is good and beautiful and true, those who tell and interpret these accounts should stress what was once called *sameness,* that certain homogeneity that was said to have come with the American experience.

Founders in Support of Sameness

Some contenders argue all this out of a nostalgia for the America that they genuinely believe once existed. Others consult historians who claim that the American founders, children of the eighteenth-century Enlightenment, projected and then at least partly realized a culturally unified republic. In terms of this reading of the national motto, the United States was established to be an *unum*, a unity, a single organic whole. It would, of course, include in subordinate ways the *plures*, the many groups who participate in the main themes. Other contenders argue that the majority religious faith of the nation—call it biblical or Judeo-Christian or Christian—should provide the one and unifying story.

Such traditions can cite important spiritual ancestors on their sides. Take, first, the founders at the time of Independence in 1776 and the drafting of the Constitution in 1787. Most of them, as they were busy trying to unite the colonies, found it important to stress sameness among the citizens. With a few major exceptions, among them the very important one of James Madison, most of the people remembered as framers of American institutions did want homogeneity of story and outlook to prevail among the colonies, later the states, and in the federal republic. They overlooked or even questioned the integrity of what we are calling the peoples and groups and subcommunities; they made little or no provision for the dissonant particular voices in the federal mix.

In those days, women had their place but not their collective voice. Similarly, some of the homogenizers wanted to convert and "civilize" the Native Americans, known to them as Indians, until they increasingly would become like everyone else in the colonies. Most of the onlookers and propagandists, however, expected the Indians to die off through disease. Or the conquerors worked to see them pushed West, where they were eventually put on reservations or killed. Jews and Muslims, further, were not present in sufficiently large numbers to be reckoned with except through theoretical formulations or in state constitutions. Their cultures did not threaten to turn any colony into a heterogeneous and thus problematic community—though of course they promoted the interests of "difference" when it came to the rights and culture of specific colonies.

A most expressive version of this impulse to promote sameness for the sake of the republic's health appeared in *The Federalist No. 2,* written for the *Independent Journal* in New York City, which was already in 1789 a place marked by population diversity. In this paper, one of the three *Federalist* authors, John Jay—who with his colleagues was trying to get the Constitution ratified by the states— foresaw and displayed the "Natural Advantages of the Union." He had often been pleased to observe that independent America "was not composed of detached and distant territories, but that one connected, fertile, wide-spreading country was the portion of our western sons of liberty." He acknowledged that "Providence has in a particular manner blessed" the new nation with a variety of soils, innumerable streams, navigable waters, and noble rivers. Then Jay, who for a moment must have forgotten that he himself had French Huguenot and Dutch ancestors, sounded English as he added—and I have marked his *one*s, his *same*s, and his *similar*s in italic:

> With equal pleasure I have as often taken notice, that Providence has been pleased to give this *one* connected country to *one* united people— a people descended from the *same* ancestors, speaking the *same* language, professing the *same* religion, attached to the *same* principles of government, *very similar* in their manners and customs, and who, by their joint counsels, arms, and efforts, fighting side by side throughout a long and bloody war, have nobly established general liberty and independence.
>
> This country and this people seem to have been made for each other, and it appears as if it was the design of Providence, that an inheritance so proper and convenient for a band of brethren, united to each other by the strongest ties, should never be split into a number of unsocial, jealous, and alien sovereignties.
>
> *Similar* sentiments have hitherto prevailed among all orders and denominations of men among us. To all general purposes we have uniformly been *one* people.[1]

Jay later became chief justice of the United States Supreme Court. He wrote only a few of the early *Federalist* papers, and may be forgotten by most Americans. But in his company, on this subject, there camped a far more determinative figure, the nation's third president, Thomas Jefferson. In his *Notes on the State of Virginia,* Jefferson manifested a fear of difference and a preference for sameness, also in respect to the stock of citizens.

Jefferson, the primary author of the Declaration of Independence, expressly desired a small republic in the interests of community and affection. In his *Notes* he wrote and responded to a "Query 8" in the form of a chapter on the "number of Virginia's inhabitants." There he contended against "the present desire of America to produce rapid population by as great importations of foreigners as possible." Then he argued for sameness: "It is for the happiness of those united in society to harmonize as much as possible in matters which they must of necessity transact together."

Jefferson thought that the emigrants from continental Europe came with troublesome intellectual and political baggage, especially after their bad experience under absolute monarchies: "Yet, from such, we are to expect the greatest number of emigrants. They will bring with them the principles of the governments they leave, imbibed in their early youth; or, if able to throw them off, it will be in exchange for an unbounded licentiousness, passing, as is usual, from one extreme to the other." Jefferson sounds like many later figures, including those of our own time, who have feared what the diversity of the newcomers—many of whom arrived through unrestricted emigration—would mean. He was apprehensive that they would transmit their foreign ideals to their children. They would thereupon render legislation that would produce "a heterogeneous, incoherent, distracted mass."[2]

Jefferson's sometime political rival and counterpart, Alexander Hamilton, spoke in similar terms for the cause of sameness. Writing in 1802, he showed fear of the influx of foreigners who must "tend to produce a heterogeneous compound; to change and corrupt the national spirit; to complicate and confound public opinion; to introduce foreign propensities. In the composition of society, the harmony of the ingredients is all-important, and whatever tends to discordant intermixture must have an injurious tendency."[3] There is little point in replicating much further the testimony of these three founders in their prime. Benjamin Franklin stressed language, custom, and religion as he looked to the Palatine and other sources of immigrants. He was apprehensive lest the Palatinate "boors" coming to Pennsylvania would "shortly be so numerous as to Germanize us instead of our Anglifying them, and will never adopt our language or customs, any more than they can acquire our complexion."[4]

The testimony in defense of the *unum* and of sameness, absent the case of Madison, would itself be nearly unanimous among the main founders. But if such leaders feared for a republic with this sort of foreigner coming, they need not have done so in their own time. The federal republic did take shape and survive. Only later did the arrival of other sorts of immigrants disturb the serenity of those who stood in the tradition that defended sameness.

Sameness in the Common Schools

Because immigrants did keep coming and the flow showed no signs of slowing, serious people in a second half-century of national life began to ask how best to promote their cherished sameness for the sake of furthering national unity. They concentrated on using public education as a means to homogenize settlers. Through complex processes that developed in the course of the decades, pathfinders invented what they called the "common school." This institution was most developed in Massachusetts but was destined to spread throughout the states. Charles Leslie Glenn has captured something of its history, concentrating on the most influential holder of the common-school patent, Horace Mann.

Glenn drew on the ideas of the sociologist Edward Shils to interpret the homogenizing impulse. According to Shils,

> the society without conflict, the highly integrated society has not only been the reverently cultivated ideal. It has also been the object of government policies . . . The Reformation settlement which declared that the religion of the ruler should also be the religion of his subjects was one sign of the desire of rulers not merely to gain the submission of their subjects but to integrate them into a single society through the uniformity of beliefs. When nationality became an object of passionate devotion . . . rulers found what was to them an almost ideal basis for the integration of the societies.

To further this, societies try to develop, alongside the central authority, a "central cultural system" consisting of "those beliefs and expressive symbols which are concerned with the central institutional system and with 'things' which transcend the central institutional system and reflect on it." For this function, the best candidate, thought Shils and in the present case Glenn as well, was a complex of educational institutions that contributed to the "formation, diffusion, and maintenance of the common culture."[5]

By the 1840s, during a time of increased immigration and also of considerable social experimentation, a democratic nation found itself searching for sameness without choosing to use a central authority to impose it. Granted, thought many leaders, education should be the builder of a culture of sameness. But who would determine what story was taught and how it was to be taught?

At this point, ironically, one of the smaller religious denominations (and the one most despised by other Protestants) had often preempted the positions of authority and filled the void. They were the Unitarians, who, fanning out from the Boston area, had developed high levels of literacy. Theirs was a society church of largely well-educated people. Many were wealthy and occupied positions of leadership; and a sense of *noblesse oblige* moved them to want to communicate across class lines. Though liberal in theology and politics, they became involved in much of the effort to develop schools for people who were not liberal in their modes. The Unitarian educator and theorist Horace Mann was most prominent among them.

The Unitarians found cultured company on some terms with mainstream Protestant denominations, notably the Congregationalists, the Episcopalians, and the Presbyterians. Yet there was rivalry among these other groups and also between them and the unorthodox Unitarians, who kept winning out, to the chagrin of the more conservative denominations.

Mann and his cohorts insisted that they were teaching nonsectarian and thus common values and beliefs. They argued that sectarianism on the one hand and atheism on the other threatened to disrupt the common culture needed in the republic. In 1838, in a lecture entitled "The Necessity of Education in a Republican Government," Mann defined education as "such a culture of our moral affections and religious sensibilities, as in the course of nature and Providence shall lead to a subjection or conformity of all our appetites, propensities, and sentiments to the will of Heaven." This enculturating would go on—if one can make a deduction based on Mann's avoidance of references—without the Bible. In any case, Glenn argues, Mann alienated the orthodox rivals.[6]

Whenever the orthodox tried to counter Mann and his version of religion, he pronounced them divisively sectarian. Because they did not go along with his moralistic version of religion, he also faulted them morally. As schools developed, he argued, "moral training, or the application of religious principles to the duties of life, should be its inseparable accompaniment." Mann regularly spoke of principle but illustrated with story. On these terms, "no community can long subsist, unless it has religious principle as the foundation of moral action; nor unless it has moral action as the superstructure of religious principle." So far, so good.

In his *Eleventh Report* (1848), however, Mann made a distinction between teaching the Bible as the boards of education would do it and the way sectarian clergy did. He thought naively that such boards could exclude "theological systems of human origin." This meant that "they may exclude a peculiarity which one denomination believes to be true," and in the process they would then "exclude what other denominations hold to be erroneous." The words *peculiar* and *peculiarity* kept cropping up in the writings of Mann, who saw himself as a generalist: "If it be the tendency of all parties and sects, to fasten the mind upon what is peculiar to each, and to withdraw it from what is common to all, these provisions of the law [that Mann favored] counter-work that tendency. They turn the mind towards that which produces harmony, while they withdraw it from sources of discord."

Most observers have subsequently agreed that Mann was more naive than ruthless in his efforts to displace the peculiar sectarians in the interest of his general religious proposals. He could not comprehend that if he wanted a religion that excluded belief in those Christian distinctives now associated integrally with Christ, that in the eyes of the conventional majority, he himself was privileging a kind of Unitarianism, which to all others looked like a "peculiar" sect.[7]

Horace Mann and his colleagues in the leadership of the common-school movement were watching or were even accidentally developing a critique of conventional religion in the schools. His now-standard version of faith and morality, orthodox critics feared, was issuing in a decline in the treatment of traditional religion and its replacement by generalized moral teaching. Indeed, religion in the formal sense *was* disappearing from educational institutions, a fact that advocates of religion in the schools have since regretted. But they do not have a means of accounting for the decline before the secular humanists, whom they blame, "took over," as they would put it, in the past half-century. In 1958, however, William Kailer Dunn made a study of textbooks through this long-ago period and spotted a trend: "The readers used in the colonies prior to 1775 devoted 85% of the space to religion and 8% to morals; those between 1775 and 1825, 22% to religion and 28% to morals; those between 1825 and 1875, 7.5% to religion and 23% to morals; and those between 1875 and 1915, only 1.5% to religion and 7% to morals." By the time of the Civil War, says Dunn, "there was little in the textbook content . . . to give the public school child an understanding of natural theology, and even less of Christianity itself." Not that public schools owed normative theology to children or had a right to impose it. But the conventional believers feared that it was disappearing from its place in the American story as a whole. And critics of the public schools as institutions forced to be secular today have to invent a particular religious past for them that did not exist, at least not on this model.[8]

Who *was* chiefly responsible for the decline of religion in the moral discourse of the early public school texts? Neither secular humanists, conspirators, liberals, ideologues, nor indifferentists are to be credited or blamed for this change. Here was an early instance of group rivalry on a wide scale, this time motivated by religion. Early on, in their jealousy, the sects or denominations blunted one another's efforts as well as those of the would-be generalists like Horace Mann. Glenn notes that efforts to fill the consequent void produced an alternative religious ethos. His conclusion, developed in ironic tones, is appropriate:

> Although explicit religious instruction was increasingly removed from the common school, largely in an attempt to enroll and thus to assimilate the children of Catholic immigrants, *the mission of the school itself became more than less truly "religious" over this period.*
>
> The common school and the vision of American life that it embodied came to be vested with a religious seriousness and exaltation. It became the core institution of American society, the definer of meanings, and

the only way to higher life—spiritually as well as materially—for generations of immigrant and native-born children alike. In close alliance with but never subordinate to the Protestant churches, the common school occupied a "sacred space" where its mission was beyond debate and where to question it was a kind of blasphemy.[9]

Why, it may reasonably be asked, was this use of "sacred space" by the public school tolerated back then by so many citizens who were not Catholic and affirmed by the many Protestant sects that did not set up alternative schools? At the same time, why was it condoned by those indifferent or hostile to religion? Glenn argues that the subversion of both secular and sectarian outlooks by the religious-appearing moralism of Mann and his colleagues resulted from the fact that "in Horace Mann's day, the moral objectives of the school were essentially congruent with those of the public, but this is no longer the case." Glenn continues:

> Mann drew upon a consensus about right and wrong that, as he often pointed out, was largely independent of the diverse religious convictions of the times . . .
> This consensus on the moral content of education no longer exists. The values most strongly stressed in public schools and, even more significantly, those ignored or subtly denigrated are in many cases matters over which Americans divide more clearly than over any theological issue.[10]

There we leave Glenn, who made no secret of his own agenda. He was eager to suggest that, following examples from the past, the United States should permit ventures like voucher systems to encourage parental choice among schools, including religious schools, for their children. Only such approaches were equitable for certain families, those families who were trying to prevent their children from being indoctrinated with values that they regarded as offensive or inadequate.

Depictions of Sameness in School Texts

To say that school leaders and writers of textbooks aspired to express the values shared by the public a century and more ago inspires the question: Which public? What kind of public was represented by the images of sameness among the people and of oneness for the nation? Those who ask such questions today argue effectively that it was easier to find and elaborate a consensus longer ago because only one population element expressed itself in the texts and was represented in them. The textbooks from the nineteenth century survive. Whoever examines them will quickly find that they portrayed a homogeneous citizenry in command, one set of people idealized. Racial, religious, and other minorities were left out or were uniformly pictured in negative terms.

Ruth Miller Elson, a historian, examined the texts in a study published in 1964, before the current round of conflict and competition among the groups in America grew intense. Numerous studies have followed. Elson's observations and ascriptions, however, have stood the test of time and bear revisiting in our own more turbulent period. With scholarly thoroughness she explored over a thousand elementary school texts, choosing elementary school examples because she recognized that high school was the experience of the few in that period. Her *Guardians of Tradition,* written in a more innocent time, provides ammunition for any whose group departed from the mainstream or from the norm held up by the caste of textbook writers.[11]

Next to the Bible, we learn, these often overlooked school texts were the most widely read books in the United States. Unquestionably they influenced the shaping of attitudes:

> However ill qualified to do so, the authors of schoolbooks both created and solidified American traditions. Their choice of what they admired in the past and the present, and what they wished to preserve for the future, was likely to be the first formal evaluation of man and his works to which an American child was exposed. The schoolbooks delineated for him an idealized image both of himself and of the history that had produced the admired American type. They were a compendium of ideas popularly approved at the time, and they offer an excellent index of concepts considered "proper" for the nineteenth-century American.[12]

Elson drew on some of the better known of the authors to support this conclusion. One of them was the dictionary author Noah Webster, writing in 1810. He said he wanted one of his books used to instill into children's minds "the first rudiments of the language, some just ideas of religion, morals and domestic economy." Seven years earlier Mathew Carey in *The School of Wisdom, or, American Monitor* argued that just as European books were "calculated to impress on their youthful minds a prejudice in favor of the existing order of things," so should American texts inculcate "American principles."[13]

Most of these books were written by New Englanders, for whom American principles were New England principles and biases writ large. Wrote Elson: "The public school was the product of New England Puritanism, and it should occasion no surprise that textbook authors were a by-product." Even the pre–Civil War South had to accept, however grudgingly, the New England version of American principles, imported because there was not much of a southern textbook industry.[14]

The homogeneity of a United States to which children owed loyalty was a constant theme. One of the earliest books, published the year the Constitution was ratified, on the virtue of having a common national father, preached: "Begin with the infant in his cradle. Let the first word he lisps be Washington." In 1828 Jesse Hopkins in *The Patriot's Manual* quoted Daniel Webster's oration at Bunker Hill: "Let our object be, *our country, our whole country, and nothing but our country.*"[15]

Authors were selective about who made up the country and how they should be portrayed. Numerous texts assigned specified and limiting roles, for example, to women. Nathaniel Heaton in his reader *The Pleasing Library* looked into the new century in 1801 and spelled out terms that were replicated hundreds of times: "The modest virgin, the prudent wife, or the careful matron, are much more serviceable in life than petticoated philosophers, blustering heroines, or *virago* queens." There were few if any exceptions to such preachments.[16]

Racial and ethnic minorities received unfair, even brutal treatment at the hands of authors who belonged to only one set of people. Thus, says Elson, "very rarely is a Jew favorably mentioned." The fabled McGuffey readers, still advertised as beneficial today and cherished by Americans who would like a return to the good old days, in 1866 quoted Jean-Jacques Rousseau with favor: "The Jewish authors were incapable of the diction and strangers to the morality, contained in the gospel." It is true that later in the century a few moderating voices were heard. But for the most part old stereotypes about Jews and their supposed greed and love of money were perpetuated on these pages for children. Jews were not on the bottom rung in some texts, however. In 1831 A. T. Lowe, in his *Second-Class Book,* said of the Greeks that they were "more barefaced in their impositions than even the Jews."[17]

A whole hierarchy of peoples appeared above the lowest, the African Americans, and all of them were inferior to those of white Western European stock, who received the best grades. People descended from immigrants who had come from Scotland, Switzerland ("the only nation of the Old World who govern themselves"), England, France, and Germany were ranked far above those from Southern Europe, Latin America, China, and Japan.

The schoolbook authors were not interested so much in reinforcing racist attitudes and spelling out the deficiencies of others as they were in elevating the American norm as they defined it. Frederick Butler in his *Elements of Geography and History Combined,* published in 1825, asked the question anyone could have answered on the basis of all these texts: "Q. What is the national character of the United States? A. More elevated and refined than that of any nation on earth."[18]

Many authors spelled out the virtues of the nation that displayed such a character, and on many occasions they credited Christianity with having produced these virtues. Although American character was not yet fully formed, the writers could explain away the surviving flaws because development was still in process in the young nation. So there could be some criticisms, quickly mitigated: "A desire for gain is the ruling passion of the people of the United States. The avidity of becoming rich, however, does not render them avaricious." This theme was common in the second and third decades of the century.

The North, as suggested earlier, was superior to the South. "In New England the population is homogeneous and native,—the emigrant does not settle there,—the country is too full of people." This was a mid-century statement, written after New England had already begun to grow more heterogeneous with the arrival of immigrants from Ireland and the European continent. The South, though in more recent times nicknamed the "Bible Belt," was then regularly criticized for being irreligious. The new West was treated with special hope and respect. A McGuffey reader in 1853 quoted Dr. Daniel Drake on the "patriotism of Western literature": "Our literature cannot fail to be patriotic, and its patriotism will be American; composed of a love of country, mingled with an admiration for our political institutions . . . because the foreign influences, which dilute and vitiate this virtue in the extremities, can not reach the heart of the continent, where all that lives and moves is American . . . Hence a native of the West can be confided in as his country's hope."[19]

A close-up view of one people, the Irish, in a randomly chosen text reinforces all these images. Picture trying to sell a text like this one by Jedidiah Morse from 1784 to metropolitan American publics today. The father of Samuel F. B. Morse, the inventor of the telegraph, is himself remembered as the inventor of some brands of nativism. In his text, Morse blustered: "The Irish are represented as an ignorant, uncivilized, blundering sort of people; impatient of abuse and injury; implacable, and violent in their affections." Morse hurried then to say that the Irish must have a better side as well. They were "quick of apprehension, courteous to strangers and patient of hardships." A schoolteacher author discussing Irish peasants in 1837 observed that "many of the people are very poor, ignorant and wicked." Only a few texts designed to be used in Catholic schools were friendlier to this generally despised immigrant group.[20]

If textbook writers ranked nations, they were even more emphatic when they measured the character and quality of races. One expects to find racism, and does find it in abundance. The point here is not to show how evil the generations of common-school textbook writers were. Our own generation has few advantages over them except those that come with hindsight and the accident of having been born later. We revisit these texts simply to depict the ways in which representatives of a cultural center, the old establishment, were able to stamp images on young minds before anyone rose to represent minorities.

The core theme appeared in a section title from a work of 1866: "The White Race the Normal or Typical Race." The author urged the children: just look at the ideals already frozen in marble by ancient sculptors. From there the writers could look with regret or disdain on their inferiors. One text quoted Justice Joseph Story: "What can be more melancholy than [the American Indians'] history? By a law of nature they seem destined to a slow but sure extinction. Everywhere at the approach of the white man they fade away."[21] The Indian did often remain a "noble savage"; noble, indeed, but still a savage who was destined to disappear.

Lines like these appeared regularly: "The religion of nature, the light of revelation, and the pages of history, are combined in the proof, that God has ordered that nations shall become extinct, and that others shall take their places." The extinction theme was consistent. This eulogy for the Indian appeared already in an 1813 reader:

> His agonies at first seem to demand a tear from the eyes of humanity: but when we reflect; that the extinction of his race, and the progress of the arts which give rise to his distressing apprehensions, are for the increase of mankind, and for the promotion of the world's glory and happiness, that five hundred rational animals may enjoy life in plenty and comfort, where only one savage drags out a hungry existence, we shall be pleased with the perspective futurity.[22]

The African American, as noted, was still lower than the Indian, though the northern textbook writers criticized the institution of slavery that contributed to the low character of blacks. The fewer southern writers justified the slave system on economic terms. Most of these texts appeared during the institution of slavery, but authors north and south had little use for African Americans, be they slave or free. As early as 1789 a text titled *Elements of Geography and Astronomy* included statements that Negroes were "a brutish people, having little more of humanity but its form."[23] When it came to defining racial traits and not pointing to injustices, the Negroes fared least well, along with their African ancestors and counterparts. Thus in a text from 1817: "Africa has justly been called the country of monsters . . . Even man, in this quarter of the world exists in a state of lowest barbarism."[24]

Elson provides scores of references for every one I have cited here, but the profile is clear, emphatic, and easily replicable by anyone who assesses other artifacts of nineteenth-century popular culture issuing from the old majority. Of course, some revision of this elementary school canon had occurred before the twentieth century. But any visiting of the old texts should support the observation that the

touted consensus of olden nineteenth-century days was not something that can or should be available to twenty-first-century educa-
tors, patriots, or planners.

History is about change, and a dynamic nation like the United
States has moved beyond such roots as these. Yet before the change
came, there had been many opportunities for one set of people, those
favored to promote "sameness," to do so—at the expense of the integrity of the moral and practical lives of their compatriots.

Those who would revert to the era of the McGuffey readers and
who would seek norms and values from the ideal of sameness proposed in the generation of founders like John Jay must not have read
these texts carefully, at least not from the perspective of racial and
ethnic minorities. Those who admire the "universalizing" impulse of
pioneers of schooling like Horace Mann will find puzzling or offensive their notions that one set of people could set the standard of
core values for all. Isaiah Berlin has made an observation that can
serve as a warning:

> One belief, more than any other, is responsible for the slaughter of
> individuals on the altars of the great historical ideals—justice or prog-
> ress or the happiness of future generations, or the sacred mission or
> emancipation of a nation or race or class, or even liberty itself, which
> demands the sacrifice of individuals for the freedom of society. This is
> the belief that somewhere, in the past or in the future, in divine rev-
> elation or in the mind of an individual thinker, in the pronouncements
> of history or science, or in the simple heart of an uncorrupted good
> man, there is a final solution. This ancient faith rests on the conviction
> that all the positive values in which men have believed must, in the
> end, be compatible, and perhaps even entail one another.[25]

Even moderate critics of the textbook tradition tend to agree that
in fashioning the American stories for today, no single set of people
ought to do the interpreting for all the peoples. The trauma is not
only caused when one elite group gets to do all the telling, all the
shaping, but when any one group takes this role. "Sameness" had its
day at the expense of differences among the diverse nations, immigrants, and races in the developing United States. Yet on the highest
level, in the Supreme Court of the United States, one last effort was

made to enforce conformity, an instance that we shall next examine. The decision, made just before World War II, illustrates the problem of attempting to impose a legal solution to the question of the one and the many, especially when one of the many radically dissents.

CHAPTER FOUR

 Forcing One Story on the Many

The common good advances best when citizens freely choose the stories they tell and hear, the symbols to which they respond, and the practices they want to follow. Yet the temptation is always strong on the part of the powerful few to try to coerce the many groups into a single mold whenever persuasion fails. One camp in particular, those we are calling totalists, who persistently favor ways of life depicted in nineteenth-century textbooks, celebrate civil religion, and promote an ideology or creed for the whole nation, have to fall back on attempts at coercion when they otherwise fail to achieve any measure of submission to them. In turn, those we are calling tribalists, people who want to turn their own group into the be-all and end-all of existence in isolation, have to try to produce conformity to the norms of their group and impose standards on members based on these. At this moment, for the sake of the present argument, the totalists concern us most. It is important to pay attention to them because various groups have made dealing with the issues of past dominance a major item on their agenda.

The Right Idea in the Wrong Context

Some people of liberal disposition, when in crisis or when addressing particular problems, have been as ready as antiliberals to attempt to coerce concurrence both in opinion, which is not really possible, and in practice and profession, which is. An incident that occurred a century after the prime of Horace Mann, an event that took place on the eve of World War II, illustrates this. Public schools again, as so often in the republic, provided the arena for contention.

As American involvement in the war in Europe loomed, officials in some public school districts, in fits of patriotism, began to make compulsory the salute to the United States flag in their schools. The Minersville, Pennsylvania, school district was one of these. The children of a family named Gobitis, with their parents' support, said that they would "stand in respectful silence" but not "bow down to a graven image," an act forbidden to them by their beliefs as Jehovah's Witnesses. The flag was such an image. A legal case resulted. The local judge, who saw no "religious significance" in the salute to the flag, ruled that if the family saw such significance, their religious freedom should be respected. They did not have to salute.

The case, however, worked its way to the United States Supreme Court, where in 1940, to the surprise of many, the district and circuit courts that had defended the Gobitis children were overruled in an eight-to-one decision. Only Justice Harlan Fiske Stone dissented. Almost at once the Court began to be criticized by law professors and journalists. The Jesuit magazine *America* and the liberal Protestant *Christian Century* rarely agreed on anything, but here they concurred in their criticism of the Court for its suppression of religious dissent.

The majority opinion in *Minersville School District v. Gobitis* had been written by Justice Felix Frankfurter, then a liberal, who in most cases wanted to extend and assure citizens' rights. He was also Jewish, and was evidently concerned lest America lose what we might call its spiritual center and thus its resolve to oppose Nazism and fascism. Frankfurter declared his support for the school board. These civil authorities had "the right to awaken in the child's mind considerations as to the significance of the flag contrary to those implanted by the parent."

In the course of making this argument for coercion Frankfurter wrote words that are particularly relevant here. He spoke of traditions and symbols—I would connect these with stories—in a coercive context. The state had a right to exact a flag salute even from people who thought such an act idolatrous:

> The ultimate foundation of a free society is the binding tie of cohesive sentiment. Such a sentiment is fostered by all those agencies of the

mind and spirit which may serve to gather up the traditions of a people, transmit them from generation to generation, and thereby create that continuity of a treasured common life which constitutes a civilization. "We live by symbols."[1]

The immediate consequence of the Supreme Court ruling included many violent measures, acts, and enforcements by school and other authorities against Jehovah's Witness children. They suffered stigma, ostracism, and even physical abuse. Between 1940 and 1943 members of this never-popular sect found their lives and limbs threatened, thanks to government action.

So disturbing was the situation that a case similar to *Gobitis,* this time from West Virginia, also was eventually taken up by the United States Supreme Court. In June 1943, in *West Virginia State Board of Education v. Barnette,* by a six-to-three majority—Frankfurter in consternation among the dissenters—the Court ruled contrary to its own decision in *Gobitis* three years earlier. This time Justice Robert H. Jackson provided the memorable wording:

> To believe that patriotism will not flourish if patriotic ceremonies are voluntary and spontaneous instead of a compulsory routine is to make an unflattering estimate of the appeal of our institutions to free minds. We can have intellectual individualism and the rich cultural diversities that we owe to exceptional minds only at the price of occasional eccentricity and abnormal attitudes . . .
>
> If there is any fixed star in our constitutional constellation, it is that no official, high or petty, can prescribe what shall be orthodox in politics, nationalism, religion, or other matters of opinion or force citizens to confess by word or act their faith therein.[2]

Frankfurter had used many terms that implied coercion: he wanted the flag salute and similar impositions of symbols to be "compulsory," "exacted," "enforced," "required," "directed," "secured," "provided for," and "promoted" by public authorities, even at the expense of the religious freedom of irritant groups (I have changed a few of the Justice's verb forms). Justice Jackson, in contrast, wanted response to the symbols and traditions to be "voluntary and spontaneous instead of a compulsory routine." The substance of what Frankfurter wanted, but in the mode that Jackson supported, shows promise over fifty years later.

Frankfurter's biographer, H. N. Hirsch, thought Frankfurter had been demonstrating "his belief in the irrelevance of religious affiliation," at least in the conventional sense. Hirsch suggested that the Justice therefore was asking the Gobitis children "to make the same choice he himself had made—to accept the secular over the religious."

Both antagonistic justices agonized over their decisions, as their correspondence with Justice Harlan Stone revealed. Stone wrote that "the case is peculiarly one of the relative weight of imponderables and I cannot overcome the feeling that the Constitution tips the scale in favor of religion."[3]

Hirsch, by posing the term "religious affiliation" over against "the secular," may have drawn the line too sharply. In some respects and with more expansive definitions of religion in mind, one might say that Frankfurter was really proposing a different *kind* of sacred sanctioning, because the flag salute takes on at least quasi-religious connotations. From this point of view, it appears to be a prime and what would have been a universal symbol in civil religion on Jean-Jacques Rousseau's governmentally chartered model.

Frankfurter would not have called his resort to symbols religious, but he certainly lent weight to their ultimate value in the added comment, "We live by symbols." He picked up this language again in *Barnette*, though now he was defensive in dissent:

> We are told that symbolism is a dramatic but primitive way of communicating ideas. Symbolism is inescapable. Even the most sophisticated live by symbols . . . The significance of a symbol lies in what it represents. To reject the swastika does not imply rejection of the Cross . . . To deny the power to employ educational symbols is to say that the state's educational system may not stimulate the imagination because this may lead to unwise stimulation.[4]

Frankfurter was aware that some critics regarded his concern for symbolism to be almost obsessive. A full generation later, in 1964, he wrote to Alexander Bickel: "You probably have heard me quote Holmes's epigram, 'we live by symbols.' [My wife] Marion says I quote it so often that she wishes Holmes had never said it, but I said I quote it so often because it is so often applicable."[5]

The Shadow of Rousseau's Civil Religion

Shadows of Rousseau's kind of state-authorized and enforced "civil religion" or a "religion of the Republic" color Frankfurter's dicta as much as they have tinged later efforts to privilege Judeo-Christian or Christian America and establish places for its expression in the public sector. *Collectivism* may be too strong a word for this, or at least a misleading one, given its association with economic ideologies like Marxism. British philosopher Michael Oakeshott used it in a more limited sense:

> By the politics of collectivism I mean an understanding of government in which its proper office is believed to be the imposition upon its subjects of a single pattern of conduct, organizing all their activities in such a manner that they conform to this pattern. It understands governing as the activity of creating a "community" by determining a "common good" and enforcing conformity to it. And the "common good" concerned is not understood in terms of tolerating the activities and choices of the individuals who compose the society, but as a comprehensive pattern of conduct imposed on all subjects alike.

Oakeshott then spoke for the "modern" who flee into a situation where the collectivist pattern prevails:

> The collapse of the communal order has left me not eager to exploit the opportunities of individuality, but lost, unprotected, leaderless and homeless. I have been deprived of the sense of belonging to a community but I have neither the intellectual nor the material resources to set up my own . . . The only escape seems to be to a morality which recognizes a "common good" or a "communal good" to which my activity and that of all others is subordinated, and to an understanding of government as the custodian and promoter of this "common good."

Oakeshott perceived this approach as having emerged long ago in the character of the "godly prince" of the Reformation. Such a figure had still been limited in Martin Luther's understanding. The prince specifically was only to establish and protect an ecclesiastical order—definitely a premodern understanding.

The collectivist pattern of governing, thought Oakeshott, had been invented in John Calvin's Geneva. The Reformed Calvinist approach was no longer an extension of medieval communal ties effected through government. It was instead an adaptation in a polity that was made up of individuals, now in the modern sense. In Geneva we saw a pattern of life, "a 'common good,' from which no person was exempt." Now "every subject, in all his activities, became the agent of a government which demanded not only obedience and loyalty, but enthusiasm and gratitude."[6] Oakeshott and almost everyone else who pays attention to the subject observed the transport of this view to Puritan England and then saw it to be central to governing in Puritan New England, when it helped shape the American ethos.

Coercion and Persuasion Today

To pursue the Frankfurter agenda, as I think is important, while avoiding his resort to civil coercion, is to explore how "the binding tie of cohesive sentiment" can be effected by voluntary means to voluntarily accepted ends. How through persuasion and example alone can agencies of the mind and spirit "gather up the traditions," transmit them, and create a continuity of a common life? How can loyalty be efficiently stimulated to permit the symbols to work their effect?

George P. Fletcher provides some clues as he surveys the changed religious-legal scene. On the legal level, he observes that privilege and prejudices have still favored the heirs of the citizens of the "old stock" in the United States. Although between 1943 and 1990 the Court demonstrated a "deferential attitude toward compelling loyalties as an expression of respect for the religious and ethnic minorities" in today's America, Fletcher documents how in this period Jews, Muslims, Native Americans, and Scientologists "fared badly" and "received short shrift" in both the state and national Supreme Courts. His main point is to note that *Gobitis*, long thought to have been left forever behind when the Court shifted its reasoning and judgment in *Barnette*, is by no means dead. Justice Antonin Scalia most notably resurrected it in his reading of the law in *Department of Human Resources of Oregon v Smith*. Fletcher writes:

Scorned as a nadir of tolerance in American constitutional law, the case [*Gobitis*] has nevertheless recently risen from the dust of decaying court reports. In 1990 a majority of five on the Supreme Court, led by Justice Antonin Scalia, upheld an Oregon regulation that denied unemployment benefits to Indians fired for smoking peyote, even though their use of the "controlled substance" was exclusively for religious purposes.

. . . As Justice Scalia argues, relying on Justice Felix Frankfurter's words in *Gobitis:* "Conscientious scruples have not, in the course of the long struggle for religious toleration, relieved the individual from obedience to a general law not aimed at the promotion or restriction of religious beliefs."[7]

Needless to say, in the argument of this book, *Smith* has to be seen as unfair to a particular religion, to the conscience of citizens, and to the interpretation of the First Amendment that had helped ensure freedom for minorities for over half a century. The decision in Smith was a dangerous departure into religious coercion.

The religious groups of America reacted instantly to the Court's pronouncement, and massively protested. Congress quickly took notice of the protest with legislation that would help ensure religious freedom. It wanted to help provide a climate in which the common good that Frankfurter sought could be pursued, but only on voluntary lines. Each phrase from his paragraph in the *Gobitis* decision is to the point of the present controversy:

First, "the ultimate foundation of a free society": I do not know whether in a metaphysical sense free societies have or need ultimate foundations. Certainly American groups and individuals would not agree on how a society would determine whether it has such a need or what this basic underpinning would be. But whoever has seen the role that a search for such foundations has played in past crises may find it appropriate to speak of such elements in the life of a republic. We can leave the deeper layers of philosophy and political science on this point to those who want to debate the details of Frankfurter's rhetoric. Such debates would invigorate the republic.

Next, Frankfurter spoke of the "binding tie." Here one can project ways in which, on a voluntary basis, a republic as a society can begin to revisit elements of the common life. The ties in a civil association connect the factions, interests, sects, and other heterogeneous elements within it. If there is to be a society at all, its citizens will discern something like binding ties—even if they have to be relatively loose.

Third, Frankfurter spoke of "cohesive sentiment." With regard to the noun *sentiment,* we can assume that Frankfurter used his terms with conceptual propriety and care. In such a case, it is important to rescue the notion of sentiment from sentimentality and other purely emotional descriptions. There is much to strip away from the term, which is regularly misused. In the final chapter I shall elaborate on terms we must begin to define now. Thus the definition of *sentimental* in *Oxford English Dictionary* is "addicted to indulgence in superficial emotion; apt to be swayed by sentiment." And *sentimentality* is "affectation of sensibility, exaggerated insistence upon the claims of sentiment."

After having taken away the addiction, superficiality, swaying, affectation, and exaggeration we are left with *sentiment.* Its current meanings: "what one feels with regard to something; mental attitude (of approval or disapproval, etc.); an opinion or view as to what is right or agreeable . . . In wider sense: An opinion, view (e.g. on a question of fact or scientific truth)." Additional definitions refer to the fact that sentiment has usually been restricted to "those feelings which involve an intellectual element or are concerned with ideal objects." Add: "A thought or reflection coloured by or proceeding from emotion."

In other words, "cohesive sentiment" has included, along with the emotional, the mental elements: whatever had to do with opinions and views, as well as intellectual dimensions. Those who invoke the word in Frankfurter's context or as I use it here are less interested in measuring the palpitations of the heart at a pep rally and more in observing considered opinion in the context of emotional response.

In his opinion, the Supreme Court justice added the comment: "Such a sentiment is fostered by all those agencies of the mind and spirit . . ." For Frankfurter those agencies were the public elementary and high schools, but by extension they can include the interest groups, the aggregates and communities that reinforce identities. To this we can add the more intimate communities—the extended family, church, neighborhood, and the like. All collective agencies of mind and spirit are implied, though, of course, the dictum did not rule out private endeavors that serve civil ends.

Then Frankfurter mentioned precisely the elements that are at issue now in controversies over the one and the many, the whole civil association and the parts in the groups. He expected that the agencies "may serve to gather up the traditions of a people." Are there such traditions? Are there any that are not subjects of conflict today? Are there any on which any two groups can agree? If there are, can they be benign and acceptable to all? Do American "peoples" form "*a people*"?

Deferring for now attempts to address such questions, we notice next Frankfurter's hope that the agencies of mind and spirit might "transmit [these traditions] from generation to generation." Here comes more controversy: how can the present generation pass on a tradition that it does not fully possess or know or know well or agree upon? To rephrase the theme for present-day contentions, how can we transmit the traditions of the *many* peoples? To the above, add all the issues concerning the instrumentalities and media to be used for transmission. They, their value, and their current conditions are also disputed. What about the schools? Families? Television? Government agencies? The particular media of separate tribes?

Frankfurter hoped that the agencies would "create that continuity of a treasured common life which constitutes a civilization." Here the contemporary critics sharpen their critical knives and pose questions. Is not "continuity" precisely what has been disrupted in late modern America? Why consider a "treasure" a heritage that includes slavery, reservations, oppression, and abuse? Where, precisely, is the notion of the "common" that might connect the various peoples, their religious differences, their gender differences, the gulfs between their classes? And where is the "civilization" itself about which dreamers spoke fifty or more years ago?

Finally: "We live by symbols." Frankfurter, recall, was drawing upon a saying of Oliver Wendell Holmes, but he was also tapping into and anticipating an extensive and profound conversation and debate that will also demand treatment.

The Incommensurable Universes of Discourse

After mentioning an agenda as full of hazards as that one is, I bring up the biggest hurdle of all. Alasdair MacIntyre specializes in the history of ethics. He has devoted himself to the problem of carrying on moral discourse in contemporary pluralist society. In the course of his pilgrimage from and back to religious faith, he began a sustained critique of what he calls "the Enlightenment Project."

Referring thus to the great eighteenth-century movement of thought that so profoundly influenced the founders and founding of the United States, MacIntyre has observed the hold that its various rationalisms still have on the higher academy. He has also been aware that in recent decades significant thinkers have begun to call into question those modes of rationality and to relativize them. Critical of forms of liberalism that were dependent upon Enlightenment modes of conceiving the rational, he has applauded the way that liberals have at least tended not to romanticize national community. They countered talk of community with concerns of "subordinate voluntary associations."

In 1981 MacIntyre charted a new course for the debate over morals in political philosophy and the realities of government in *After Virtue*. Picture MacIntyre addressing the scene of "the one and the many" described here. He saw the "agencies of the mind and spirit" in the form of contentious interest groups. They argue about rights: to abortion, free speech, pornographic expression, public worship, resources, compensatory "affirmative action" to set old grievances right, homosexual expression, therapeutic programs for victims of abuse, and more.

Unfortunately, as MacIntyre heard them, most speech from these groups was unrelated to forms of reasoning congenial to Enlightenment thought or to natural law patterns of Aristotle's ancient Greece or to Thomas Aquinas's medieval Catholicism. Whoever naively employs anything like such modes of thought in speaking to these collectivities is quickly dismissed. When someone says, for example, "that is unjust" or "that is wrong," persons who speak from the interest groups usually say something that can be translated to "I have an emotional reaction against that kind of activity or assertion."

Critics in the spirit of MacIntyre's *After Virtue* must survey the scene of the communities and other groups that share life in a civil association like American society. Most of them would undoubtedly concur in his judgment that many citizens in their various competitive groups do inhabit incommensurable universes of discourse, universes that lack a basis of comparison and hence an ability to communicate. What assumptions, after all, does a pro-choice absolutist share with a pro-life absolutist, especially if both speak from the viewpoint of groups that repudiate even the notion of seeking a middle ground? How can one begin any communication about the rights of homosexuals or about a vindication of their ways of living among members of a community bonded specifically in order to oppose gay and lesbian styles and homosexual interest groups? How can a discussion be started between Indians who insist on treaty rights to land and waters claimed by non-Indians for centuries and those non-Indians who now "own" the land and waters? Is not the whole Frankfurter project doomed along with that of the Enlightenment? How can "the one and the many" or "the many and the many" do more than stumble in disarray and fail to address moral issues?

For MacIntyre, "the new dark ages . . . are already upon us." The barbarians "are not waiting beyond the frontiers; they have already been governing us for quite some time. And it is our lack of consciousness of this that constitutes part of our predicament." MacIntyre was using his book to sound the alarm, to warn us that our disrupted moral discourse has left us "already in a state so disastrous that there are no large remedies for it."

In his response to MacIntyre, Jeffrey Stout selected key themes that relate to our subject. Stout quoted MacIntyre's earlier book, *Short History of Ethics,* which pointedly describes our scene:

> It follows that we are liable to find two kinds of people in our society: those who speak from within one of these surviving moralities, and those who stand outside all of them. Between the adherents of rival moralities and between the adherents of one morality and the adherents of none there exists no court of appeal, no impersonal neutral standard. For those who speak from within a given morality, the connection between fact and valuation is established in virtue of the meanings of the words they use. To those who speak from without, those who speak from within appear merely to be uttering imperatives which express their own liking and their private choices.

MacIntyre later criticized himself for having included some leftover traces of modernist hope. More recently he turned more pessimistic: "The most striking feature of contemporary moral utterance is that so much of it is used to express disagreements." In the better older days Westerners could use Aristotelian and other frameworks to seek agreements on "man-as-he-could-be-if-he-realized-his-*telos*," man's goal and his fulfillment.

Stout agreed with much of MacIntyre's analysis but was both less nostalgic about the presumed good old Aristotelian days and less despairing about the present. He agreed that of course there is not complete agreement on the good; hence moral discourse is not easy. Agreement is unattainable. But Stout questioned whether it ever was; yet despite this disagreement through the ages, past societies were often productive. In part that was the case and can be so now because of the possibility of some "overlapping consensus" between those who inhabit what MacIntyre thought were simply incommensurable universes of discourse. Stout countered: "Most of us do agree on the essentials of what might be called the provisional *telos* of our society."

> Only very rarely, if ever, are human societies of any size and complexity united in perfect agreement on the common good. Ours certainly is not. But it is still possible for us to recognize the unfortunate effects of religious warfare, invent ways of talking and living with one another that make such effects less likely, *and tell stories to justify those ways to one another*, just as it is still possible for us to carry on with our moral reasoning in many other ways, relying throughout on agreements we do have. [Emphasis added.]

Stout listed some of these agreements, for starters. Of course, he continued, "we do not, in our public discourse, presuppose the existence of a specific sort of God, related to us and our land in a certain fashion. Nor do we share a single, essentially unitary canon of texts, exemplars, and models to serve as a rational constraint on what can count, for us, as justified or true in ethics."

All this did not mean, however, that MacIntyre was right when he argued that we cannot engage in rational moral disputation. Throughout, wrote Stout, "MacIntyre takes insufficient heed of what I have called a language's capacity for hermeneutical enrichment." Moral languages never have been and are not now static systems.[8]

I have introduced MacIntyre here as the most informed critic of the Enlightenment rationalism on which much of the argument for liberal republicanism was based—before the groups devoted to identity politics and interests came to reset the terms for moral and spiritual talk in the United States. A fleshing out of what Frankfurter alluded to in *Gobitis* can be a creative if partial address to MacIntyre, even as the notion of an "overlapping consensus" can be for others who are also seeking consensus at the base of liberal society.

The Commensurable Possibilities in Storytelling

Ironically, MacIntyre, the same philosopher who portrayed the collapse of one system and the jeopardy of its offspring, offered some positive and constructive approaches compatible with what Frankfurter hoped for. These also address, if they do not fully satisfy, the interests of groups that despair of the common good and insist on their own boundaries and claims.

Among these approaches are those devoted to the narrative self. Recall MacIntyre's summary, where he contended that "man is in his actions and practice, as well as in his fictions, essentially a storytelling animal . . . the key question for men is not about their own authorship; I can only answer the question 'What am I to do?' if I can answer the prior question 'Of what story or stories do I find myself a part?' We enter human society, that is, with one or more imputed characters—roles into which we have been drafted—and we have to learn what they are in order to be able to understand how others respond to us and how our responses to them are apt to be construed."

The human can in part choose to fabricate a self. But in many ways such a person has inherited some elements of an identity, a kind of prepackaged self in the context of which the person makes the choices. MacIntyre himself pays tribute for their formative influence to the intense groups and intimate communities that also later help complicate talk in a pluralist world. Thus he relates self to community: "I inherit from the past of my family, my city, my tribe, my nation, a variety of debts, inheritances, rightful expectations, and obligations. These constitute the given of my life, my moral starting point." Clearly, "I" am in some sort of continuity—Frankfurter hoped for us to discern that—with what I have been in my group. So MacIntyre must ask:

> In what does the unity of an individual life consist? The answer is that its unity is the unity of a narrative embodied in a single life. To ask

"What is the good for me?" is to ask how best I might live out that unity and bring it to completion. To ask "What is the good for man?" is to ask what all answers to the former question must have in common. But now it is important to emphasize that it is the systematic asking of these two questions and the attempt to answer them in deed as well as in word which provide the moral life with its unity. The unity of a human life is the unity of a narrative quest.[9]

This self is located in tradition, which for MacIntyre is not a traditionalist or backward-looking concept. Two of his respondents, Stephen Mulhall and Adam Swift, have summarized tradition in ways that again reveal how compatible his prefiguring is with what Frankfurter was enjoining:

> A tradition is constituted by a set of practices and is a mode of understanding their importance and worth; it is the medium by which such practices are shaped and transmitted across generations. Traditions may be primarily religious or moral (for example Catholicism or humanism), economic (for example a particular craft or profession, trade union or manufacturer), aesthetic (for example modes of literature or painting), or geographical (for example crystallising around the history and culture of a particular house, village or region).[10]

Note that MacIntyre did not include race, gender, ethnicity, class, or interest in the catalogs of those who are bearers of tradition. These elements usually are the contemporary bases for forming identity and are most contended for in pluralist republics today. Such a gross omission could mean that MacIntyre simply overlooked the obvious, the most visible and audible of the subgroups. That is not likely, because he was busy making a pessimistic case, and references to these subgroups would have helped confirm it.

More likely, he saw tradition borne along not by anything so generically broad as one's gender, race, or class. Instead, the traditions that form the narrative self are more particularized than those that the advocates of identity politics are spelling out. Yet one can take MacIntyre's concepts of the narrative self, tradition, and practices and relate them to the prescript of Felix Frankfurter, as we shall later, in the last part of this book.

However, this time around the advocates of the common good, if they are serious, will promote it through persuasion and seek voluntary responses, rejecting once and for all the coercion to which the Supreme Court justice resorted a half century before, the way of force that remains forever a temptation among those who are powerful or who would become so.

The Many

There was once, so Schopenhauer tells us, a colony of porcupines. They were wont to huddle together on a cold winter's day and, thus wrapped in communal warmth, escape being frozen. But, plagued with the pricks of each other's quills, they drew apart. And every time the desire for warmth brought them together again, the same calamity overtook them. Thus they remained, distracted between two misfortunes, able neither to tolerate nor to do without one another, until they discovered that when they stood at a certain distance from one another they could both delight in one another's individuality and enjoy one another's company. They did not attribute any metaphysical significance to this distance, nor did they imagine it to be an independent source of happiness, like finding a friend. They recognized it to be a relationship in terms not of substantive enjoyments but of contingent considerabilities that they must determine for themselves. Unknown to themselves, they had invented civil association.

Michael Oakeshott

CHAPTER FIVE

Plural Possessors, Single Intentions

Before Americans coined and began to use today's concept of "multiculturalism" to describe features of their manyness, they experimented with the concept of "pluralism" as a way of trying to do justice to the fact that their oneness contained many elements. Since in years to come diversity will continue to mark national life, citizens will struggle with both concepts. It will become evident that the notion of pluralism as it was invented after World War II applies well only to some aspects of civil existence in the United States. Too narrowing, too controlling to be always fair to the situation of the richer diversity apparent today, such pluralism deserves examination by those who would seek the common good in a new century.

Around the middle of this century, American leaders experimented with a model that focused on religion—Protestant, Catholic, Jewish, secularist—and not on ethnicity, race, gender, or other group designators that divide the nation today. And most citizens evidently welcomed the experiment, because it allowed them to be the "one nation, under God, indivisible" that Congress declared them to be in 1954, while it also began to recognize the enduring internal differences that had not fused in a great melting pot. It is impossible to understand today's conflicts without having some comprehension of this mid-passage through pluralism, and we shall spend some time tracing it.

Another way to put this theme: America was not always seen as John Jay had seen it, made up of a single people with only sameness in the plot of its story. In the middle of the twentieth century, citizens briefly improvised a way through which they could try to do more justice than before to the variety of peoples, while holding on to some notion of national coherence. Their experiment can be called *consensus pluralism*. Those who advocated it contended that there must be *some* philosophical *consensus* if the various groups in America were to coexist and interact. At the same time *some* recognition of *pluralism* was necessary, but it could not test the consensus too radically.

Pluralism as it emerged in discourse around 1950 was an effort by those who had generally represented sameness before but were now in teamwork with some of those who had not been included. They worked to incorporate diversity and still preserve national cohesion. They wanted to achieve this at the least moral expense and with a minimal risk, lest a new model would lead to moral anarchy. Their own model was designed to suggest to formerly marginal minorities that they were regarded as equal participants in the center of American life, however limited in practice their realization of such equality might be in every case. The consensual pluralists did not take up the toughest issues, like race and gender, with which later generations have had to deal. To the mid-century leaders, religious differences appeared to be the great troublers of the peace. Therefore religious pluralism became their test case.

Defining the New Pluralism

Those who take for granted the term *pluralism* may be surprised to find that before the middle of this century it rarely showed up in American library indexes. When on rare occasions it did appear, the reference was to two main earlier definitions that were irrelevant to the public theme. First, the term referred to an arcane philosophical notion about "plurality of worlds." Second, in the works on metaphysics and in the book titles of thinkers like William James, pluralism was posed against monism as a way of speaking of the universe in philosophical terms.

Populist and political pluralism, however, began to show up in a coinage of the secularized Jewish philosopher Horace Kallen. In 1924 he had begun to speak of *cultural pluralism* as a way of preserving heritages while encouraging their civil interaction within a single republic. Through the efforts of thinkers like Kallen the term worked its way into currency and at mid-century first showed up in indexes such as the *Readers' Guide to Periodical Literature*.[1]

It might fairly be asked: why spend time with a stop-action camera focused on a passing experiment that lasted in pristine form for only a decade or two? The answer is complex but suggestive of many possibilities for understanding and dealing with issues in the present. For one thing, the still influential senior generation in America and the nostalgic juniors today project focused and vivid images of this postwar period. For many those years have become "the good old days." From that time many measure the values concerning national consensus, moral absolutes, patriotism and loyalty, family values, cultural norms, and the like.

Second, the sudden rise and fall of this model of consensus pluralism shows that citizens had not found—as they have not yet found and may never find—permanently satisfying ways to connect "the one and the many" in American life. Studying past attempts to do so illumines present efforts and contentions. So pluralism becomes the focus by which one is readied to deal with ever more contentious heterogeneity.

My own involvement with the term goes back to a reading of the *Christian Century* in 1951. A cover headline of that magazine became one of the early references to a modern use of the term in the *Readers' Guide to Periodical Literature*. The editorial heading read "Pluralism— National Menace."[2] It happened to introduce an anti-Catholic editorial, but it could as well have been an anti-Zionist one.

The *Christian Century* editors at that time still favored their own image of sameness, an image that fused latter-day Protestant and late-in-the-day Enlightenment beliefs about the meshing of religion and reason, churchly and civil power, and the projection of one people's ideals onto others. The editors were not racist; in fact they pioneered among white Protestants in promoting civil rights and racial integration. But they wanted African Americans to be integrated into the white America that these editors best knew. They also expected Jews to be, as they might have said, "just like us." Such liberal Protestants measured the worth and character of the various peoples in America by the degree to which these could be assimilated to old liberal Protestant ways.

By the time I joined the staff in 1956 the magazine's traditional anti-Catholicism remained only as a subtheme. It did not wholly disappear until the Second Vatican Council between 1962 and 1965. Its old anti-Zionism, still vigorous in editorials written at the birth of Israel in 1948, had begun to be replaced by a theme of "balance" in Middle Eastern affairs that was unsatisfying to all sides. But overall, the appreciation of pluralism within the United States was growing, and in qualified ways it had come to dominate the magazine's editorial positions even as the *Century* extended its influence to propagate what I am calling consensus pluralism.

Something similar happened a few years later in respect to pluralism in the case of Catholicism. That change is easy to document because in 1964–65, through actions promoted by Americans at the Second Vatican Council, the Catholic church altered its positions on religious freedom and pluralism. Most Jews, of course, found pluralism to be advantageous and worked to advance it even as their leaders welcomed new opportunities to contribute to consensus.

The suddenness of such changes suggests why it is dangerous to type sets of citizens as being permanently locked in one or another position vis-à-vis sameness and pluralism. The nation is too kinetic, its forces are too fluid, the minds of its citizens are too full of ambiguity, and its recent historical record is too full of changes for us to suggest that there can be no possibilities for future experiment.

Pluralism in the Sociology of Religion

From these early references it can be seen that through the 1950s and into the 1960s the term *pluralism* found favor chiefly among analysts who concentrated not on racial, ethnic, class, or gender differences but on the varieties of religions in America. In his decisive book *Protestant, Catholic, Jew,* Will Herberg argued that essentially three religious family groups represented three ways in which citizens found their identities in the United States.[3] Yet ironically and also positively, he saw that the three essentially supported a single consensus. He saw the product to be a kind of religion of the "American Way of Life."

The consensus pluralism noted by Herberg was not confined to the pages of books. It was realized in hundreds of campus "Religious Emphasis Weeks" and thousands of local forums during Brotherhood Weeks. In most cases the Protestant-Catholic-Jew triad reflected broad public sentiment and for a time provided a standard model, though the Eastern Orthodox Christians might grumble a bit about their exclusion. Muslims were still too few to be reckoned with.

Herberg did not differentiate much *within* these three giant groups. He and most of his colleagues hardly noted that forms of Protestantism with which he was less familiar, movements called fundamentalist, Pentecostal, or evangelical, provided for millions of citizens a separate base for identity, locus for loyalty, matrix for values, or source of power. These movements differed from and often opposed what was not yet named mainstream or mainline Protestantism, about which Herberg was most knowledgeable. He also included virtually no depictions of African-American versus European-American Protestant tendencies, portrayals that came to be common only a decade later.

From reading Herberg and his portrayal of Americans self-identified as Catholics, one could hardly have sensed that Catholicism behind its façade was divided into an enduring mélange of ethnic factions. If there was protest from within against the homogenized picture of American Catholicism in 1955, it must have been muted, or at least Herberg did not notice it. The profound internal differences were not to be exposed to non-Catholic view until the 1960s, the time of the Second Vatican Council and a new scholarly emphasis on ethnicity.

Some signs of change came early in the 1960s. Herberg himself took a new turn and identified with a neoconservative subcluster when he became religion editor of William F. Buckley's *National Review*. And Gerhard Lenski wrote *The Religious Factor*, discovering and defining in it what strikes anyone today as being obvious: that there was no single Protestantism.[4] At the very least, as far as the expression of communal depth was concerned, African-American Protestantism was in many ways a separate reality. Given this observation, America was, then, a complex of a four-faith pluralism.

The Historians and Consensus

The case of historians themselves provides one way to grasp a sense of cultural change. In the present instance: during the 1960s the prevailing schools of social historians began to devote themselves to narratives of conflict in the American past. In the eyes of these revisionists, most of their immediate predecessors belonged to a school they called consensus history. These were criticized for having all too willingly provided overly neat images of the American past, images most useful for waging ideological conflict with international communism during the Cold War. Such historians were faulted for having homogenized the American past, having downplayed the nation's moral flaws, and having minimized the stories of slavery, the effects of reservation policies on Indians, past and current class struggles, and ongoing racial tensions.

In 1975 Bernard Sternsher summarized the differences between the two schools in his *Consensus, Conflict, and American Historians,* a work that provides us with another reference book, as Herberg's did twenty years earlier.[5] Sternsher commented most extensively on the historian Louis Hartz on the liberal side and Daniel J. Boorstin on the conservative side among the consensus-minded historians. He first analyzed their works that dated from 1953 and 1955. In the final portion of the book he referred to New Left critiques of consensus, those that had been written by William Appleman Williams, Howard Zinn, Martin Duberman, and Barton J. Bernstein, in books dated between 1968 and 1970. They reflected an American academy very different from that of Hartz and Boorstin and company hardly more than a dozen years before.

It is remarkable that most of the groups that have received attention in the 1980s and 1990s do not represent what were the main issues for either the consensus- or conflict-minded historians of a decade earlier. Some of their debates had to do with "givenness" and sameness in American history. Others in a long catalog dealt with chronicles of Cold War domestic disputes and foreign policy battles; the role of ideology and nonideology at universities; the place of political parties; the exception to consensus that was the Civil War; capitalism, violence, the class system, and the like. Sternsher made no mention at all in 1975 of any camp of gender issues represented by feminists or homosexuals. Religion was fading as a problem for the consensus-minded.

Race, which, like gender, has subsequently come to be seen as a main establisher of difference among groups as they face others, received only a paragraph or two of notice.[6] Sternsher did take note of the new literature on ethnicity, but it was as yet unintegrated into the broader approaches to American historical writing. The ethnic emphasis was beginning to show up in textbooks, so the author did point in a new and right direction. Still, the scholarly world he described appears to be far removed from the later scene of conflict between the various groups as they vied with one another and against the concept of consensus or national unity. His depiction of this transitional moment provides a useful summary of trends:

> Since the publication of Nathan Glazer's and Daniel P. Moynihan's *Beyond the Melting Pot* in 1963, scores of new historical studies of immigrant ethnic groups and blacks, as well as reprints, have appeared and this surge has reached the classroom. The titles of three anthologies compiled for college students connote sympathetic concern for losers and resentment at the conduct of those who have defeated them: Melvin Steinfeld, *Cracks in the Melting Pot: Racism and Discrimination in American History* (1970); Thomas R. Frazier, *The Underside of American History: Other Readings* (1971), which considers Indians, immigrants, poor whites, blacks, and women; and Paul Jacobs, Saul Landau, and Eve Pell, *To Serve the Devil* (1971), which underlines the plight of Indians, blacks, Chicanos, Hawaiians, Japanese, Chinese, and Puerto Ricans.[7]

Two Kinds of Ethnic Life

Sternsher was right to associate the ethnic revival with the work of Moynihan and Glazer and others who followed them. But to understand the subsequent period, we have to make some distinctions. Ethnic groups, after all, had been vividly on the scene and resplendently different from one another in America for centuries—certainly having been more disparate than they had become by the 1960s and 1970s.

Note the distinctions between what I would label "Ethnicity A" and "Ethnicity B."[8] Ethnicity A is reflexive. People are simply "in" ethnic groups and give expression to their ethos. Ethnicity A is what America used to display so extravagantly. Jews back then talked Yiddish and lived in ghettos, not in suburbs, whence they later went to universities to read books about their ancestry and its faith. Ethnicity A is what America had when people of Central and Eastern European descent knew no recipes but their own, while others did not even know how to find their ethnic cafés. The guidebooks to ethnic dining had not yet appeared.

Ethnicity B is more of an academic expression of uprooted people who seek to locate themselves in vestigial and blurred traditions. It appears when rootless people in assimilated and mainstream cultures become anxious about their identity or become concerned about their potential loss of identity. Ethnicity B is what citizens capture and exploit, for example, if they are "one-eighth" members of a minority that makes its claim in or against the larger society. Ethnicity B often represents a search for power by members of one group against other contenders. It depends not on an influx of new immigrants but on the rediscovery or fabrication of an identity based on what is left of a people's traditions, now thinned, after the passage of generations.

To its successors and critics, the ethnic revival of the early 1960s after the years of the Protestant-Catholic-Jew-secularist pluralism seemed to resemble manufactured versions of the same undifferentiated American way. The new ethnicity was an often beautiful means of providing an element or more of identity for grandchildren of people who had had no trouble with their own. It began to provide a base for the political moves in legislatures or on campuses some years later.

Upon the arrival of Ethnicity B some Americans donned dashikis and had their hair cut Afro style, as their parents and grandparents had not. *Black Elk,* a poet's rendering of a Native American vision, became popular among non-Indians. Meanwhile Native Americans themselves recovered and articulated cultural visions of their own life that had been disdained or submerged, sometimes by force, in the past, when their grandparents had been moved to reservations. Now they could choose to be partially assimilated to "white" ways.

In many respects this Ethnicity B belonged more to what Ernest Gellner has called the decor of life than to its substance.[9] Not that it did not grow from and branch out into humanistic expressions. As vestiges of traditional cultures progressively disappeared and immigrant cultures eroded, it became credible for those who inherited any part of such cultures to make efforts to recover and revive them. Sometimes this retrieval could only be aesthetic or superficial, as in efforts at historic preservation or in the revitalizing of fading buildings whose plastic façades needed removal if authenticity was to be partly represented.

At other times in this period shattering events served to quicken more profound ethnic expression. When the very existence of the Jewish people was threatened (as was the case when Israel was almost defeated in 1973 and has been the case in the face of intermarriage between Jews and non-Jews), it became urgent for those so minded to rescue, retain, and project Jewish cultural artifacts. When it was discovered by Jewish leaders that power vacuums were developing while the touted national consensus or center did not hold, what had been decor got reexamined. Now it became part of the substantial dimension of Jewish culture, and it was mined for political power.

The dream of a realized pluralism coexisting with national consensus was tested but not destroyed by the ethnic revivals just described. People spoke of interfaith tensions but not of intergroup divisions that issued in mutually exclusive movements. While it lasted, the experiment provided the public and some of its more notable thinkers with opportunities to address the tensions. Since elements of that earlier style of pluralism remain, some of the experiments tried and lessons learned around mid-century become instructive in our more recent times of profound conflict.

The Problems and Gifts of Pluralism

Pluralism in a republic can be conceived of as a problem as much as a promised gift. It does make conceptualization of the common life difficult. It is easier to conceive of life in simple terms in Shi'ite Islamic Iran or the Sudan, or in the island nation of Japan, than it is in biethnic places like Northern Ireland and Canada. And conflicts involving only two groups of people are sadly easier to define than are tensions within diverse republics anywhere.

Philosophers and theologians in the time of consensus pluralism attempted to contribute to theories of the one and the many. They still were seeing religion as a main divider of peoples and their world views. The Catholic theologian John Courtney Murray, for instance, wrote in support of religious freedom. He considered it to be a necessary corollary of pluralism in a republic even before he and his colleagues helped get the Catholic bishops at Vatican II to go on record in support of such freedom. Murray stands as a mid-century advocate of pluralism.

As a theologian, however, with a self-confidence about his knowl-edge of God that many others lacked, the Jesuit famously averred that "religious pluralism is against the will of God." Then he went on realistically to remind readers that pluralism, however, "is the human condition; it is written into the script of history. It will not somehow marvelously cease to trouble the City.[10]

A parallel to the conceptual problem for Thomist theologians like Murray is an existential one for those with whom I would side. Some are Madisonian in their appreciation of the republican values of fac-tionalism. Madison argued that in respect to freedoms, a large repub-lic offered a case of "the more, the merrier" or at least "the more, the more free." Yet people of my commitment, while agreeing with Mad-ison, may also be advocates of ecumenism.

At the Second Vatican Council in 1964, whenever I tired of hearing four or five hours of Latin discourse in the morning, I would exit St. Peter's and then sit and drink coffee in the Via della Conciliazione with Joseph Lichten, an American Jewish observer. We would watch 2,300 purple-clad bishops emerge from the cathedral at lunchtime.

Over coffee one day Lichten asked how I could be *for* entente and concord among Christians but also *for* the survival and exercise of freedom on the part of many interests and factions and denomina-tions in the republic. We both recalled how James Madison had ar-gued that the security of a republic lay in the diversity and multi-plicity of sects, factions, and interests. Yet as a believer I was under mandates and guided by promises to seek the highest measure of Christian unity possible. Lichten asked: Would not the realization of any part of that ecumenical effort lead to a diminution of pluralism? Wouldn't it decrease the number of competitive and exclusive sects, just as it would create a larger bloc or tribe of Christians who could be a threat to smaller components in the republic, like the Jewish minority?

I daily assured Lichten that this time around the impulse to bring Christians together was not being exercised in a triumphalist or an-tagonistic spirit. Popes John XXIII and Paul VI plus the Protestant and Orthodox ecumenical leaders were embodying, exemplifying, and setting forth guarantees that Christian unity did not mean that the church would henceforth be better organized for crusades and inquisitions or for persecutions of minorities. But the historical rec-ord was not completely reassuring. Whoever wanted to live with both republicanism and Christian ecumenical and evangelistic drives would inevitably have to engage in a balancing act.

Back home in the United States, we heard daily reports of how, more and more, heterogeneity or pluralism was complicating the lives of the republic and the individual. Little wonder that many wearied of diversity and tried to create a homogeneous republic congenial to their own ideology. Meanwhile, many others resisted such systems of power and took refuge in absolutist and separatist subgroups. Lewis Coser and other sociologists who study the groupings of true believers point out how much easier it is to keep one's group together and energized if it can demonize the competitor or enemy. For such movements, leaders need a devil more than they need a god.[11]

Living agreeably with pluralism and enthusiastically with ecumenism could also breed indifference in a believing community. It has been pointed out that Christians were more easily motivated to undertake overseas missions in the past than now. Back then missions-minded Christians found it easy to fire up support for missionaries who told them how bad the Buddhists overseas were. It is harder to inspire them, however, when the one being fired up lives next door to a good Buddhist.

Often the ideologues, the demonizers, or the missionaries in their various groups will be recognized as having the most dogged commitments of anyone in a republic. "By God, at least they believe in *something*," mutters the awed observer who is weary of indifference. In the face of this, one may well argue that in fact it takes more dedication to sustain the dual commitments that go with genuine pluralist life than to have a single commitment and the obsessions that can come with it.

If pluralism is a problem for the republic and the individual, it is also a problem for those groups that share a polity. Indeed, the expressiveness or militancy of some racial, ethnic, religious, gendered, and class movements in the recent past is often born of impatience with pluralism. In some of its civil forms pluralism befuddles and infuriates particularists. They keep being included in the web of tolerances within a society, but they do not often feel that they are heard there. Too easily they are dismissed as one or another of the quaint luxuries that are allowed to survive but not to have a voice in the modern republic.

At other times the exclusivists become bewildered and infuriated because they sense they are getting no hearing at all. Until recently, for example, those who represented the gay in the closet or the member of a despised religious group belonged to this category. Still others are wary, lest by being truly accepted as partners, they will be tempted to move toward the presumed center of national life. In the process, their members may lose their identity. They may be lost to the subcommunity through the mixed marriages that follow acceptance. Or they may be blurred into society in general, having followed the choice to kick over the traces or having made the attempt to join a cosmopolitan association that rejects separatism.

The Lord's Song in a Pluralist Land

The thought of John Courtney Murray inspired such musings in the minds of many who thought about the future of particular groups in a republic. In 1964 the ethicist Paul Ramsey approached the issue from the opposite side. He preached on a root problem when he asked in an article title, "How Shall We Sing the Lord's Song in a Pluralistic Land?"[12]

Ramsey invoked a biblical allusion to ancient Israel. God's people wondered how they might stay together and worship in Babylon, the land of their exile. There, elders feared, their language would sound muffled, incomprehensible even to themselves. In another generation these exiles might intermarry with the daughters and sons of their captors. They would forget who they were and become bewildered.

These worries were real to Ramsey in his own "strange" (because more pluralist) nation. What some critics used to call "repressive tolerance," Ramsey feared, would lead other Americans to grant "the Lord's people" their time for singing the Lord's song and the place for their shrines—though not on public land. The larger society might treat any particular group with amusement or bemusement. It would then move on to watch another in the long list of American interest groups or else become concerned about other matters entirely.

A pluralist society might not kill dissenters with silence, but it could stifle their distinctiveness by accepting them prematurely and genially. To be healthy, a group needed to stand against many interests of the whole society, or even of rival groups. Of course, people with relativist perspectives might ask someone like Ramsey, "How do you know yours is the Lord's song?" and go on, not very poetically: "My

Lord is not your Lord. My Lord's song is not your Lord's song. Yet we are citizens and have to get along. We might even gain something valuable out of joining together."

One more question: how seriously should one take the claims of any particular chorus when so many alternative sets of singers advertise themselves as "the Lord's"?

Groups worry, then, that positive involvement with others in a pluralist society may weaken commitment to their own group. This is less likely to be the case in matters of racial and ethnic contact than in religious or ideological involvements, but it is a threat to leaders in all cases. As long as one occupies a tribal place on one side of a mountain and is "pluralistically ignorant," these problems do not arise. One can always hear portrayals of the evils of the other tribe but have no more contact with it than across battlefields during raids and forays. As long as one is in a ghetto and has no intimate involvement with others, it is easy to inspire conflict and prevent intermarriage or reject the entertainment of ideas uncongenial to one's own tribe. Where there is ignorance one can portray monsters at the edges of the moral map. Thus the cartographer Hartman Schedel long ago drew prototypes for those who reject unfamiliar elements in modern pluralist society. In 1493 at the edges of his own map of the world (following the practice of Gaius Julius Solinus [fl. A.D. 250]), he drew fanciful beings and wrote *haec incoluerunt monstra,* "here be monsters."[13]

If ignorance can create imaginary monsters, knowledge and interaction can potentially humanize "the other." Yet this knowledge can also "de-monsterize" the other and thus confuse one's own identity and blur the boundaries of one's group. That is why some tribes and subgroups in recent decades have insisted more strenuously than ever before that they must be separate, exclusive, untainted.

The moment we find groups being exclusivist about their place, their blood and soil, their interests, and even their ideas, we find problems for any who have notions of a common humanity or of the common good in a republic. And when, on the other hand, people do recognize the interchangeability of ideas and do encourage the interaction of groups, the leadership of movements bent on control of their own know that ties of loyalty can be weakened. They do not want to take the risk.

One who listens can make a good case that some of the intense exclusivism and some of the separatist claims by groups within pluralist societies have been exaggerated, and that this occurs for a clear reason. Leaders fear the diminishing of loyalty in groups that tolerate tolerance and that place a positive value on responsiveness and empathy. Statistics underscore the trend: ecumenical communions tend to decline, while most standoffish and aggressive ones prosper in a pluralist world. Positive interaction that does not produce indifferentism can be hard to sustain in large social movements, as their agents and their rivals well know.

The Legacy of Pluralism

One of the problems inherited from the period when moderate pluralism was the norm concerns the necessity and difficulty of rising above chaos and then starting and sustaining argument. A republic made up of many interests, if it seeks justice, must encourage argument. A classic statement of this issue also came from John Courtney Murray, who gathered his mid-century writings into a book, *We Hold These Truths,* in 1960. During those years he had discerned four major religious groups—Protestant, Catholic, Jew, and secularist—and then had worried about how they could participate in one republic.

Murray, whose Jesuit tradition stressed the value of the *disputatio,* believed that a republic thrived on argument. He contended that groups had to recognize some measure of consensus among themselves before there could be any true disagreements, disagreements being the basis of arguments. Otherwise, the contenders would turn out to be barbarians and not civil persons. They might think they were engaging in argument when they were really involved in confusion. Murray went on to say:

> As we discourse on public affairs, on the affairs of the commonwealth, and particularly on the problem of consensus, we inevitably have to move upward, as it were, into realms of some theoretical generality— into metaphysics, ethics, theology. This movement does not carry us into disagreement; for disagreement is not an easy thing to reach. Rather, we move into confusion. Among us there is a plurality of universes of discourse. These universes are incommensurable. And when they clash, the issue of agreement and disagreement tends to become irrelevant. The immediate situation is simply one of confusion.[14]

The sophisticated Jesuit, proposing his own reading of the "self-evident truths" of American life, did so more even than he always recognized on the basis of natural law, particularly as mediated through Catholicism. To non-Catholics or to any critics of natural law, however, such generalizing and universalizing proposals looked like one more form of particularism, and they could not build on it.

Incommensurable Universes of Discourse Revisited

The Murray critique that referred to "incommensurable universes of discourse" has been sharpened, as we have seen, in more recent times in another almost instantly classic analysis by Alasdair MacIntyre. His famed book title, *After Virtue,* was a kind of pun. Americans as he saw them were going "after virtue," craving a way to argue and pursue it. But chronologically, he mourned, they were living "after" the time when they could talk sensibly about virtue. Lacking a common philosophy, they had to reduce their viewpoints to emotion. For one group to say "abortion is wrong" meant, in the hearing of others, "we have an emotional reaction against abortions and do not want you to perform any." Argument therefore ended before it began, though conflict never ended.[15]

Even those who did not share MacIntyre's pessimism about groups that could not communicate or agree on norms often did agree that some of his portrayals were accurate. Americans in their religious, racial, ethnic, and gender subgroups did indeed come to live in those "incommensurable universes of discourse." They might as well have been expressing their emotions and preferences in different languages. The result: a Babel that would only grow more confusing as group tensions continued to unfold in the United States.

No doubt it had been easier to find measures of consensus in a past that had been dominated by both a Puritan-Reformed-Protestantism and a particular form of Enlightenment thought. By the time Murray wrote about pluralism, there may no longer have been any describable center in national life and thought. But there endured some traces of an ellipse with two poles. Citizens had once disagreed enough over what this common religious ethos and this philosophical bent meant to engage in a Civil War over their implications. But the people in the Union and the Confederacy presumably also understood better what they were fighting about than would citizens living in times of more chaotic pluralism.

While making numberless revisions and seeing many transformations, the people devoted to these two poles within the ellipse here exercised enduring power. The writers of textbooks, drafters of laws, agents of voluntary associations, and leaders of religious institutions drew on them. Reform causes, down through the civil rights movement near our own time, have drawn on both, despite their other differences. Reformers have often effected a loose kind of synthesis between the poles.

From the Enlightenment culture the liberal republic adopted the notion, first of all, that civil argument must assume some form of secular rationality as a basis for communication. You cannot expect others to comprehend and take seriously your offer to argue by starting with "Last night an angel came to me and imparted this truth, which I insist you accept." Or "The gods have spoken in this revelation, and you have to respond and use it alongside your own canon of revealed divine truths. You may even have to let it displace your own." Never.

Second, a civil society favored the notion that such a republic must relegate religions and philosophies to the private sphere. It must see them as matters of apparent indifference for the sake of tolerance and concord. And, finally, a republic must allow for and encourage extreme individualism and not make the "common good" the be-all and end-all of existence.[16]

From the biblical tradition as embodied in Western Christianity and Judaism, meanwhile, this combined culture also promoted general but often strong notions that America was a chosen nation. Consequently it had a moral mission both among other nations and when administering its own affairs. Somehow it lived by a divine covenant and must be a steward of the gifts of the creator. And it must live responsibly "under God," a God who willed that the nation be just.

Mere, Utter, and Civil Pluralism

What must be apparent to anyone who reflects on pluralism and manyness is that any vital republic *must* reflect on them. The notion that one can simply accept pluralism as pluralism, in a pattern that I call *mere* pluralism, means that the observer does no more than remark on and accept the presence of the whole range of racial, ethnic, religious, gender, and class contentions. The act of merely accepting diversity in the makeup of republican life leaves a vacuum for others to fill.

Similarly what we may call *utter* pluralism, which refers to a drastic variety unaccompanied by any reflection on the part of the participants in or observers of the culture in question, tends to work against the notion of a civil society. A set of ground rules or some understood approach has to commend itself, if there is to be a third alternative, *civil* pluralism, one that represents what James Madison calls the "permanent and aggregate interests of the community."

The reality of diversity in a civil society forces one or more of several options on citizens who wish to move beyond mere or utter pluralism, beyond merely observing that there is variety and then letting the game be played by others. It makes clear that free people have the right and the obligation to choose their levels and kinds of commitments and the measures of what they might borrow from other groups or, through barter, might extend to them. Awareness of this reality reinforces the notion that both the general republic and the subgroups make bids for loyalty, spell out kinds of truths, and stipulate ground rules for coexistence and interaction.

Leadership in such a republic asks for people to consider how they and their values cohere and how they are mediated. But still another question inherited from the period of experimental pluralism within consensus is one that has come to be urgent: how do the groups themselves coexist, and how do they make contributions to the common good? The examples of Lebanon and Bosnia, among others, alert many to the dangers of tribalism unchecked by republicanism. The failure of the Soviet Union and similar regimes illustrates that authority is incapable of suppressing difference and diverse commitments when totalism prevails.

What is sought is a means of doing some justice in a new situation to the *unum* and the *plures,* to the common good and the particular groupings and interests. This at a time when advocates of each tempt partisans to choose and make a total commitment to one or the other.

A Positive Role for Acquiescence

Such a pursuit of efforts to do justice to both the one and the many, the whole and the parts, the civil association and the voluntary associations, has to begin with fresh motivations and reconceptions. Nicholas Rescher has indicated one approach worth exploring, while offering his own critique of the enduring search for consensus. His philosophical language is necessarily somewhat abstract and compressed, but it will reward the reader who is patient with its demands. And his conclusion figures into what follows in later chapters here.

Rescher listened to two kinds of voices. He heard the consensualists saying, in effect, "Do whatever is needed to avert discord. Work always and everywhere for consensus." Rescher posed this over against the pluralists and sided with them, as I do. The pluralists urge, "Accept the inevitability of dissensus in a complex and imperfect world." Then they strive to make the world safe for disagreement and to keep the processes and procedures tolerable and, one hopes, productive.

Rescher pictures four main reactions to pluralism. He calls them skepticism, syncretism, "indifferentist relativism," and "perspectival rationalism or contextualism." Skepticism and syncretism are the easiest to grasp but are of least concern to us here. They urge: either accept *no* alternatives in the search for truth or accept *all* of them. Practically they amount to the same result, a kind of "God's eye" view of reality that is not of much use to any human.[17]

More relevant for Rescher and for us is the third choice, indifferentist relativism, which argues that "only one alternative should be accepted."[18] But such a choice results not from rational cogency but from taste, personal inclination, or, in the context of this book, from the social traditions of the groups to which one chooses to belong. More can be said for this alternative, since it need not run counter to efforts to make some rational claims and justifications in a republic.

Rescher, however, argues as do I for what he calls contextualism or perspectival rationalism. The contexts for one's thought and endeavors in the social world, he says, can be (1) humanity as such; (2) culture, civilization, and tradition; (3) the transient practices and procedures adopted by parochial groups; and/or (4) one's personal situation (that is, character, disposition, idiosyncratic experience, and so forth).

At no level among these is choice entirely random or haphazard. It is "constrained and rationalized" by any number of factors in the "situational concreteness of a particular individual's particular experience," for example, the consequences of membership in a group or a community. Also, rational cogency *is* likely to be an element in any dialogue with members of other groups. "Nothing in perspectival pluralism as such compels us to see our cognitive commitments as *mere opinions*," says Rescher.[19]

One question is particularly relevant: "Is consensus required for a benign social order?" There is a negative side to any answer implying a "yes": consensus—sometimes forced, sometimes the result of mass delusion, and sometimes the result of rational decisions with unintended consequences—has certainly issued in malign tyrannies and totalitarianisms. On another, much milder front, consensus can be "an impediment to creativity and innovation . . . an invitation to mediocrity . . . a disincentive to productive effort." Rescher then adds a novel idea:

> What matters for social harmony is not that we agree with one another, but that each of us acquiesces in what the other is doing, that we "live and let live," so that we avoid letting our differences become a *casus belli* between us. ACQUIESCENCE is the key. And this is not a matter of *approbation,* but rather one of a mutual restraint which, even when disapproving and disagreeing, is willing (no doubt reluctantly) to "let things be," because the alternative—actual conflict or warfare—will lead to a situation that is still worse.

Rescher's choice of a story to illustrate his theme is memorable. In 1866, immediately after the Civil War, General Robert E. Lee of the defeated Confederacy had to testify before a Joint Committee on Reconstruction of the U.S. Congress—obviously, hostile territory. The victors pressed Lee to say whether the former Confederates agreed with the plans and programs of the victorious Union, which now meant the government in Washington. They also wanted to know whether the former Confederates were "friendly towards the government of the United States." In response, Lee was careful to say, "I believe they entirely *acquiesce* in the government."[20]

Rescher comments: "The difference between *acquiescence* and *agreement* cannot be shown much more clearly." Note that acquiescence is not really the same as *compromise*. It is a way of disagreeing but moving on in a "live-and-let-live" manner. It does not find a place between positions or a synthesis so much as a motive for moving on or avoiding the worst.

In sum, Rescher adds, consensus is "no more than one positive factor that has to be weighed on the scale along with many others." It is an "inherently limited good much like money." If consensus comes "at the right price," fine. But it does not merit unqualified approbation and is not the be-all and end-all of civil life.[21]

For all the efforts to find a halfway house between totalism and tribalism, between America conceived as one and the same or as made up of mutually exclusive interest or identity groups, the discovery and refinement of the notion of pluralism after the 1950s turned out to be unsatisfactory to many citizens at a certain stage.

They consequently came up with a new image of polity and practice. In it, the subgroups that made up the larger society had to all but reject even the concept of the one. In reality, as they saw it, the concept was a mask for privilege by a dominant elite. Their reaction also called them to distance themselves from one another, as the subgroups inside the model of pluralism had not done. Many were on the verge of proposing and venturing upon the scene of a more acutely disruptive way of describing the relations of the "one and the many."

As one aspect after another of presumed consensus disappeared from the 1960s through the 1980s, until encysted groups began to turn their backs on one another and to oppose the idea of any national common ground, it had not yet become acceptable or urgent enough for many citizens to suggest, in a spirit of conscious and reasoned acquiescence: "Let's get on with it." For the moment, for the decades, they stood apart in patterns of definition and with passions of militancy unanticipated at mid-century. They were inventing patterns and ways of life that challenged the older pluralism, and, with it, every idea of a grand narrative and any stories that might promote national cohesion or easy identification with the larger human family. In many zones of national life, tribalism prevailed.

CHAPTER SIX

The Exclusivists' Stories

Those who aspire to express oneness and those who guard their identities in their many groups could contribute to the common good if they were genuinely and regularly interactive. Instead they have in recent decades turned exclusivist and often belligerent. Americans have always been in conflict over the differences among the peoples who make up their nation. A country that has experienced the reality of slavery and racism, of reservations and repression, and of competing ideologies and interests cannot look on trends since the 1960s as wholly novel. The newer conflicts have to be seen against the background of many experiments with metaphors, some already mentioned: the nation of immigrants and interests as a melting pot, a salad bowl, a mosaic, and, in the middle of the twentieth century, as we have just seen, as a pluralist society.

In that more recent case, especially in the 1950s, the differences among mainly religious groups of citizens did not lead to profound societal disruption. One reason was the fact that most citizens were believed to share a measure of consensus on the important matters of national life. The more recent rejection of this form of pluralist society by militant and exclusive groups—I am now speaking of the period of the 1960s into the 1990s—has been described as a novel and overdue attempt to oppose dominance by old elites. These forceful groups made their way by attacking the real or presumed power and attitudes of the established privileged few.

Meanwhile those who did the rejecting expressed the hope that they might become ever more secure in their own identities. Each could then be more focused than before in their loyalty to fellow members of their group and more empowered in the whole society.

"The Collective Concrete Other"

Observing that isolated individuals lacked power and identity, some in these recent decades have insisted that citizens be seen chiefly in clumps and clusters. Nancy Fraser has contended that each group is a "collective concrete other" and that people should be encountered "less as unique individuals than as members of groups or collectivities with culturally specific identities, solidarities and forms of life."[1] Citizens then relate to one another through neither atomized individual nor universalist standards and norms. Fraser spoke in a period when the "other" took on specific roles in defining what or who is against my group. "Collective" stressed that people are seen in groups by people in groups. And "concrete" accents the awareness that the idea of a group or a people is not as compelling as the actual contact with or brush up against them.

For most such advocates, the collective concrete others make their appearance within a hierarchy of rights. Thus another advocate of identity politics, Iris Young, criticized the notion that every one of these collectivities has equal rights to protection and for expression. She and many with her have insisted that some groups are especially disadvantaged and are simply victims. Their members therefore deserve and must demand special treatment. Young wrote that "because there is no unsituated group-neutral point of view, the situation and experience of dominant groups tend to define the norms" that are promoted as universal in the present context. In the future, therefore, instead of settling for equal treatment, she thought that the currently disadvantaged need compensatory advantages, special rights.

Those who argue for this position would no doubt present their own list of these favored groups. The catalog proposed by Young is predictable, matching many of the categories already mentioned in connection with Gerda Lerner, Reinhold Niebuhr, and Harold Isaacs, but expanding. These include "women, blacks, Native Americans, Chicanos, Puerto Ricans and other Spanish-speaking Americans, Asian Americans, gay men, lesbians, working-class people, poor people, old people, and mentally and physically disabled people." Each of these, argued Young, would need "institutional mechanisms and public resources" to support the "self-organization of group members" and give them a sense of "collective empowerment." In this situation, "decision makers are obliged to show that they have taken these perspectives into consideration."

Iris Young thereupon called for something that many find hard to envision or are unready to welcome. She demanded a "public [that] must be constituted to decide which groups deserve specific representation in decision-making procedures."[2] Questions arise at once: Who educates and informs? Who convokes and inspires such a public to action? What are the rights of dissenters within that public? Further reservations come to mind: Would all the clusters of women, for instance, wish to be seen as part of one collective concrete other? Are all women in need of the supports Young describes, and are all willing to accept them?

Other examples: Who authentically and representatively speaks for the blacks: those who cluster around Justice Clarence Thomas and columnist Thomas Sowell on the right, around Minister Louis Farrakhan at an extreme, or the novelist Toni Morrison, or the Reverend Jesse Jackson? Do groups matriculate and get status only within such a complex of collectivities? Do any of them ever "graduate" out of it? What happens when these groups compete with one another in their appeal to rights? Who decides who is to be favored and supported? Will all people in a collectivity agree with all other members on what the issues are and how to relate to them? What about intermarriage: when a black marries a white or a working-class person marries a white-collar professional, what happens? Does the one newly related to a member of a collectivity acquire the rights, or does the one already in the group marry out of them?[3]

To raise such questions is not to dismiss the issues raised by Fraser and Young. But just as there are problems with overestimating the measure of consensus in America, so there are conundrums for those who celebrate dissensus of groups in the nation.

The Movements of the Groups

Keeping such questions in mind, we get on with it and observe what has happened. Consensual pluralism at mid-century had been marked by a simply envisioned matrix of religious groups. Succeeding and replacing this was a more complex but still informal polity, one that did not focus on religious groups.

With this new arrangement came the voices of a set of exclusive and often militant groups. They intended to disrupt any notion that citizens could trade on and work for any notion of a common good. All addresses to the common fabric, critics within the intense groups contended, would turn out to promote the interest of long dominant groups that wanted to hold onto or regain their power.

The newly realized pattern developed during the decades after 1965 or so. This is not the place to present a chronicle of this change and development.[4] Instead, where reflection on narrative, not narrative itself, is the concern, I shall only outline the main features relating to the "collective concrete other." For example, this new pattern was manifest in the militant groups of the mid-1960s whose leaders set out to counter the notion that all individual citizens could fit into a homogenized national whole or unity. A good instance is the perception by militant African Americans that the liberal notion of racial integration propounded by whites would not satisfy blacks. Thus when movements advocating racial integration were most favored during the then-fading civil rights movement, James Baldwin asked in the face of the structural situation: "Do I really *want* to be integrated into a burning house?" A new postintegrationist structure was needed, said many who responded in sympathy with Baldwin.[5]

The frustrations that came with failed policies of racial integration in the South and in American cities more generally led Malcolm X to pour fuel on the national "burning house." Instead of endeavors toward racial integration, there now came calls for separatism. Black radicals insisted on separate development by African Americans. They made little positive reference to the common good or the national whole.

At that moment, within the latter half of the 1960s, one often heard strident voices and read or heard many exclamations: "Black Power!" "Uhuru!" "Sisterhood is Powerful!" "Chicano Power!" "God is Red!" These began as rather individualized and cryptic cries by the initial and often most belligerent leaders. They knew that they would not get the attention of Americans by seconding the motion, adding a nuance, or suggesting a subtlety.

After the agitations there characteristically emerged leaders who possessed pedagogical and organizational skill. They were mentors and tutors who gave voice to a generalized belief that could help a group broaden its interest and constituency without losing its boundaries. Such belief, in the American instance, makes it possible to achieve the desired result. According to Neil Smelser, it identifies "the source of strain, attributes certain characteristics to this source, and specifies certain responses to the strain as possible or appropriate." These beliefs, says Smelser, could be voiced with hysteria or hostility or wishfulness; they could be norm-oriented or value-oriented.[6] And so they were, in various hands. Such growing and spreading generalized beliefs are seen by members of each group as belonging distinctively to it. At such a time members of movements focus, usually negatively, on others. These others are the different ones, the demonized alternatives.

The dissenters raised clenched fists against the "establishment." The military-industrial complex. White America. Straight America. Male chauvinist America. General Custer's America. The America of coopted potential allies. The people who made up these powers were seen as either corrupt leaders or meek and blind citizens. The ordinary people who refused to dissent or revolt, it was said, had been beguiled by "repressive tolerance" or capitalist corruption. They were described as people made captive by the numbing signals of mass media, enslaved by traditional creeds, afraid of a counterculture, or blighted by the seniority of those dominant in the larger society.

Usually a specific incident served as a catalyst for group organization. Thus in Greenwich Village in 1969, a police raid galvanized gay men to form a movement and reinforce their collective identity. Then the choice by President Richard Nixon in 1969 to bomb Cambodia as a step in prosecuting the war involving its neighbor, Vietnam, produced or enhanced temporarily coherent subgroupings of campus dissenters. Incidents involving the FBI and Native Americans at Wounded Knee on the Pine Ridge reservation in South Dakota in 1973 served to unite the American Indian Movement, giving it a clear enemy and helping to provide it with an agenda and a set of goals.

In line with a pattern described by Smelser, the groups next mobilized for action, even while bearing what he called the marks of "the onset of panic, the outbreak of hostility, or the beginning of agitation for reform or revolution. In this process of mobilization," he added, "the behavior of leaders is extremely important."[7] Thus the feminist groups moved into militancy when their leaders gave them plans for action. A Chicano manifesto appeared. Racial and ethnic subgroups made demands for studies programs, curricular changes, separate centers. Two African-American athletes at the 1968 Olympics refused to salute the American flag but stood with fists clenched, symbolizing their defiance of the American ethos as a whole. Caucuses in religious denominations insisted on quota systems, obstructed parliamentary procedure in meetings, and made demands for representation on all church councils. Tensions within Protestant-Catholic-Jewish circles and within each denomination grew fiercer than the conflicts among them had been just after mid-century.

Change in America occurs rapidly, and trends reverse themselves unpredictably. Since the mid-1960s some of the movements and groupings born a generation ago have already disappeared. Their moment passed. Some disintegrated into patterns of indiscipline, insignificance, or anarchy. (Some years ago there *was* a book with the oxymoronic title *Patterns of Anarchy*.) Others accommodated to a new culture. Some of the radicals moved to Wall Street, repudiating their earlier ways. The dashiki was abandoned for all but ceremonial occasions, and the business suit among those seeking the M.B.A. became a common uniform for those who earlier had intensely pursued interest-group life.

Most of the movements, however, entered a political arena where compromise or acquiescence ought to have a timely role, and have now come into a second stage. The leadership in all cases has aged, often having along the way become less focused, more resigned, and sometimes partly ready to deal with ambiguity. Some leaders have sputtered in frustration over failed intentions. Others have been more ready to seek mediating solutions to problems. Still others have been frozen or fossilized in postures that appear increasingly irrelevant to their successors and competitors.

Today the prefix *post-* often gets attached to various movements. One hears regularly of *postfeminism,* and David A. Hollinger has spoken at length of an emergent *Postethnic America.*[8] Leaders of feminist or ethnic movements do not like being thought of as growing somewhat obsolete, of course, but all causes do pass through phases, and these are not turning out to be exceptions. Many efforts to assert the continuing relevance of movements at their various stages often serve only to point to their growing irrelevance. Where the assertions are too defensive they often foreclose possibilities of conversation with others or listening to criticism of one's own movement.

It would be foolish to expect every mentioned subgroup to be content with following the same timetable or acquiring identical forms; each likes to think of itself as unique. Yet the comparativist finds some common features. Members of the various subgroups, moreover, whether or not they accept the precise observations of their own group's changes, give evidence that they see such stages and changes among their rivals or in the shifting strategies of the hierarchs, patriarchs, and establishments that they challenge.

Whether or not all groups follow similar patterns, it is obvious that history does not stop for any of them, dependent as they are for their status, power, and morale on the situations of other subgroups. So it is not easy for them to sit still, nor is it profitable for them to see themselves as sitting still. More important than asking about a group's stage is the question of how dynamic it is. If it is not dynamic, it will be figuratively frozen in amber, the relic of a past.

Elites in each group depend on popular expression by ordinary people within them. Whoever sets out to write a group's history is certain to find that the articulators of such subgroup identity typically are not, for example, the members of an African-American or Hispanic or Appalachian white underclass. Ordinary Hispanic-American citizens do not spontaneously and independently organize or vote. The Native Americans on reservations for a century have lacked power on their own to acquire more power. The leadership of most groups instead has tended to be made up of middle-class, well-educated, tenured, bestselling authors or others, securely employed, who try to keep in mind and represent the lower-class, less-educated, unemployed, or insecure fellow members of each of their groups.

The subcultures posed against one another, often in their self-definition and even more frequently in the eyes of those against whom they turn their rhetoric, turn out to be in classic terms Manichaean. Their members draw emphatic distinctions between "us" and "you" or "them." For those who believe in God, the absolute line is drawn between God and Satan; for Christians, between Christ and the Antichrist; for anyone, between good and evil, with no middle ground on which to negotiate differences. Trauma results.

The Crucial Role of Suffering and Victimhood

Crucial in every subgroup's account has been the theme of suffering on the part of its ancestors or its current members. Spokespersons among them make the claim that they have been exploited, victimized, and dominated by other groups. Usually the dominators are seen to be elites who claimed to speak for the good of the whole society. In all the relatively homogeneous sets of complaints and claims, leaders in the various groups have spoken or acted consistently on several themes. I listen especially for the religious dimension. This perspective is often overlooked in humanistic and political discourse, but it is especially revelatory.

First, they say, our subculture has been misused or suppressed by the dominators. Hence we have suffered trauma, so we must enjoy a privileged situation during recovery, if it ever comes.

Second, our subculture has values of its own. Born of our suffering, these are different from and superior to "yours," although you were long positioned to voice and display yours, while until recently we were not.

Third, because we have been depressed while our values have been neglected and suppressed, we seek liberation from suffering and must state its terms on our own. Our values need articulation, and we alone can offer it. Thus Black Theology, in its first articulations by its founders, insisted that God is black. God in the imagery of whites had to be painted over or replaced. In the work of the Nation of Islam and in the early expression of some Christian theologians, pioneer articulators insisted that not only could blacks alone do theology for African Americans. More than that: only African Americans could write theology, especially Christian theology, at all. In that reading, the gospel was always and only about liberation from suffering and oppression, and white America had always been on the side of the oppressors.

Early feminist theologians often similarly argued not only that one must be a woman to write theology for women, but that, given the patriarchy that had produced the suffering and victimization, only a woman could write theology at all, so vast and long and inclusive had been the power and abuse of the male establishment. Men could only misinterpret Jewish or Christian community insofar as women embodied it.

Representations of oppressed cultures had to be realized by the people in them. Thus for the casting of the play *Miss Saigon* in New York in 1993, it was insisted that the role of the heroine be played by someone of Asian descent, as had not been the case in the London cast. In part the argument was political and financial: Asian actors had too few chances to be in the spotlight and bring home a paycheck. But this claim was often enshrouded in a parallel but culturally more controversial one: only persons of Asian descent could get inside an Asian role; only they could be empathic enough to express the depths of Asianness in America because of the suffering endured by immigrants from across the Pacific. In this as in so many other cases, the message really came down to "move over" or "move out." Male patriarchs have ruled long enough and, it was reasoned, had done so from positions of such dominance that they could never be empathic with sufferers. They could never write effectively about black or women's or Asian imaginative literature—or even about such groups' rights or consciousness or history at all.

In many of these cases and for all these reasons, the other, the different, had to be demonized or marginalized. Thus, for example: the pre-Columbian Native Americans in these celebrations were romanticized for their presumed gentle way with nature, self, other, and the environment. The horrific accounts of what whites did to Indians documented the suffering induced by their interactions.

Yet in later, critical appraisals, there have been good reasons to present a realistic picture of victim peoples that has to include their nonromantic side, too. Many people who lived in what are today Central and South America were ritually killed by members of their own peoples. There are reports of Aztec rites occurring shortly before Columbus's time in which tens of thousands were sacrificed. The claim that all the Native Americans were always environmentally conscious and protective also hardly survives scrutiny.[9]

As the exploitative ways of those long dominant in the culture came to be called into question, a consistent range of critiques emerged. Life, argued the realists, is always messier than the defenders of diverse and mutually condemnatory cultures suggest. The strategies that advocate separation and exclusion on the part of various groups are in many ways ineffective and futile. It is hard to keep groups truly sealed off, thanks to mass media, mass higher education, the market, mixed marriages, cultural amnesia, self-hatred, and the setting of a premium on universalizing instruments of technology; "McWorld" is always there to counter "Jihad," as Benjamin Barber's book title puts it.[10] There is always more interaction than is commonly acknowledged among groups, more blurriness among them, more messiness of mixed imageries where boundaries of a group and others meet.

Other counterattacks against leaders of identity politics allege that groups often fabricate their heritage and credentials for the sake of advantage in contemporary involvements. Thus in a family where assimilation has been going on for generations, a person of one-eighth Jewish descent suddenly chooses to become fully a Jew. She changes the decor of her home and the practices that go on in it, even as she sends money to and prays for Israel. Some such Jews have the passion of new converts, which can be at odds with the compromising sagacity of the well-weathered participants in the Jewish tradition.

Politics versus Humanism in Group Relations

One of the more telling critiques separates the political power moves of the groups from their humanistic ideals. An attempt to gain power for otherwise unheard groups must create huge artificial clusters of subgroups and individuals if it is to be effective. But these *en masse* renderings cannot do justice to the diversities in each supergroup. The humanist needs close-up pictures of a phenomenon in order to discern the rich human varieties inside any tribe.

Such humanistic outreach recognizes that individuals, even alienated ones who choose isolation, are not describable apart from subcultures. There have been Catholic identity-group advocates who try to speak for the whole one-fourth of America that is self-identified as Catholic. Yet charismatic Catholics are quite distinct from anti-charismatic fellow believers. Catholics who respond to the liberal theologians Hans Küng and Rosemary Ruether are quite different from Catholics who align themselves with Pope John Paul II; this latter group may not even accord Catholic status to members of the liberal subcommunities within the church.

Thus also Thomas Merton, the Trappist monk, cannot be seen simply as a Catholic; he was a Trappist, and thus a member of a very distinct subgroup. Further, for some years he chose the isolation of the hermitage. Therefore his writings are not comprehensible apart from the context of Cistercianism and the community at the Abbey of Gethsemani in Kentucky, where his hermitage was both enclosed and set aside. Mystics may try to transcend ordinary boundaries of social existence, but their writings make best sense when they are *located*—as within Buddhism, say, or within the circle of those influenced by medieval spirituality or by ancient occult faiths.

Most identity politics defines groups too broadly and thus misses the texture of life and the profound interests of most people it tries to incorporate. The novelist who wants to deal with the experience of a second-generation family of migrants from Mexico to San Antonio will bewilder readers if he renders this family generically Hispanic. Yet in identity politics, *Hispanic* is supposed to cover this family and many other kinds of people from Mexico, Cuba, Puerto Rico, Central America, or Spain. What sense can one make of the San Antonio people if they are observed as belonging to the same community as the right-wing and wealthy Cuban exiles in Miami, who are also labeled Hispanic?

Doing Justice

The novelist needs to deal with the thickness of experience. So does the historian. The broad political categories invented to encompass a people not only did not help clarify anything; instead they created confusion. Both sets of people just mentioned may consent to be typed Hispanic over against European American for political reasons. But in the humanistic context, the people of Mexican and Cuban descent are hardly recognizable to or often recognized by each other.

The alternative close-up approach breaks down the massive political blocs in order to do justice to people as they were and are. It allows for more clarity of definition than do panoramic clustering visions of the good victim groups versus the bad oppressor groups. Different members of an aggrieved group in close-up view are seen as partly transcending their limits, even while they affirm many aspects of the larger group's existence.

Through the course of the years members of the groups in question are seen to be free to move in or out of them. The close-up approach invites others in, just as the bloc approach is forbidding. Upon entering a scene, one is beckoned to observe what can be noted on comparable levels among other peoples. For instance, in many aspects of life, the nineteenth-century Chinese laborer in the mines or on the railroads may have more in common with Indians on reservations or sharecropping blacks than with a wealthy Asian American, with whom they putatively share community.

If a goal of the humanities is to help the participant imagine what it is to be someone else, somewhere else, then the particularizing and idiographic approaches serve more honestly and are more helpful than those that homogenize. It will be difficult to locate someone socially or morally if he is merely described as an oppressor in power because he is a European male. This Euro-American may be an unemployed Finnish miner in the Upper Peninsula of Michigan, or the son of an Okie who fled Oklahoma in the drought, as John Steinbeck portrayed in *The Grapes of Wrath*. He may live in a Newport mansion, in a sod house as my grandparents did in Nebraska, or under a bridge. The purpose of reading about others is not always and only political, so the bloc approach is misleading.

Finally, in this context, group separatism, especially when its mode is exclusivist as opposed to enriching, does not allow for the growth of empathy and understanding on humanistic lines. On many campuses there have been debates about replacing a canon of Western literature or "subverting" it with literatures from outside the West. The participants in such debates have been at it so long that they have worn one another down and yet still are far from a solution or compromise. Here humanistic empathy has a role to play.

A case in point: my own historical inquiry has concentrated on the Abrahamic spheres of faith. Yet for decades I have been surrounded and influenced by colleagues who study African, Asian, and other religious contexts. My borrowing from them would not make me an expert in their worlds. So I would be listed as a student of the West, mainly of Europe and America. Such a listing, however, does not diminish my curiosity or my sense that I must learn from others to do some justice to them while enlarging my own perspective.

A story: it happened that my colleague Anthony Yu was translating a work from the Chinese often called *The Monkey*. In English the work turned out to be four volumes, *The Journey to the West*.[11] The lead characters include a monk and a monkey. Through my slow reading of volume one, I was bewildered by the characters, genre, context, and intent. When volume two appeared, the pace picked up. Still I was bemused by the novel's mix of what Westerners would call the sacred and the profane, the holy and the picaresque, the transcendent and the immanent, the grave and the humorous, the rational and the irrational, and the religious and the secular. All were jumbled and irreverently juxtaposed.

After a year or two of effort I was finally emboldened to say: "Anthony, *now* I think I've got it! *The Monkey* is the *Don Quixote* of the East." His canon-enlarging comment was designed to extend my education which, henceforth, I hope to continue: "Marty, you're halfway there. *Don Quixote* is *The Monkey* of the West!"

Pedagogically the awareness that grows from such encounters can be minimal and has limits for curriculum writers. One cannot in a lifetime read more than a sampling of all the great Asian and African and other literatures including those produced in the West. But even if one could read the whole canon of the West in the form of the Great Books and enhance it with readings of fiction and poetry termed classic, vast worlds of literature from everywhere would remain "out there." The intercultural, empathic exercise itself may matter as much as the substance of the books. And it is this exercise that is thwarted by group exclusivism.

I do not want to focus on knowledge, awareness, and empathy only in respect to literature; that to many can be seen as a luxury. The issues to which such literature points are also life-and-death matters. That evidences of the diversity of groups are important far beyond politics and the academic world is evident in any number of spheres. One illustration is the medical world. Decisions made concerning euthanasia, termination of treatment, or "do not resuscitate" orders at the end of life; concerning in vitro fertilization and abortion before or at the beginning of it; in respect to organ transplants, sexual matters, and approaches to physical suffering in between—all these are culturally conditioned. Infibulation, female circumcision, a practice of some of the cultures that are now represented in the American immigrant mix, has to be reckoned with by people who cross group boundaries. Lobbyists for children's causes have seen animal sacrifice among Haitian immigrant parents who practice Santería.

The conventional approaches in the model of consensual pluralism allowed for the respecting of minor differences between groups. But they tended to reduce all these interpretations of meaning and decision to a thin Western academic philosophical model. Thus medical ethicists were taught to work only with a short list of principles drawn from a canonical list of Western philosophers, typically from thinkers named Aristotle and Hippocrates, Mill and Kant, Ackerman and Rawls. Such students were prepared to deal with a philosophical or ethical quadrilateral of themes that were supposed to be applicable in all situations and groups: autonomy, justice, nonmalevolence, and beneficence. Yet in the thickness of American religious and cultural experience almost no patient families ever think in such terms. They want to know what their good doctor, their good minister, their good aunt, their good book, their good God, their good group determines to be right or wrong.

To mention this kind of situation in metropolitan America, where the medical researchers may be Jewish, the nursing staff Filipino, the surgeons Pakistani Muslims, and the psychiatrists Hindu, is to draw predictable yawns. Everyone knows how diverse is the population and how varied are the stories in complex cities. Mention it as I did in a small eastern Iowa city during a seminar on the subject, and the speaker may be greeted with suspicion: "Of course, that is how things are in places like Chicago or Detroit or New York, where you have all those Black Muslims and Iranian fundamentalists and Sikhs, but here . . ."

During subsequent minutes that day, the staffs from a half-dozen other small city hospitals began describing the cultural mix. Gypsies. Do you have Gypsies in the metropolises? You "do" nothing gynecological with Gypsies unless their queen is on hand to legitimate it. Have you Amish in Chicago? We have them here. They may defer medical treatment until something catastrophic occurs, but when one faces decisions, the company that Amish people keep is determinative. Down the road for some was Fairfield, Iowa, and its Transcendental Meditation University founded by devotees of the Maharishi Mehesh Yogi. The devotees may try to levitate and will certainly meditate their way through medical treatment.

The list kept expanding. Of course there were Christian Scientists and Jehovah's Witnesses, with their enclave approaches to things medical. Orthodox Jews lived in one of the larger cities. Where is the oldest mosque in America, the Muslim worshiping community with the longest lineage? In Cedar Rapids, Iowa. This is not the place, of course, to canvass the whole "Churches and Synagogues" section of the Iowa phone books, or to provide an ethnic census yearbook, but only to illustrate the practical significance of the concerns on which I have been reporting.

Here again, however, one must draw closer than before to subgroups and the enduring fixed center of the medical-ethical concern: the patient. She more likely than not is part of a group or subcommunity and is conscious of that. (I argue that everyone, including an old stock Anglo-Saxon, is part of a group, but that is not the present point.) Is *this* patient of a sect in Islam that opposes birth control? Is this a dissenting Catholic whose conscience does allow for an abortion? Will this Christian Scientist family bring in a terribly ill child for medical treatment at a certain stage? Should a court intervene temporarily to take a Jehovah's Witness child from its parents in order to give it a blood transfusion, and thus try to save its life?

Acts such as stereotyping, reading the books of groups' leadership, and letting the representatives of blocs speak may do injustice to the transcultural concerns on the one hand and the microinterests of subcommunities on another. Many of the people mentioned in these three paragraphs would be lumped together as European Americans by those in other groups. Is it helpful to cluster them as a single dominant enemy group?

The Literary Portrayal of Sufferers

Given the educated and elite characteristics of the leadership and the main followers in groups, one would expect to see the movements defined by a literature. Ellen Charry has often observed how "scriptural" and canonical groups become. She confines herself to the religious dimensions of groups, which are also defined by race and gender. Charry writes:

The last two decades [the 1970s and 1980s] witnessed the rise of re-

ligious movements grounded in interpretations of the histories of oppression of specific groups . . . From their inception all these movements have been practically oriented. Each aimed to expose the trauma
perpetrated against his/her community by the dominant ruling class
and to rectify wrongs . . . In most cases, the texts selected are those
which deal with the communal trauma being addressed by the critics.
Thus, trauma literature . . . is being interpreted by and for the community in what I will call privileged reading.[12]

Citing the work of David Bleich, Charry agrees "that reading contributes to self-enhancement by altering one's self-image or lifestyle
and facilitating greater psychological and social adaptability." And she
also concurs that there is a "social dimension of knowledge." This
meant that "the authority for such a perception lies only in the influence of that interpretive community which claims that perspective
which is its accepted way of making a sense of what it reads."[13]

In such reading, says Charry, "the individual self is a representative
of a community which shares interpretive strategies because it holds
a common fund of experience, knowledge, opinions, concerns, and
education." Interpretation thus goes on between "people who already
agree with one another."[14] For Charry and for us this means that
"membership in the community of the traumatized gives the community and its representative critics a singular claim on its own literature."

> The substance of this claim is that membership in the traumatized
> group provides individuals with the ethos by which to interpret and
> benefit from its literature. By ethos I mean the attitudes, values, opin-
> ions, outlook, and style of communication which characterize the com-
> munity. While individuality may be encouraged, in the work of privi-
> leged criticism, individual autonomy is structured within the limits of
> the hermeneutical framework agreed upon by the community.

Those engaged in privileged reading from within the interpretive
community find that the community's story of trauma "destroys the
chaos, isolation, and anomie which otherwise threaten." Such reading
"provides social location, meaning, and direction" and helps members
"to overcome the consequences of the trauma through personal transformation."[15] Black power. Chicano power. Sisterhood is powerful.
Slogans like these suggest sources for such personal transformation.

Religion definitely enters in. Charry contends that "critics from traumatized communities are using the literature produced by the experience of trauma to create normative structures establishing discrete and autonomous religious communities as comprehensive alternatives to mainline religions." Translation: They use stories to thicken their communities, distance themselves from others, and reject alternatives. A fair number of orthodox Christians of liberal persuasion have regarded many of these expressions as being incompatible with Christianity. Some women's groups, for example, have been described variously as "pagan," "goddess-worshiping," and the like. Interpretations arguing that *God is Red* or *God is Black* or *God is Only She* are also seen as deviations from mainstream religions and sometimes as repudiations of them, even if the reading of the stories and claims goes on within subcommunities of these religions.

In a brief *tour de force* of comparisons, Charry signaled that the interpretive subcommunities relate to their chosen texts the way ancient religious traditions did. Each reading has first an "ecclesiastical function," in which the subcommunity shapes the canon, while the canon reciprocally or circularly contributes to subcommunity formation. Second is a "hermeneutical and theological function," which scriptural readings also elicit in Buddhism, Islam, or Judaism. And there are homiletical, kerygmatic, and catechetical functions. That is: leaders interpret, theorize, preach, proclaim, and routinely teach the main lessons of these texts. They even issue a kind of invitation to make a decision of the sort one associates with evangelistic calls.

Pastoral functions are next, says Charry, featuring as they do "therapeutic guidance, encouragement, and succor in the transformation of personal identity." As in the case of classic religions, one finds even a set of apologetic functions: boundaries are placed around the privileged readers and the interpretive community. These lines are drawn against all other interpretive communities and against the whole national community. It is at this final boundary-setting stage that the alienating, exclusive character of many subcommunities becomes problematic.[16]

Thus from Charry's reading of Carol Christ's canon, *Diving Deep and Surfacing,* an anthology of feminist writers, we learn that the editor Christ, with women only in view, "counsels not the search for loving relationships but the rejection of men as the only way for women to protect themselves from the traumas of patriarchy." Also, "the relation between the feminist and the male world is a complete stand-off, and anger is the means of communication between them. Reconciliation is nowhere in sight," and "the male reader is left to ponder his loss." Carol Christ's canon thereupon counters that of Christianity: "God or goddess is self."[17]

As with feminist exclusivism and over-againstness, so with womanism, a particular form of African-American feminism. Charry notes that the theologian Delores Williams has proposed a canon of writers. She is less extreme than Carol Christ, and she allows some potential for transformation not only of the self but also of the other, yet, says Charry,

> Williams is not interested in helping white readers atone for their sins so that they can feel good about themselves again. She is interested in having her sisters experience the full strength of their moral fibre. Yet although the nonprivileged reader must stand at a distance, s/he is perhaps allowed to reflect on her/his own behavior and responses under the scrutiny of the privileged author and critic yet in the privacy of one's favorite reading chair.

In other words, there does not seem to be a way for the excluded *ever* to be included in the positive concerns of the traumatized community and the company of its interpreters.[18]

Still another sample instance is the canon of the theologian James Evans as it appears in still another anthology. He does not repudiate Christianity, webbed as it is into African-American experience, but, says Charry, he "appropriates its doctrines to the new canon of scripture to create a paratheology that mediates a coherent construction of African-American spirituality to both privileged and nonprivileged reader alike."[19] Evans at least opens a window on the privileged interpretive subcommunity. However, one could adduce many instances of African-American literature and canonical formation that have simply been exclusive and rejecting.[20]

Charry then raises several questions that one could easily enlarge to chapter or book length and that belong on the agenda here. First, does not this literature risk "*institutionalizing* the suffering in the name of trying to transform it"? The potential result: tribalism. Second, does not the set of functions of such literature "reinforce the prior polarization between the community and the outside world"? And is there not "also the psychological risk of institutionalizing the status of the victim"? Charry elaborates: "By suggesting that trauma is the only starting point for identity, might the critics not inadvertently assume or reinforce a victim mentality as the community's norm?"[21] My elaboration would ask: does not literature that is written out of the situation of trauma and is developed consistently on its basis, with an exclusivist and distancing aura, assign too much continuing power to the thrall of the victimizer, the oppressor? If so, does this do justice to the integrity of independently expressed life in all these communities?

Charry moves toward a couple of other suggestions. I would enlarge on her observation that if a literature has depth, clarity, passion, and the potential of being classic, it cannot be confined within the apologetically defined subcommunity. Much profound literature grows out of trauma, and all is deeply rooted in particulars. We all read Toni Morrison or Fyodor Dostoyevsky or Willa Cather, not to learn how to be a black woman or to learn the geography of Russia or the ethos of Cather's Nebraska or Santa Fe or Quebec, but to learn what it has been and what it is to be human somewhere else in another time in a community not our own.

And Charry offers a kind of theological postscript from the larger religious—in her specific case, Christian—context. Literatures that grow out of a subcommunity's traumas reject universal intentions or reconciliatory ideas. They leave behind major theological problems for Christians (or members of other traditional communities) who might be tempted to appropriate the central focus of these trauma literatures:

> The result of the canonization of these alternative scriptures is the substitution of biological, ethnic, and cultural identity for traditional faith in God. That the appropriateness of this decision is taken for granted is seen in the fact that no [one of these critics] discussed the implications of leaving traditional God-talk behind. But the decision is momentous, for to jettison even the hope that God calls us beyond the healing of our own pain is to end up with Feuerbach culturally contextualized . . .
>
> And is there not a possibility that in elevating the particularities of suffering, with its inevitable companion anger, to the center of religious

reflection, each community may develop an exclusive claim on its own suffering that inures it to the suffering of others and blinds rather than sensitizes it to its own complicity in that suffering?[22]

The concerns in the first of these two paragraphs involve theists in particular; those of the second have a bearing on pluralist civil communities and those who seek to spread reconciliatory words across boundaries of community, to stimulate empathy or sympathy in pursuit of the common good. They do not or need not attempt this at the expense of the stories that, like most profoundly humanistic ones, deal with sufferers and suffering within specific communities.

But if the concept of *community* is too intimate and its expression too profound to apply to interactions between most people and peoples, some other term has to be available to suggest measures of openness, interaction, and responsibility. The concept of *association*, I will contend, serves best.

CHAPTER SEVEN

Association over Community

Most of those who propose efforts for the common good describe the goal in terms of community, as in "national community." While they may do this with the best of intentions and will, and while some features of community offer much to a society, true national community is never to be realized. This does not mean, however, that mere individualism and group exclusivism are the only remaining alternatives. Through the centuries numbers of public philosophers have proposed an option that includes other valuable features of community and that can be realized. It also serves to connect individuals and groups in enduring if ever-changing ways. Although different thinkers have used different images and metaphors, they tend to come down to one idea: association.

Why Association, and Not Community?

I will argue that in both patterns, it is the dream of realizing various forms or sizes of community itself that has produced many of the current dissatisfactions and contributed to many problems. To begin, it must be recognized that true community is too intimate, too thick, too rich, and too demanding to be realized in something as public, broad, thin, and undifferentiated as a free and complex republic. At the same time and for the some of the same reasons, the word *community* suggests an unrealizable and artificial model for the larger racial, ethnic, religious, gender, class, and other interest groups in the United States. Each of these "proximal identification" groups has to embrace too many subgroups for the concept of community to serve well. These interest groups are too much the product of coalitions between people who need one another for some purposes, but who can find too little common ground for others, to be zones where community prospers.

Community has its place, but this place is more likely to be recognized or at least pursued on ideological or creedal levels in global connections. Among these are communities within Christianity, Judaism, or Islam whose members agree to extend expressions of loyalty to their belief systems, because these are occupied with issues of ultimate concern. Or community can be more easily and truly realized in small or local phenomena: family, clan, tribe, friendship circle, college, neighborhood, or caucus. Today we need to recover and emphasize a different word and concept that will attract aspirations and energies. *Association*, especially as in *civil association*, has come to be called upon once again by numbers of public philosophers in recent years to serve this purpose.

Association implies an entity that is looser and more dependent on voluntary impulses than community. It allows for the company of strangers who will or must seek common purposes but who do not share all the dimensions of life with these others. One can take smaller risks with association than with community but still have the proper yield for the purposes that the nation and the groups alike aspire to fulfill. Here I shall do some borrowing, citing major figures with a design to work a single effect: to point to a long tradition of models that can guide Americans beyond the present experience that has created such a trauma for civil life. Here as elsewhere in the book I risk what Montaigne in *On Physiognomy* feared: some may assert "that I have merely gathered here a bunch of other men's flowers, having furnished nothing of my own but the string to hold them together." But the design is intentional and integral to this project: to try to help bring about and exemplify a kind of conversation among disparate voices that converge on a single theme.

Of Porcupines and "Civil Association": A Theme from Michael Oakeshott

Let the concept of association, then, be connected with both the *unum* and the *plures*, the one and the many, the nation and the groups. An image from Arthur Schopenhauer, borrowed via Michael Oakeshott and familiar from our earlier epigraph, stimulates a vivid way to think of this choice of concepts. It may seem bizarre to compare American citizens to a pack of porcupines, but the observation that goes with the summoning of those creatures makes risk with such an image worth taking.

> There was once, so Schopenhauer tells us, a colony of porcupines. They were wont to huddle together on a cold winter's day and, thus wrapped in communal warmth, escape being frozen. But, plagued with the pricks of each other's quills, they drew apart. And every time the desire for warmth brought them together again, the same calamity overtook them. Thus they remained, distracted between two misfortunes, able neither to tolerate nor to do without one another, until they discovered that when they stood at a certain distance from one another they could both delight in one another's individuality and enjoy one another's company. They did not attribute any metaphysical significance to this distance, nor did they imagine it to be an independent source of happiness, like finding a friend. They recognized it to be a relationship in terms not of substantive enjoyments but of contingent considerabilities that they must determine for themselves. Unknown to themselves, they had invented civil association.

Schopenhauer spoke of moments like our own by bringing up that image of porcupines. So we adjust our metaphoric spectacles and look at their company. Times of crisis or trauma, he infers, are like the cold winter days, when the animals knew they had to be "wrapped in communal warmth." In the philosopher's terms, they were not able "to do without one another."[1] The historian of the recent past might document similar moments when Americans especially needed one another. Thus they together fought the World War II or faced an ideological and military enemy during the Cold War. Thus they also have gone through economic depressions and natural disasters while struggling with crises of values and moral breakdown.

In one of these crises, its encounter with the Shi'ite Islamic fundamentalist government in Iran in 1978–79, the United States, with its internal diversities and lack of ideological focus, appeared to be at a disadvantage. Some Americans immediately insisted that the United States was hampered because it could not mobilize people around a single clarified ideology or creed. Many citizens showed frustration, often with good cause, over moral relativism at home and its apparent negative consequences abroad.

One faction among the ideologues was resentful of those they described as secular humanists or liberals. Some were advocates on the religious right who spoke up for legislation that would privilege what it calls "Christian America." At other times in American history there have been serious championings of the notion that the government should provide an ideological framework of often quasi-religious cast to promote virtue and morality among citizens. In a typical promotion of such an idea, George Will once advocated a relation of the state to the spiritual and moral fabric under the title *Statecraft as Soulcraft*.[2]

These fabrications of course are satisfying in the eyes of their promoters. At least momentarily and superficially, they appear to others to have positive features. But on closer examination citizens have found themselves, like Schopenhauer's porcupines, to be "plagued," in "calamity," or suffering "misfortune." The record of governmentally coerced civil religions and ideologies anywhere in the world, or of privileged particular faiths in other nations throughout this century, has not been encouraging to such citizens, especially if they cherish the rights of dissenting minorities. A state overtly supportive of religion, it is often observed, also tends to corrupt religion.

Continuing the porcupine metaphor, these citizens, as individuals and especially in groups, similarly could not tolerate intimacy or enjoy too much proximity to each other. They were, in Oakeshott's retelling, "plagued with the pricks of each other's quills." Therefore, figuratively "they drew apart," not being able on such terms to "tolerate . . . one another." That is where the various groups were left, out in the cold and not together.

Oakeshott, we see, employed the example of the porcupines to depict civil association, a model that allows for both the need to "huddle together" and the occasion to "draw apart." These movements can serve as models for citizens in their national and subnational groupings and as individuals.

Citizens would do well to see their polity as an "association of associations," one that lacks what Oakeshott called metaphysical significance. Such a civil complex does not encourage them "to imagine [their situation] to be an independent source of happiness," like a friend or God or ultimates and absolutes. Such an association of associations does, however, allow citizens to choose to be "wrapped in communal warmth, [and to] escape being frozen." There may well be frequent times in the life of the nation when individuals and groups in special ways cannot "do without one another."

Contrary to the notions of those who promote the model of a great national community, the concept of civil association along with that of an association of associations does necessitate that the citizens and their groupings "stand at a certain distance from one another." But it dare not lead them to forget civil responsibility, as militant advocates of individualism or of exclusive groupings urge them to do. They may even enjoy aesthetic and emotional yields when they stand at that certain distance. Oakeshott was right to observe that they may then "both delight in one another's individuality and enjoy one another's company."

The Voluntary, Not the Coerced

In this image and proposal two main themes emerge. First, the elements of common life that *are* broadly realized dare not belong to the *coercive* aspects of national life. The porcupines choose their postures and positions by instinct and voluntary judgment, not under the whip of a commissar or master porcupine. The situations in which the porcupines find themselves are not prescribed by the government, whether the government acts on the basis of citizen or representative balloting, executive order, or judicial decision. Calamity, in fact, results when they are so prescribed.

Such elements of life together, however, may well be assets when realized in the *persuasive* dimensions of that same national life. They are at such times offered by articulate leaders. Some use the bully pulpits of government; others are rhetoricians, artists, and exemplars in the voluntary sector and in the private domain. Citizens then freely choose to accept or reject the messages and concepts. The assets are seen as "contingent considerabilities that they must determine for themselves," not as part of formal or legal "civil association."

Because we shall make much of the notion of an association of associations, we keep the instructive image of the dialectically active porcupines in mind. Then we can take a moment to see what their observer Oakeshott more formally proposed under the concept of civil association. His was a minimalist definition of government, in the end a bit too stringent and spartan for many tastes, including mine, especially when it comes to addressing the purposes described in the Preamble to the Constitution of the United States. But for what we might call the spiritual aspect of national life and the zone of the soul in groups, it has much to say. In Oakeshott's words:

> Civil associates may, at choice, enter into relationships of affection, of discourse, of gainful enterprise, or of playful engagement, but in respect of being civilly associated they cannot be either required or forbidden to do so; they are required only to subscribe to the conditions of *respublica* . . . In short, the civil condition and a state understood in terms of civil association postulates self-determined autonomous human beings seeking the satisfaction of their wants in self-chosen transactions with others of their kind.[3]

Oakeshott was mindful of the many "others of their kind" who promote affection, discourse, enterprise, engagement, and satisfaction in the *res publica*. He wrote in the United Kingdom but would have been especially made aware of these others in the United States, where they are especially organized, articulate, often exclusive, on occasion militant:

> Indeed, there is no end to the variety of the minorities of interest into which they [citizens] may circumstantially compose themselves or the collocations (sex, family, race, profession, hobby and so on) in terms of which they may from time to time recognize themselves.[4]

Oakeshott spoke elsewhere of other kinds of inventions in modern society such as "enterprise associations." These are purposive. They serve as means to ends. They are chosen by the individuals who make them up and who manage them in order to promote various programs. The civil association, in contrast, is not an association of focused purposes or precise wants but one of broadly accepted and acknowledged rules, code-named the complex of laws, *lex*. Its practice can be conceived in its entirety as the *res publica,* the public order, the republic. In this *res publica* citizens are capable of making a distinction, of drawing a line, between what belongs to the public or is compulsory and what belongs to the private or is voluntary.

It is this line that is relevant to our present topic and to the American scene. Oakeshott argued forcefully against the notion that the nation as civil association can be defined ideologically or creedally:

> If, for example, the common purpose in civil association is said to be the common . . . devotion to a set of religious beliefs which prescribe substantive conduct, then these are unquestionably substantive ends capable of being jointly pursued; but the force and meaning of the adjective "civil" is to seek. What is being identified [then] is . . . a religious community and we are left wondering why any [such] should be called *civil* association.

Later, although he himself was a religious person who was at home with Christian imagery, Oakeshott added, "Whatever the civil condition may be it is not the New Jerusalem or Grace Abounding." He did know what community in other circumstances could look like, and he spelled out some examples:

> Thus, the fraternity that gathered in the garden of Epicurus, the communities of early Christians joined in charity and in the expectation of a momentous event, a monastic order, a brotherhood of *illuminati*, the Moravian communities inspired and financed by Count Zinzendorf in eighteenth century England, settlements of simplelifers disenchanted with the squalor of urban existence, kibbutzim, Abodes of Love, Children of Light, fraternities joined in millenarian expectation, nudist colonies, or even persons associated in the enjoyment of a highly integrated communal life for its own sake; monks for the cowl.

Oakeshott seemed to regard some of these communities respectfully and good-humoredly. He did not see them as representing a difficult problem for accommodation by the republic when it is conceived as a civil association. Such accommodation "is well within the character of a state understood in the terms of *societas*." But the state could not itself be the kind of corporate association that took on the character of community. Oakeshott listed ten categories that we can flesh out: sex, family, race, profession, hobby, region, kinship, genes, or organic or so-called social integration.[5]

On today's American scene, we encounter the following communities or putative communities, among others. Sex: straight/gay, feminist/masculinist. Race and genes, region, relations and kinship: Euro-, Afro-, Native- Hispanic-, Asian-American, in the approximately six hundred self-selected variations citizens used to identify themselves in the "ethnic" category in the 1990 United States Census. Propinquity: rust belt/sun belt, urban/suburban. Profession (and class): knowledge class or new class/underclass. "Organic or so-called 'social' integration": Christian (by being born again)/everybody else. The variations within these categories are almost numberless in contemporary society. Each bids for attention.

An Association of Associations: The Legacy of Althusius

The participants in this associative model for a republic, while promoting the good of the whole society, find they must also be alert to affirmations of the integrity of the groups that make it up. My reference point for such a model has long been the work of Johannes Althusius (1557–1638). He was a Calvinist political scientist and a critic of Hobbes, to whose *Leviathan* he opposed his own interests in a pluralistic polity. Althusius came up with his own formula for the dialectic of powers. Association is again central for him:

> Politics is the art of associating men for the purpose of establishing, cultivating, and conserving social life among them. Whence it is called "symbiotics." The subject matter of politics is therefore association, in which the symbiotes pledge themselves to each other, by explicit or tacit agreement, to mutual communication of whatever is useful and necessary for the harmonious exercise of social life.

Althusius, with so many of these thinkers, distinguished between civil associations and those he called natural, or what others called organic or integral. His reference to the family is most clarifying:

> The private and natural symbiotic association is one in which married persons, blood relatives, and in-laws, in response to a natural affection and necessity, agree to a definite communication among themselves. Whence this individual, natural, necessary, economic, and domestic society is said to be contracted permanently among these symbiotic

allies of life, with the same boundaries of life itself. Therefore it is rightly called the most intense society, friendship, relationship, and union, the seedbed of every other symbiotic association. Whence these symbiotic allies are called relatives, kinsmen, and friends.

Althusius reflected the instincts and heritage of late medieval Europe. People then were used to thinking in terms of human rankings and orderings. So he piled up hierarchies of mediators between the individual and the republic. These included the *collegia,* the guilds or corporations, along with professional, ecclesiastical, and other associations, as well as the city, which is also a public. Then he too spoke of what I would call an association of associations: "The public association exists when many private associations are linked together for the purpose of establishing an inclusive political order. It can be called a community, an associated body, or the pre-eminent political association." As for this connecting: it can occur independently of a political unit such as a republic, a sovereignty. But ordinarily it will be located in what is here called a commonwealth. We read further:

> And these symbiotic associations as the first to develop can subsist by themselves even without a province or realm. However, as long as they are not united in the associated and symbiotic universal body of a province, commonwealth, or realm, they are deprived of many of the advantages and necessary supports of life. It is necessary, therefore, that the doctrine of the symbiotic life of families, kinship associations, collegia, cities, and provinces precede the doctrine of the realm or universal symbiotic association that arises from the former associations and is composed of them.[6]

In this connection we come across Althusius's notion of a republic as a *communitas communitatum,* a community of communities. A modern commentator, Robert Nisbet, calls this the author's all-important idea.[7] Equally important is the notion that the associations are in symbiotic relation to one another, the many, the *plures,* and the whole commonwealth, the *unum.*

Much of my argument here turns on this choice. The idea of *symbiotes* suggests relationships that cannot exist in the world of totalists and tribalists. Totalists envision that the central authority of the commonwealth should dominate. Tribalists envision that it will dominate but should not. They have little interest in the commonwealth. They have little investment in anything beyond their own tribe, their self-enclosed group, except when they need to make negative references.

Now, instead of the proposal that would see a commonwealth as a community of communities, we follow the connection implied by Althusius of an association of associations. This choice of association over community is not minor or arbitrary. It allows for distinctions among groups when they are in political modes, which means when they are seeking power and rights and justice. It is also appropriate when they embody traditions that are of interest for their literary, philosophical, and religious dimensions.

The large power clusters and groups on the scene of identity politics today do not serve well as communities, with all the implications of communion summoned by that term. To suggest that they do only confuses the scene. David Hollinger has been helpful here. In *Postethnic America* he speaks of an "ethno-racial pentagon," "a 'quintuple melting pot,'" replacing the 'triple melting pot' made famous by Will Herberg's book of 1955, *Protestant-Catholic-Jew*": "On application forms and questionnaires, individuals are routinely invited to declare themselves to be one of the following: Euro-American (or sometimes white), Asian American, African American, Hispanic (or sometimes Latino), and Indigenous Peoples (or sometimes Native Americans)."[8] Usually this pentagon appears complete with hyphens. But to what community, the complex citizen asks, do I belong, bearing my hyphen, as a Native-, African-, European-, Asian-, or Hispanic-American? Or as a feminist or masculinist or homosexual? As a member of the middle class, or an agent of a knowledge class or new class? As a mainstream Protestant or evangelical?

In all these cases I have good reason to be in an association with others. The communities to which I belong—my sorority or fellowship, college or congregation—that come close to providing intimacy, profound agreement, and communion may be parts of such an association. But the spokespersons of the interest groups and clusters in identity politics want the large groups *themselves* to be communities. They present these as thick, impenetrable, impervious to impulses from others, and incapable of receiving positive influences from those in other groups.

In summary, using the form of interaction Althusius proposes, and choosing one of two sets of concepts that provide for interacting, we speak of this republic as an association of associations, *not* a community of communities.

From Aristotle to Burke

Althusius, however, is not the only political philosopher who dealt with models of the one and the many. The search for metaphors and images goes back at least to Aristotle. When the *res publica* possesses all the defining power, as Aristotle thought it did in Plato's *Republic,* other powers are aborted. Over against such a situation, and more congenial to the argument of this book, is Aristotle's critique of Plato's monism. In the second book of the *Politics,* Aristotle, perhaps slightly overstating the case, sees Plato reducing everything in the *polis,* the political state, to a unity. No, says Aristotle, commenting on Socrates in Plato:

> The error of Socrates must be attributed to the false notion of unity from which he starts. Unity there should be, both of the family and of the state, but in some respects only. For there is a point at which a *polis,* by advancing in unity, will cease to be a *polis,* but will none the less come near to losing its essence, and will thus be a worse *polis.* It is as if you were to turn harmony into mere unison, or to reduce a theme to a single beat. The truth is that the *polis* is an aggregate of many members.

Again, Aristotle reinforces his point:

> Is it not obvious, that a state may at length attain such a degree of unity as to be no longer a state?—since the nature of a state is to be a plurality, and intending to greater unity, from being a state, it becomes a family, and from being a family, an individual; for the family may be said to be more one than the state, and the individual than the family. So that we ought not to attain this greatest unity even if we could, for it would be the destruction of the state.[9]

In today's America, the groups of the oppressed or those who claim, with or without good reason, to have been oppressed and distinctively victimized and who then express themselves as caucuses and coalitions, whether as movements to change curricula or ensure voting rights or whatever, are normally what Aristotle calls aggregates of many members—even aggregates of aggregates. Not communities of communities.

This can easily be illustrated. An African-American middle-class woman may suffer discrimination because of her race. She has reasons to participate in an aggregate with others to fight off discrimination. Although she cannot shed her skin color and genetic makeup, she may choose to link up with one as opposed to another of the African-American entities or racially mixed communities to find communion. She may thereupon choose for her spiritual communion to be in a community called the Nation of Islam or the National Baptist Convention or the racially mixed and once-racist Southern Baptist Convention. She may join the National Association for the Advancement of Colored People or the Chamber of Commerce. She may be a member of a Democratic caucus or may belong to the Justice Clarence Thomas fan club. Each may provide community or be a community, but taken together under the genus African American, they will be an association, loosely structured, containing many contrarinesses and disparate elements. So from Aristotle we might learn to speak of the commonwealth as an aggregate of aggregates.

Robert Nisbet, in a work on political community, once provided a catalog of some of the options for symbiosis in commonwealths. It is worth revisiting some to enlarge the current repertory of images and options. Thus Edmund Burke provided one example. In England, reacting against the French Revolution, Burke feared the encroachments of the *unum,* the central organ of what he called civil society. He could not picture leaving the individual isolated and powerless, so he used two images.

In one setting he spoke of associations or aggregates as platoons. One is not simply a member of the large, sprawling, amorphous, civil army; one finds immediate company and strategic value in a platoon. Burke had no problem fitting the platoon into a hierarchy of relations, though there are good reasons to draw back from such usages in the American republic with its preferred egalitarian intentions.

More fitting is his image of inns. Burke had seen that in the sweep of the French Revolution the inherited corporations, estates, guilds, churchly districts, and other spheres of loyalties had been destroyed.

He mourned their general loss and argued that wherever possible their vestiges and counterparts should be nurtured. But then he proposed:

> We begin our public affections in our families. No cold relation is a zealous citizen. We pass on to our neighborhoods, and our habitual provincial connections. These are inns and resting-places. Such divisions of our country as have been formed by habit, and not by a sudden jerk of authority, were so many little images of the great country in which the heart found something which it could fill. The love to the whole is not extinguished by this subordinate partiality.[10]

The whole interrelates with subordinate partiality in potentially creative ways today. These often get overlooked when the nation encroaches on the individual or when the defense of subgroups is too strident and exclusive.

A Domestic Influence: Founder James Madison

In the new United States James Madison, as influential on this front as any of the national founders, kept the concept of the *res publica* minimal, chaste, and almost as nonpurposeful as did Oakeshott. Because much of my argument relates to the models of the two, it is important at this moment to notice one significant difference between them. James Madison in *Federalist No. 10* and *No. 51* spoke up clearly and forcefully for the rights of faction and interest. He discussed how they act and should act and how nonmembers in the larger republic might deal with them. But he did not want faction members to lose sight of a theme that bursts through in *No. 51*: "Justice is the end of government. It is the end of civil society. It ever has been and ever will be pursued until it be obtained, or until liberty be lost in pursuit."[11]

Because Madison does not often speak of the aim of government, some have overlooked the very clear message he relayed. Because Madison writes economically with little repetition, many do not know how deliberate and judicious he reveals himself to be. Some readers of Madison believe that too much is conventionally made of *Federalist No. 10* as a charter for pluralism at the expense of its cognate or cousin, *Federalist No. 51*. Why have a government and why protect the interests and the individuals in it unless government has a goal?

William B. Allen has challenged the centrality of *Federalist No. 10*, in the interest of promoting the positive elements in *No. 51*. He quotes the latter as the keynote, where Madison wrote, "In the extended republic of the United States, and among the great variety of interests, parties, and sects which it embraces, a coalition of a majority of the whole society could seldom take place on any other principles than those of justice and the general good." Notice "justice and the general good." Allen criticizes those who "fail to take seriously *Federalist 51's* invocation of justice," using as an "operative analogy" the claim that "justice inheres as fully in the arguments of *The Federalist* as piety inheres in the *Torah*, although neither is frequently mentioned in either."[12]

Allen also adduces as part of the Madisonian project Madison's draft of a farewell address he wrote for George Washington in 1792. Madison was in that project as enthusiastic as Jay had been about "America's providential advantages and achievements" and as ready as Jay to see it as the "theatre of our fortunes." Madison wrote of America: "All its essential interests are the same: while its diversities arising from climate, from soil, and for other local & lesser peculiarities, will naturally form a mutual relation of the parts, that may give to the whole a more entire independence than has perhaps fallen to the lot of any other nation."[13]

To the end of pursuing justice, Madison therefore had to worry about the unrepresentativeness of the electorate in his time. Although he did not take up the subject of women's suffrage—debate over it was still more than a century off—he did concern himself with slaves and nonfreeholders:

> In proportion as slavery prevails in a state, the government, however democratic in name, must be aristocratic in fact. The power lies in a part instead of the whole; in the hands of property, not of numbers. . . . In Virginia . . . the slaves and non-freeholders amount to nearly 3/4 of the State. The power is therefore in about 1/4. Were the slaves free and the right of suffrage extended to all, the operation of the government might be very different.[14]

On many occasions Madison did elaborate on issues relevant to the topic of the common good. Often he spoke of the aggregates and associations in a negative cast, as factions, parties, interests, religious sects, and the like, again, all within a page or two of the *Federalist Papers*. His factions were intense interest groups: "By a faction, I understand a number of citizens, whether amounting to a majority or a minority of the whole, who are united and actuated by some common impulse of passion, or of interest, adverse to the rights of other citizens, or to the permanent and aggregate interests of the community."[15]

The key term as Madison dealt with faction, interest, and sect, was not the same that we found in the writing of John Jay in *Federalist No. 2*. Madison chose "different." A register of Madisonian usages in just a page or two of *Federalist No. 10* includes "different opinions," "different . . . faculties of acquiring property," "the possession of different degrees and kinds of property," "different interests and parties," "different opinions concerning religion," "attachment to different leaders," as well as "different classes of legislators."

Let it be noted that in protecting the factions, interests, and sects, Madison was not viewing them as favorably as do the advocates who lead them today and, for that matter, as I often do. Madison treated them less as assets and more as problems for a republic to address as it wanted to protect majorities, minorities, and the republic itself. "So strong is this propensity of mankind to fall into mutual animosities," he wrote, "that where no substantial occasion presents itself the most frivolous and fanciful distinctions have been sufficient to kindle their unfriendly passions and excite their most violent conflicts." And Madison regularly spoke of the "mischiefs of factions."[16] He also had more concern for propertied interests, including his own, than we need to elaborate upon here.

Note that Madison made a distinction within the world of differences, interests, and factions. Factions were numbers of citizens "united and actuated by some common impulse of passion, or of interest, adverse to the rights of other citizens, or to the permanent and aggregate interests of the community." He did not in those lines allow for the possibility that a faction of citizens might only *appear* to work in ways adverse to the rights of others. Nor did he make much of the similar possibility that while inconveniencing some others, a particular faction might be working on the logic of rights and freedom for the good of the whole. For a modern instance, the civil rights organizations appeared to be working adversely to the interests of the white people of Birmingham, Alabama. The civil rights faction inconvenienced others, but it prevailed and worked in the end *for* the interests of the majority and of other factions.

Further, Madison drew a distinction among factions based on passion, including religion (and presumably today he would add gender and race), on the one hand, and on interest, especially economic, on the other. A republic could take care of the latter rather easily. In discussing the former he used such language as "zeal," "ambitiously contending for pre-eminence," "inflamed . . . mutual animosity," "vex and oppress," "unfriendly passions," and "violent conflicts."

It is clear that Madison was here expressing his dark view of the limits of human nature. Factions rose essentially not because people had regard for the civil society but because they were selfish. In the process of giving expression to such views, Madison employed language of the sort used by those who today oppose the expressive racial, ethnic, religious, gender, and class interests in society. Incidentally, in twelve of the *Federalist Papers* Madison used the word *passion*, usually with negative associations. In twenty of the twenty-nine papers attributed to him he used the word *reason*, but not always favorably. Reason could be "fallible," expressive of "self-love," and worse. Still, Madison thought, the republic had to worry more about passions in factions than about reason in their interactions.[17]

Mary Ann Glendon has pointed to a striking feature in the language and concerns of the national founders. They spent energy on the *unum* of the republic, the *plures* of the states, and the factions that could disturb the peace of both. Similarly, they took pains to protect the rights of individuals and call forth responsibility from them. But they tended to overlook the contributions of positive mediating forces. Glendon suggests a reason why they do not get mentioned:

> In the beginning, that is, at the Founding, there was no particular reason for American statesmen to pay special attention to families, neighborhoods, or small associations. These social systems were just there, seemingly "natural," like gravity on whose continued existence we rely to keep us grounded, steady, and attached to our surroundings. In all likelihood, the Founders just took for granted the dense texture of eighteenth-century American society, with its economically interdependent families and its tightknit communities.

These founders, says Glendon, could not have pictured how the growth of the federal government, the disintegration of families, the decay of great cities, and the economic dependence of many Americans on large, bureaucratic public and private organizations would take up the space of the old, more intimate associations.[18] It could well be that the late modern groups devoted to special interests and identity politics gained the credibility they often manifest as they filled the space between the individual and the central authorities, when small mediating associations atrophied or disappeared.

Alexis de Tocqueville on Associations

Not many years after James Madison, however, these associations still were vital forces, as we see in the case of Alexis de Tocqueville, a visitor to America who addressed in classic terms the problem of the one and the many in the republic. He also preferred the term *association* to *community*. While other commentators on association feared governmental centralization under revolutionary forces, monarchs, or bureaucrats, Tocqueville saw how social egalitarians might turn out to overstress the *unum* of a democracy.

> The foremost or indeed the sole condition required in order to succeed in centralizing the supreme power in a democratic community is to love equality, or to get men to believe you love it. Thus, the science of despotism, which was once so complex, is simplified, and reduced, as it were, to a single principle.

Democracy could become authoritarian and totalitarian if unchecked and if bureaucratization had full sway. The hope for America and for democracies in general, Tocqueville thought, involved the dividing of authority and the finding of ways to provide checks against central administration and expansive bureaucracy. He added to this his hope for local agencies but, most of all again, for the freedom of people to form associations. In his case, too, there was fear of the too-powerful *unum* and the too-weak individual, posed against each other. Then, between them:

> At the present time the liberty of association has become a necessary guarantee against the tyranny of the majority . . . There are no countries in which associations are more needed to prevent the despotism of faction or the arbitrary power of a prince than those which are

democratically constituted. In countries where such associations do
not exist, if private individuals cannot create an artificial and temporary substitute for them I can see no permanent protection against the
most galling tyranny; and a great people may be oppressed with im-
punity by a small faction or by a single individual.

The French visitor came to admire the cultural, social, and non-
political institutions that emerged. He then praised, no doubt over-
praised, the American versions collectively:

> There is only one country on the face of the earth where the citizens
> enjoy unlimited freedom of association for political purposes. This
> same country is the only one in the world where the continual exercise
> of the right of association has been introduced into civil life and where
> all the advantages which civilization can confer are procured by means
> of it.[19]

Can and Should the Nation-State Provide Community?

Most of these thinkers spoke of the components of a republic as
associations more readily than as communities. Community for them
is offered and attainable only in circumscribed, momentary, and partial ways within marriage, the family, circles of friendship, religious
congregations (often local), and in cells of people devoted to a cause.
Against those who overadvertise national community or the community of their large clusters or groups, Glenn Tinder, in a work
informed by theology and observation, called community itself a
"tragic ideal." In some contexts, his statement may sound extreme,
but its astringent and economical view of community is helpful here.
Tinder spoke favorably of many aspects of the quest for it but then
argued the extreme case that can inform more moderate observations:

> Community is not only alluring, however, it is also unattainable. Man
> is not capable of community—not, at least, in any full and stable form.
> No doubt relationships of communal quality can be realized occasion-
> ally and in limits by a family, a town, a university, or even a nation.
> But no historical institution can be purely and simply a community.
> . . . Full community is unattainable partly because man is a natural

being; he lives in space and time, and he dies. To a surprising extent man's spatial, temporal, and mortal nature is ignored in writings on community . . .

Even so, our natural capacity for community is often far in excess of our moral capacity. The tendency of every person to subordinate everything to his own pleasure and preeminence—a tendency that is subtle and enduring, although often disguised—frequently forecloses whatever communal possibilities nature offers.

Add to these natural and moral obstacles a third, Tinder's "axiological," which has to do with the value of persons.

To say that man is spatial, temporal, and mortal, after all, is to say that he is finite, and this implies that the natural values he embodies are limited both in degree and duration . . . If there are any who achieve moral perfection they are so rarely encountered in daily life as to be irrelevant to the problem of community. In sum, no one commands more than qualified respect. The communal impulse capable of fulfillment only with those one respects and only in proportion to one's respect for them, is correspondingly inhibited.[20]

Tinder's theological assumptions about human nature lead him to a more limited set of expectations than many might share. But his strictures are good reminders about the difficulty of using the political order to fulfill the need for community. Once again, the concept of association for the society and the larger aggregates of groups seems vastly preferable.

Agencies of Intermediation

Robert Nisbet offered a conclusion after listening to many testimonies:

I found not only a philosophy of history that stressed the deep conflict between the political state and other, rival forms of association, ranging from kindred to local community and religion, but, with this, the idea of *intermediation*. Major groups which fall in between the individual and the sovereign state become intermediating influences between citizen and sovereign. They are at once buffers against too arbitrary a political power and reinforcements to the individual's conception of himself and his own powers.[21]

In such an account as Nisbet's and, derivatively, mine, there has to be a villain. Jean-Jacques Rousseau serves in this role. Rousseau's *Social Contract* celebrated the total state and left nothing important outside of or free to be against the state. Naturally, then, he would rule out intermediate associations. According to Nisbet, "Rousseau hated all associations, 'partial associations' which might intervene between the individual and his total absorption by the state, the General Will state, of course, and he proscribed them." He even invented the notion of a "civil religion" that would reinforce the state as *unum*, this one thing.

In opposition Nisbet posed a tradition of the American founders along with such witnesses as Edmund Burke, Alexis de Tocqueville, and "their intellectual descendants who relish the plural, differentiated, particularist and decentralized state in which the freedom of individuals is buttressed by the autonomy of all the groups and associations which prevent man from becoming an inert particle in sandheap-mass."[22]

So we return for one more moment to Tocqueville. His views were to remain most applicable to the American situation in his time and remain so in our own. He developed them by comparing France under the Old Regime with the America he observed. Of France: "Though the nation came to seem a homogeneous whole, its parts no longer held together. Nothing had been left that could obstruct the central government, but, by the same token, nothing could shore it up."[23]

This book, like so many in its genre, could be seen as a set of footnotes to Tocqueville, but in a very different situation. In our time the feared antagonism is less between the groups than among advocates of each and of those who aspire to articulate interests of the common good. There is here less fear of despotism—though one always has to keep despotic possibilities in mind—than of individualist anomie and intergroup anarchy.

Yet our argument refuses to grant to the larger community the power of the whole that Rousseau and his many American sympathizers have promoted. What is needed instead is the dialectic or conversation between the voices of the groups and of the larger community, a dialectic that does not submerge differences nor envelope or enclose those in the differing clusters and leave them alone in their exclusivism. They are, in Althusius's terms, symbiotes who interact, imparting life to each other and drawing on each other. As such, they promote association in pursuit of the common good.

The One and the Many

The ultimate foundation of a free society is the binding tie of cohesive sentiment. Such a sentiment is fostered by all those agencies of the mind and spirit which may serve to gather up the traditions of a people, transmit them from generation to generation, and thereby create that continuity of a treasured common life which constitutes a civilization. "We live by symbols."

Felix Frankfurter

CHAPTER EIGHT

 Argument, Conversation, and Story

The American struggle for the common good will advance not when citizens agree on absolutes, adopt a creed or philosophy, impose a dogma, or frame answers to all questions. Those who persist with dreams of totalism may try to impose one set of norms and attempt to coerce national community into shape, but they will fail. They lack constitutional grounds in a free society for their efforts and, should they abrogate republican polity, the inability of governments in unfree societies to impose their ideologies and then command assent suggests that such an approach would also founder here.

Left without a creed, however, citizens do find reasons to pursue the common good along with some elements of common life. They are always free to use persuasion to gain others' assent to their approach. Voluntarily they can promote the "binding tie of cohesive sentiment." In such efforts, dogmas and philosophies have had notably less effect than have symbols and stories.

Stories Survive and Serve

Max Lerner observed that "men possess thoughts, but symbols possess men," and his insight is helpful here as well. Lerner was opposing the notion that governments could live solely by rational appeals. His statement can be translated to "People possess stories, but stories possess people." Stories can generate symbols, and symbols often take on mythic and storied form.[1]

The idea of "possession" has been a constant throughout these chapters. Who, we have asked, possesses the American story and stories, the myths of the civil association and of the groups that make up national life? Lerner introduces a reciprocal note that needs stressing. Why continue to pay attention to stories at all, especially if leaders of many of the tribes that make up the nation insist that there is no grand narrative, or at least none they will accept for background or for purposes of uniting them? Given the issues that arise when narrative is mentioned, there are good reasons to ask: why story?

A comparison between the history of America and the longer history of Jews is to the point here. Dan Jacobson once discussed the story of the stories in a popular book of that title. Not a believer in the God of Israel, Jacobson was still engrossed with the story of God and God's chosen people that has animated Jewish history and somehow helps sustain Israel and Jews even today. Though convinced, as many Jews are not, that "Yahweh is wholly a human creation," Jacobson was especially drawn to the question of the power and ageless hold of the Yahweh story and of Israel's chosenness. In the South Africa of his childhood, the novelist had seen the power of this Jewish story when it was transferred to non-Jews. Supporters of apartheid used it as a grand narrative to provide a rationale for seeing themselves as the elect and chosen people of God, a people who could set the terms of life for others.

Jacobson subsequently mused about how the societies that developed along the Nile and the Tigris-Euphrates long ago had been "bound to be more powerful and hence more expansive" than any that perched on the rocky slopes where Judea and Samaria were founded. He added: "The rest—the 'facts' of conquest and enslavement—duly followed." The drama of his conclusion relates to our theme:

> Only, the Hebrews had a story to tell; their conquerors did not. That was the sole advantage they had over them. And what an advantage that has turned out to be, all said and done! *Toutes proportions gardées,* something similar might perhaps be said about the myths adumbrated by some of the great modern writers. Their diagnoses of the ailments of our civilization, and the causes and cures they propose for these ills, may all be quite wide of the mark. Probably they are. The fact that they are believed to be accurate, however, does give them an objective importance which it would be pointless to deny.[2]

"The great modern writers" of whom Jacobson was speaking in-cluded Karl Marx, whose diagnoses of the world's ailments may still be believed by some. But Marx's cures have been unceremoniously rejected. Jacobson's company of writers, as recently as 1982, also still included Sigmund Freud, whose legacy is often now seen to be based on fundamentally flawed analyses. Do Jefferson and Jackson, Tocque-ville and Lincoln, and others who have pondered how the one and the many relate in America belong to such a relatively obsolete com-pany as well?

The totalists of republicanism do not think so, of course, nor do many in the separate groups that share space in America. The leaders of many of these groups find reasons to reject any common story as it has been told to date. The winners, the dominators, the oppressors, they insist, are the ones who formerly and exclusively told what they considered and wanted to be the common story. Therefore, their op-ponents declare, such a story cannot be trusted; it will only victimize them.

To this one must counter with a line from nineteenth-century Ger-man historians: you overcome history with history. So with narrative and myth and symbol: you overcome story with story. You break the spell of myth with another myth. You come out from under the dom-inance of a symbol not by rejecting the symbol but by seeing that another interpretation of it gets heard. Think of the current circum-stance that includes critiques and retellings by African Americans of slave narratives; by Native Americans of reservation life; by Hispanic Americans of indignities against immigrants; by women, gays, and the poor of assaults and other mistold or untold portions of their stories. The accounts of Jefferson and Jackson, Tocqueville and Lin-coln all sound very different to wary citizens than they would have a third of a century ago. But the stories themselves have not disap-peared. In fact, those who criticize them often pay these stories the highest compliment by the attention they give them, neglected as they have been by most others.

Attacks on the traditions that possess us are often vicious, and the dismissals of the stories are often vehement. African Americans can, and some of their writers do, regularly criticize Jefferson for having been a racist, which he was, and for having kept slaves though he knew better, which he did, though he was troubled about his practice. Or they may turn against Lincoln for having given a higher priority to saving the Union than to freeing the slaves, though he was a leader in both. Andrew Jackson cannot be forgiven, nor should he be, by Native Americans for his part in Indian removal and in producing the Trail of Tears.

The groups have to tell their own particular stories of their chosenness, whether in their victimhood or as liberated peoples. They add to this telling their own interpretation of what is often thought of as the general story of the United States. For others to try to silence them when they bring up the plot of their particular stories would be somehow dehumanizing. The larger society, if it has integrity, develops illness and experiences crisis when it tries to distort or ignore such stories. The German Catholic theologian Johann Baptist Metz, in "A Short Apology for Narrative," connects the theme of story with memory in ways appropriate to mention here:

> As Theodor Adorno observed, "Forgetting is inhuman because man's accumulated suffering is forgotten—the historical trace of things, words, colours and sounds is always the trace of past suffering. This is why tradition is nowadays confronted with an insoluble contradiction. It is not present and cannot be evoked, but as soon as all tradition is extinguished, inhumanity begins."[3]

Unless Native Americans or Jews or the descendants of slaves speak up and tell their own stories, the legends will not be heard. Of course, the person who is not a member of one or another interpretive community may well replicate the concerns embodied in such storytelling communities. Doing such imaginative reconstructing is much of what narrative art is about. But unless an ethnic, racial, or religious group remains vigorous and finds ways to tell at least its central mythic stories, they will go neglected or be traduced by other tellers. And if those in communities profoundly shaped by memories of suffering (and often, of course, by the reality of continuing oppression and victimization) do not retell and reinterpret the central myths of the republic to include their experiences and vantages, inherited privileged readings will prevail and cast their spell.

My purpose here is not to propose the muffling of the groups in either venture but to see whether it is possible to move from models in which exclusiveness on the part of the once-excluded always has to prevail. Can there not be enrichment of each group by other groups, and of the whole by the parts in a symbiotic society? The stories of suffering are too important to be the possession alone of those descended from the sufferers. Certain ways of telling the stories can help lessen or end oppression for all. Metz quotes Martin Buber on the power of story:

> The story is itself an event and has the quality of a sacred action . . . It is more than a reflection—the sacred essence to which it bears witness continues to live in it. The wonder that is narrated becomes powerful once more . . . A rabbi, whose grandfather had been a pupil of Baal Shem Tov, was once asked to tell a story. "A story ought to be told," he said, "so that it is itself a help," and his story was this. "My grandfather was paralysed. Once he was asked to tell a story about his teacher and he told how the holy Baal Shem Tov used to jump and dance when he was praying. My grandfather stood up while he was telling the story and the story carried him away so much that he had to jump and dance to show how the master had done it. From that moment, he was healed. This is how stories ought to be told."[4]

Those moved by that story find in it an illustration of the current point as well as a story itself and a corollary point. This instance comes from a subcommunity, Hasidism, and from a broader community, Judaism. But it is too good to be kept by and for such groups only. Telling it and acting upon it can enhance and humanize others of vastly different orientations. But who should tell the stories, and to whom are they to be told?

The Concept of Symbiotes

Here I return to Johannes Althusius and his concept of the *symbiotes* and argue that many of the particular stories of each of the groups can be told for all. Each group reinterprets the stories that are told more generally, for the sake of all. They are symbiotes. Where symbiosis does not occur, trauma results.

In 1933 the *Oxford English Dictionary* lexicographers spoke of *symbiosis* as "living together, social life" but had to mark the word obsolete and rare. Then they hurried to the biological definition, which has analogies in the political sphere. Symbiosis is the "association of two different organisms . . . which live attached to each other . . . and contribute to each other's support." Then in finest print the dictionary writers add, and we can emphasize, that symbiosis is "also called *commensalism* or *consortism;* distinguished from *parasitism,* in which one organism preys upon the other." And the *Supplement* to the dictionary, dated 1987, adds, "Hence symbiote, a combination of two symbiotic organisms." By analogy, symbiotes are each of the *plures* acting upon one another and each acting in relation to the national *unum.* Symbiotes are the many to the many and the many to the one, the groups to the groups and the groups to the civil association—and in every case we can add, vice versa.

Good news about the word is evident in the 1987 *Supplement:* the lexicographers found reason to delete "obsolete, rare" from the definition "living together, social life," which is our usage. And the dictionary writers found many recent examples to flesh out the definition of symbiote. Thus an illustration from 1951 turns on the reality of the tribes, quoting Raymond Firth's *Elementary Social Organization:* the *symbiote* "is most evident in the case of an African tribe having its members intermingled with those of other tribes and in symbiotic relationship with them." The African tribal model in such a case deserves translation to the American situation of groups and their stories.

It is surprising that the dictionary writers did not know or cite the translation from 1964 by Frederick S. Carney of Johannes Althusius, where the Latin original *symbiotici,* "those who live together," was translated "symbiotes." In the most sustained use of the term, Althusius described the symbiotes both as "associated" co-workers or as "participants or partners in a common life," as we have observed Americans partnered in various relations based on gender, religion, class, interest, and the like.

Althusius himself recognized two kinds of symbiosis. One was the "natural" version, as between "married persons, blood relatives, and in-laws, in response to a natural affection and necessity, [who] agree to a definite communication among themselves." Such, Althusius added, is called "the most intense society, friendship, relationship, and union, the seedbed of every other symbiotic association," when these symbiotes are called "relatives, kinsmen, and friends."

The intense subcommunities of racial and ethnic groups often display such a character, by analogous extension. The "civil association" is the other sort of symbiosis. It bears a different character and exacts less intense involvement by the familial symbiotes. Here belongs the collegium, "a gathering, society, federation, sodality, synagogue, convention, or synod," when it is in the private sector. But there are also public associations.[5]

Identity groups must be in some measure differentiated from each other and, in many cases, are somehow in competition—how can they reach across their boundaries to other intense subcommunities with their stories? How can they do so without being overtaken by them, or assimilated, or rendered so indistinct and tolerant that they lose their purposes?

The American Jewish community leadership typically asks this as it sees half the Jewish marriages today undertaken with non-Jews and knows that only one in twenty of these will produce a convert to the Jewish community. Should leaders stress such unions' alienation from or assimilation to the larger community? Should Jews tell stories of their difference and their experience of alienation or of their success at "fitting in"? Should religious bodies proffer stories of their difference, in a free-market competition? Or should they risk being ecumenical but therefore almost inevitably more bland and nondescript than if they were standoffish? Here is another case where the storytelling and story-hearing communities need to step carefully and find fresh models.

Achieving True Conversation

How do communities make these moves? They do so as groups just as we see individuals doing so, through various modes of speaking, listening, and acting. Here I draw upon and will extrapolate from the ideas of two thinkers with whom we converse in other chapters, Ernest Gellner and Michael Oakeshott. They are quite different: Oakeshott's "modes" are "arrests of experience" of an individual. Gellner's image is "modular man," a kind of human being that he sees making up modern national society. Gellner's point of reference is the furniture store's "modular furniture," where new bits can be added and "the whole thing will still have a coherence, aesthetically and technically." In the old style "if you want coherence you have to buy it all at once, in one go," making an irrevocable or expensively revoked commitment. The totalist in civil society asks for such a commitment. "What genuine Civil Society really requires is not modular furniture, but modular man," Gellner asserts. His modular man sounds like Tocqueville's voluntary associational type:

> He can combine into specific-purpose, *ad hoc,* limited association, without binding himself by some blood ritual. He can leave an association when he comes to disagree with its policy, without being open to an accusation of treason ... The moral order has not committed itself either to a set of prescribed roles and relations, or to a set of practices. The same goes for knowledge: conviction can change, without any stigma of apostasy.[6]

Obviously, such a level of commitment is not what is expected in intensely religious or ideological communities. But many of us are members of numbers of partly contradictory associations that allow for plural belonging in patterns that change through time. Now, any group that stresses primordial ties, as in the case of "blood and soil," or any that asks people to be ready to die for the cause, is threatened by and will resist the appearance of modular humans. How can one be both civilly associated and intensely subcommunal? Here I introduce the theme of "modes" of experience, first through Alfred Schutz and others, and then through Oakeshott.

For some years I have been taking issue with those who see all plural commitments as "all or nothing" rivalries within the original group and, one might add, the individual person. Thus Sidney E. Mead, posing the American "religion of the Republic" as he defined it (in terms too expansive to be described as totalist) over against, for example, Christian particularism, insisted that all forms of religion involve deciding emphatically on "this or that." He thereupon reported on surveys of opinion and was bemused by Americans' responses where "two theologically contrary views, each rooted in age-old antagonistic theological traditions," were demonstrably "held simultaneously by conservative Christians in the republic."

In Mead's view such citizens must be "religiously and intellectually split." He thought they would have to choose between religions—or risk jeopardy to their republic. In fact, however, many citizens do show devotion to the "religion of the Republic" as being expressive of the looser "civil associational" model *and* to their particular churches or other agencies of profound belief.[7]

Moderns had been forced to learn how to live with what Robert Bellah called "multiplex consciousness."[8] Alfred Schutz noted that humans may have commitments to various "nonparamount realities" and various "universes of discourse" or "provinces of meaning." Think of civil association and intense community as analogues to the following:

> All these worlds—the world of dreams, of imageries and phantasms, especially the world of art, the world of religious experience, the world of scientific contemplation, the play world of the child, and the world of the insane—are finite provinces of meaning. This means that (a) all of them have a peculiar cognitive style . . . ; (b) all experiences within each of these worlds are, with respect to this cognitive style, consistent in themselves and compatible with one another . . . ; (c) each of these finite provinces of meaning may receive a specific accent of reality.

Schutz cited William James, who observed the human relating to various spheres, various realities. Each of these was a "world" which, "*whilst it is attended to,* is real after its own fashion; only the reality lapses with the attention." James recognized the need for focus: "*My experience is what I agree to attend to.* Only those items which I *notice* shape my mind—without selective interest experience is an utter chaos." James wrote that all know what attention is—the kind of attention I believe groups can devote to realities beyond their own: "It is the taking possession by the mind, in clear and vivid form, of one out of what seem several simultaneously possible objects or trains of thought. Focalization, consciousness are of its essence."[9]

Schutz then developed his own concept of "multiple realities," those "worlds" to which one can be attentive. Thus as a Hispanic American I may be attentive with one kind of intensity and awareness to my Pentecostal or Catholic church. With another mode of being alert I respond to the stories of my Salvadoran group of refugees. They are immigrants to the United States who have undergone the intense bonding experience of political persecution and ultimate escape. On a different level, the same "I," through a more generalized association with "Hispanic Americans" in political causes, finds another set of stories valuable. And upon embracing and acquiring citizenship I became part of another set of attachments and stories.

It may be that my priest or pastor, with special theological warrant, will say that loyalty to Christ and the Church means the disdaining of other ties. My fellow refugees may see my bonds with them weakening as they and I acquire additional and new if less profound stories. Those organizing Hispanics for votes will see my other commitments as rivals. Now the issue also arises: in which political party will we put energies, and whose stories will we share? Not all will go the same way. The jingoist defender of constitutionalism might not want me to be loyal to any of the groups along the way. Yet I and all my fellow citizens who are not wholly given to totalism or tribalism somehow do negotiate with all these groups and associations, these storytellers and stories.

Schutz knows that "I" am busy: "The interests I have in the same situation as a father, a citizen, a member of my church or of my profession, may not only be different but even incompatible with one another," so I have to be alert and keep making choices about attentiveness.[10]

A rendering into the plural of Gellner's "modular man" and Oakeshott's "modes" of being for one person has been my own central focus. I believe that groups as well as individuals can be shown to have various "modes of experience." One can see evidence of this by comparing "the minutes of the meeting" of any such group from times of its political infighting to the face it presents when dealing with external rivals. Both may be authentic and true to the vision and purpose of the group, but they are very different modes.

Oakeshott's "modes" was a designation well poised for life in a pluralistic world, away from the whole, the *unum*, the dream of the totalist. Oakeshott detailed these in *Experience and Its Modes*. One may present one's self, or the life of one's group, through an infinite number of modes; Oakeshott concentrated on history, science, and practice. Modes are particular, consistent ways of viewing the world, thanks to the focus of attention. There are no floating realities; each must belong to a mode. Each issues in its own language or universes of discourse.[11]

As a philosopher, Oakeshott is most interested in modes of expe-

rience as personal and abstract,[12] while here our interest is more political and concrete, focusing on the embodied experience (especially
embodied in groups) and level of expression. A poet's testimony
should help make the point clearer. Paul Valéry was trying to define
the modern person, in an essay from 1932, "The Politics of the Mind."
However we hypothesize the existence of premoderns—and there is
no point in romanticizing notions of simplicity and wholeness among
them—the modern person as Valéry described her confronts plural-
ities of "worlds" in Oakeshott's sense of that term. The modern person, the citizen, voter, candidate, taxpayer, common person, inhabits
worlds that partly contradict the portraits provided by contemporary
biology, psychology, or even psychiatry:

> if a civilization's *age* is to be measured by the number of contradictions
> it contains, by the number of incompatible customs and beliefs to be
> found in it, all modifying each other, or by the multiplicity of philos-
> ophies and systems of aesthetics that coexist and cohabit in the same
> heads, it must be agreed that our civilization is one of the most ancient.
> Do we not constantly find several religions, several races, several po-
> litical parties represented in one family . . . and in one individual a
> whole armory of latent discord?

This questioning leads to Valéry's attempt to define the modern
person:

> and this is what makes him modern, [he] lives on familiar terms with
> many contraries waiting in the penumbra of his mind and coming by
> turns onto the stage. That is not all. We seldom notice these inner
> contradictions, or the coexisting antagonisms around us, and only
> rarely does it occur to us that they have not always been there.[13]

The concept we need here is that of "many contraries waiting in
the penumbra of his mind." Many a citizen has made the judgment
that Christopher Columbus was a fanatic, a crusader, a self-deluded
messianic sort, a manipulator. He was someone who began the course
of those who were agents of virtual genocide and slavery, plus the
accidental bearers of disease. Yet from another angle, in a different
mode, Columbus will be perceived differently in the mind of the same
person who might also "happen to be" an Italian American, a Cath-

olic, an admirer of outstanding seamanship, and someone who believes that murderous impulses were also present and vigorously
acted upon in the hemisphere before the Europeans arrived with Columbus.

Similarly, an African American, perhaps a civil rights worker, can
consider Thomas Jefferson to have been inconsistent, not prescient.
Jefferson would be seen to have been exploitative in holding slaves
and an unimaginative racist, in one mode of perception. Yet the same
person who has heard or told these stories has often turned around
and seen Jefferson as the author of a Declaration of Independence
that served her well when she was arguing for the application of
rights to all citizens.

A third person may be a lesbian activist who, for the sake of focusing her energies, will not be in coalition with men, straight or
gay—but in another mode and toward a different end may be an
ardent Catholic, restless but still "there" in a patriarchal and hierar-
chical men's world. Such people are not being self-contradictory. They
are addressing different situations and companies out of the center
of a relatively coherent personhood. None grasps experience whole,
but always through a preoccupying mode, with a focused intent.

The Difference between Argument and Story

So people in the various groups may live in partly incommensurable
universes of discourse, and yet find it valuable to interact in ways
other than through military force or in cultural conflict. Often these
symbiotes will interact through the exercise of political power, which
means finally through argument. People do not only tell stories. They
have to find principled and pragmatic grounds for promoting justice,
and they will always meet resistance. But even there, stories will help
them. Instead of reaching for guns they reach for argument, and the
telling of stories from different perspectives is a form of argument.
One cannot have a republic without argument.

The various groups and subcommunities that make up the American civil association certainly do argue: they do this through their
politicians and their own advocates and agents. Some of their argument is mindless and storyless. That is, it represents mere staking
out of claims and some preemptions of privilege and power. But the
history of argument between the groups and within the nation is rich.

In an argument, one somehow "knows" a proposition (call it an "answer"), defends it, and tries to convince or defeat the other. On those terms, an abused black lesbian can argue that her own group has experienced the greatest victimization, and it may be hard to argue with the claim. But most argument on such terms is hard to assess and has to be considered more as witness than anything else.

So those who stress modularity and the modes of experience that occur to individuals and groups tend to move, as Oakeshott does, to the model of conversation. If argument is impelled by the answers, conversation is moved and marked by the questions. Conversation does not have to be seen as soft, (merely) tolerant, muffled and mumbling, wishy-washy, or nice. But it differs from argument in that it is more open to the use of story to advance understanding, even if the stories are not always of shared experiences. I will not be able to share the experience of the Holocaust the way children of survivors do. The case of exposure to sexual abuse is similar, if I have not suffered it. But I can be humanized by the stories of those whose groups carry accounts of such suffering with them or who even have experienced them personally.

David Tracy has described conversation over against argument as "another kind of game," where "we learn to give in to the movement required by questions worth exploring":

> The movement in conversation is questioning itself. Neither my present opinions on the question nor the text's original response to the question, but the question itself, must control every conversation. A conversation . . . is not a confrontation. It is not a debate. It is not an exam. It is questioning itself. It is a willingness to follow the question wherever it may go. It is dia-logue.

You may not convince me of anything if you try to quantify suffering, for example, by presenting comparative statistics on your social class's limited access to medical care. You may do that as well, of course. But that reasoned approach, supported by arguments from Aristotle or Immanuel Kant, John Stuart Mill or John Rawls, is not as likely to move me and my group as will stories of the fates of those denied such care. Tracy continues:

> When human beings converse, they may converse, of course, about themselves. They may exchange their narratives, expose their hopes,

desires, and fears. They may both reveal and conceal who they think they are, and who they think the other may be—the other now become the conversation partner . . .

Conversation is a game with some hard rules: say only what you mean; say it as accurately as you can; listen to and respect what the other says, however different or other; be willing to correct or defend your opinions if challenged by the conversation partner; be willing to argue if necessary, to confront if demanded, to endure necessary conflict, to change your mind if the evidence suggests it . . . [These] good rules . . . are merely variations of the transcendental imperatives elegantly articulated by Bernard Lonergan: "Be attentive, be intelligent, be responsible, be loving, and, if necessary, change."[14]

Michael Oakeshott relates conversation to the concept of modes: the various "worlds" are brought together across the boundaries of subcommunities as an "unrehearsed intellectual adventure." In this case, argument belongs to what Aristotle calls *proairesis,* purposive undertaking; conversation belongs to the voluntary sector, where life is lived *sub specie voluntatis.* In conversation

there is no symposiarch or arbiter; not even a doorkeeper to examine credentials. Every entrant is taken at its face-value and everything is permitted which can get itself accepted into the flow of speculation. And voices which speak in conversation do not compose a hierarchy. Conversation is not an enterprise designed to yield an extrinsic profit, a contest where a winner gets a prize, nor is it an activity of exegesis; it is an unrehearsed intellectual adventure. It is with conversation as with gambling, its significance lies neither in winning nor in losing, but in wagering.[15]

From these remarks it is clear that both the mode of argument and the mode of conversation are necessary among civil associations and groups. When issues of justice are at stake, "winning and losing" are important. But when the cause is gaining empathy for another group's story, humanizing other elements of "the whole" by recounting a narrative of suffering, then the conversational model, not the confrontational, is what is needed. The quotation also suggests why leaders of totalist or tribalist groups are put off by conversation. Often in the cause of rejecting hierarchy they exemplify it; in attacking another's profit, they seek to advance their own. But many in groups find benefit in getting their story told and in hearing the other's, wagering on the benefits of the outcome for both.

Haunting all such talk of story in a pluralist society, of course, is still the reference of Alasdair MacIntyre and, before him, of John Courtney Murray to "incommensurable universes of discourse." What happens when groups are so alienated from one another and from civil association that they do not want to hear or cannot hear, and if they did listen, would repudiate all stories but their own— what happens, in other words, when the excluded turn exclusive? Trauma is the result. When the rejection of all other groups is willful, as in the case of leadership that has so great an investment in monologue, solipsism, and self-reinforcement as to have lost all motive or interest in hearing the other, not much can be done.

Still, if it is hard to picture a society in which everyone would want to converse, to enter the world of others, it is just as hard to picture a society in which the majority of citizens have no commitment to participating outside their own separatist groups. All kinds of voluntary groups have overlapping memberships, and one person may belong to several groups whose boundaries are not coextensive. Many citizens, it seems, are taking part in civic association even as they seek lively groups for more intimate and intense life—or go their own individualist ways. Successful recruitment to the conversation from this sizable cohort is likely to be of more aid to the republic and the groups in it than is listening to strident attacks by the militants who confirm their own mandarin cohorts, alienate everyone else, and create backlash.

To assert all this is less productive than to examine the way stories can be told and treated in all their ambiguity. A myth or a story that does not contain ambiguity or evoke some ambivalence is likely to be a very forgettable piece of propaganda. It is striking to see that the histories designed to give due attention to the excluded or once-excluded must revisit all the focal myths of the tradition that is being questioned or attacked. We can see this by reference to the founding myths of Columbus and then of the Founders; the texts of the Declaration of Independence and the Constitution; the myths that come with the emancipation of slaves and Lincoln's desire first to save the Union; our opening myth about the space shuttle *Challenger*. The list could certainly be extended, perhaps even indefinitely.

A sample text is that of Ronald Takaki, *A Different Mirror: A History of Multicultural America*. Takaki has as his mission to call into question the presumed single American story as it got enshrined and encrusted in the tellings of people of European descent. How different will it look in the hands of the "others," the "different," who hold up a different mirror? Critical as it understandably is of the old received tradition and its custodians, the book is not a book of exclusions but of enrichments. Yet to make any sense of it, one must revisit all the central stories that Takaki wants to move off of center stage. Almost as set as the framework of the biblical canonical stories are the plots of books like his. Columbus. Slavery. Reservations. White ethnic history. Hispanics and the Mexican War. The Chinese in the Gold Rush. Eastern European Jewish immigration. Chicanos and the border. Northern blacks. The Holocaust. Japanese Americans in concentration camps in the West. Martin Luther King and civil rights. Had Takaki chosen to include gender, religion, and class in his "different mirrors," there would have been the same relativizing of the standard or canonical plot chapters, with its subversion of their single set of meanings, but still a revisiting of the tradition even as he supplemented it.

Takaki begins with the problem of the one and the many, citing E. D. Hirsch: "If we *had* to make a choice between the *one* and the *many,* most Americans would choose the principle of unity, since we cannot function as a nation without it." Hirsch would accumulate and share symbols. Only thus "can we learn to communicate effectively with one another in our national community." The *New York Times* looks on when such claims are made and reflects, as it did during a curricular battle in New York in 1990, "Essentially, the issue is how to deal with both dimensions of the nation's motto: 'E pluribus unum'—'Out of many, one.' " Takaki quoted Rodney King following the riots in Los Angeles in 1992, after the police who had beaten him were acquitted: "Please, can we get along here? We all can get along. I mean, we're all stuck here for a while. Let's try to work it out." This was a translation of John Courtney Murray's call for civility against the barbarians when he defined a republic as people locked in civil argument. Takaki, however, seized the moment after Rodney King's plea to ask, "But how should 'we' be defined? Who are the people 'stuck here' in America?" The Los Angeles "we" differed from the national "we." In Los Angeles blacks represent only 13 percent of the population, but Hispanics number 40 percent. Takaki wants the Asian, Native American, and Hispanic stories told: "The telling of stories liberates." He quotes Tomo Shojis, an elderly Nisei woman, who called on her fellow Asian Americans to learn about their own roots: "We got such good, fantastic stories to tell. All our stories are different."[16]

Takaki's history reveals more of the values of shared narrative, jostling as they may be to received tradition, than of an off-putting anthology of exclusions:

> While our stories contain the memories of different communities, together they inscribe a larger narrative. Filled with what Walt Whitman celebrated as the "varied carols" of America, our history generously gives all of us our "mystic chords of memory." Throughout our past of oppressions and struggles for equality, Americans of different races and ethnicities have been "singing with open mouths their strong melodious songs." . . . Our denied history "bursts with telling." As we hear America singing, we find ourselves invited to bring our rich cultural diversity on deck, to accept ourselves. "Of every hue and caste am I," sang Whitman. "I resist any thing better than my own diversity."[17]

The language may be a bit romantic and florid, but it suggests that the attempt to bring many ethnic perspectives to a single history may well enrich the republic, not lead to self-exclusion.

Whoever compares a book like Takaki's with the heritage of McGuffey's readers and the nostalgic renderings of American "sameness" may come to the realization that the often-cited tradition to which John Jay referred two centuries ago is by no means the most familiar part of the emergent canon. Thanks to efforts by people like Takaki for many years, the parallel set of stories has become part, almost the privileged part, of the canon.

Picture an examination of a high school class: what are these young people likely to know after watching television, attending public school? Is any white Protestant social activist as well known to them today as Martin Luther King is? Is any male Catholic's career as familiar a part of the story of activism as Dorothy Day's? Any northern male Catholic novelist as familiar to today's collegians as Flannery O'Connor or Toni Morrison? Any contemporary music issuing from northern Europe as familiar as the music coming from Mexico or the Caribbean?

High school students may have heard that there was a *Mayflower,* that John Winthrop and others talked of a "Citty upon a Hill," or that a weird, severe man named Jonathan Edwards wanted us to see ourselves suspended as a spider above a flame, with hell in the distance. Beyond that, could the rest of the New England stories be as familiar a part of secondary education as is that of Malcolm X and the Nation of Islam? Are the stories of white settlers of the West today any longer as familiar as the plot of *Dances with Wolves* and its lesser clones? Are there real worries that today's America overremembers the best-known mainstream Protestant ministers of the mid-nineteenth century, people like Horace Bushnell; or do Joseph Smith of the Mormons, Mary Baker Eddy of Christian Science, and the countercultural and utopian communalists go neglected? Just the opposite. It is time to notice how drastically the presumed canon has already changed and to reward the students who excel in this new curriculum.

When conflict over texts and curricula heats up, one reads all kinds of analyses of the motives of leaders. In all cases, obvious plays for power on the part of the leadership have to be noticed. Mere devotion to ideology, be it leftover Marxism, revised Freudianism, the reworked Enlightenment, Judeo-Christianism, or Christianism, is a demonstrable motivator, as revealed by numerous texts written by partisans. Many of the charges imply group narcissism or solipsism. Such people look into Takaki's different mirror and find it made up of many mirrors. They look only into their own. But other uses of the mirror are possible.

Myths against the World's Indifference

If the conversation is to be advanced, a search for motives other than self-portrayal is also profitable. Among the most compelling clues that I have come across, clues that can be followed through careful reading of texts by those who want their group to be heard, were those offered in a work on myth by Leszek Kolakowski. He wrote *The Presence of Myth* in 1966, but Polish authorities suppressed it and it did not appear in English until 1989, in a context very different from the one in which he wrote.

One listens, says Kolakowski, to the stories of sufferers, victims, the oppressed, or those who have endured and sometimes triumphed. These are stories designed to illumine and display a group's experience. In the course of time it becomes clear that the tellers were addressing what Kolakowski calls the "phenomenon of the world's indifference." The victims of the Holocaust went almost unnoticed by the world at large. Survivors and heirs cry out against posthumous indifference.

The horrifying accounts of brutality against slaves rarely give reference to the name of someone whose heirs were compensated, whose grave one can visit. The world looks on, indifferent. The ignominy and deprivation suffered by Japanese Americans rounded up into camps from 1942 to 1945 was not balanced by the few dollars grudgingly doled out to survivors decades later. Indifference. Homosexual men and women suffer stigma and are asked by society to change what they see as their fundamental nature, to "stay in the closet," and certainly not to band together. They are subjects of the world's indifference. So are the anonymous people who suffered on the Trail of Tears or whose hearts are buried at Wounded Knee. Cemetery stones erode, descendants move away and forget, and everything is subject to transience. So the organized indifference on the part of dominant or rival peoples is especially infuriating.

Kolakowski speaks of the role of myth against the world's indifference. Why be indifferent? "The simplest answer is that we are running away from suffering." And what does all suffering have in common? "That from which we flee is the experience of the world's indifference, and attempts to overcome this indifference constitute the crucial meaning of human struggle with fate, both in its everyday and its extreme form." Thus "in dying and in the death of our loved ones, what is most acute is precisely that they become indifferent towards us, absorbed irrevocably in the place whence they ostentatiously demonstrate a complete lack of interest in us."

We can do nothing about all this. Kolakowski speaks instead of the living company we keep: "we all know that we live only thanks to various kinds of nonindifference in our encounters with people: thanks to solidarity, trust, love, and friendship."

Kolakowski notes how intense and ecstatic the communion of the intimate group can be. "Identification with other people or groups of people," almost on the model of sexual communion, suggests this:

> Flights from the indifference of the world via edifices which enable us to be absorbed in communal life through identification with family, tribal, or national groups is not by any means worthless; but it does seem that in this respect the all-or-nothing rule prevails, that therefore partial or fleeting identifications do not truly exist.

So such endeavors do not truly satisfy efforts to overcome the experience of the world's indifference. They are efforts to "conceal this experience from ourselves in a complex system of arrangements which distract life in daily facticity." Here is where myth comes in. "Myth, be it religious or philosophical . . . has the power of removing the world's indifference."[18]

Thus the early nationalists in America had to render the Constitution a part of sacral mythology and thus Abraham Lincoln spoke as he did at Gettysburg and elsewhere. This is why the long-term custodians of national traditions in the school texts had to invent an America that never was. This is also why those who would subvert the invention choose myths that sometimes create unrealistic pictures of the daily lives of oppressed and excluded people. This is why advocates of the Judeo-Christian legacies had to combine them and name the combination a tradition, though it had never existed elsewhere. This is why they had to engage in great theological leaps in order to fabricate a set of values for the tradition—while overlooking the lethal elements in the mandates of both the Hebrew scriptures and the New Testament.

The question remains, in the face of the potential misuse of story and myth, in the name of both the *unum* and the *plures:* how can we minimize the damage the stories can do, given the ambiguity and the "dark side" locked into the stories? The advocate of pluralism sees the best safeguard in the interaction of groups that hear and tell them. The best possibilities for common life issue from their conversation and from conversation's self-correcting character. The possibilities are most slender when people restrict all value-creating signals to those of their own group. Common life happens most often when one engages in acts of "plural belonging." George P. Fletcher in his essay on loyalty uses the image of intersecting circles:

We typically find ourselves in a set of intersecting circles of loyal commitment. In the United States and indeed in virtually every modern culture, we are members of multiple groups that demand our loyalties. A typical American is a member not only of a family but of an ethnic group, a profession or trade, a particular firm, a church or religious community, the alumni circles of high school and university, and perhaps an amateur athletic team or the fan club of a local hockey or basketball team. Add to this list the special loyalties of veterans and the politically active, and you generate a picture of the typical American caught in the intersection of at least a half dozen circles of loyal attachment.

Viewing recent change, Fletcher adds:

> Despite the vast immigration of Hispanics and Asians in recent years, the coming out of gays and lesbians, the new assertiveness of feminist, Jewish and black leaders, one is hard pressed to impose on the cultural patterns of the United States the kind of enclaving that has existed for centuries in other countries. The pop culture of TV sitcoms, McDonald's, Peanuts, and Superman, the Dodgers, hating Saddam Hussein, feeling compassion for Magic Johnson, pondering the credibility of Anita Hill and Clarence Thomas—these are constitutive cultural experiences affecting virtually all Americans. Those who claim cultural rifts in the United States comparable to the endless tribal clashes of Eastern Europe, Asia, and Africa miss the beat of American life.[19]

It is this characteristic that makes both totalist and tribalist leaders so suspicious of conversation and multiple belonging. To build confidence in stories that promote the cohesive sentiment in a republic without doing injustice to the groups that share life in it, we will focus next on the realization of a common space, the arena for its stories and their explanations, and then on what we will call "constituting" myths that all Americans somehow share, however much they disagree on their meanings.

CHAPTER NINE

Storied Places, Where Healing Can Begin

Argument is necessary if there is to be justice in a free society. Conversation is urgent if citizens are freely to associate with one another within such a society. The telling and hearing of one another's stories provide motivations for such associating and promote empathy among the individuals and groups that make up the same society. But argument, conversations, and storytelling have to have some substance, some content. Merely to engage in these may be preferable to not engaging, because each helps keep the republican process going. But as mere procedures, they would soon lose their capability for advancing the common good. Whoever listens long and reaches far into the past and into the experiences of the lively individuals and contending peoples will find that a primary, even primal, topic is the common space, the shared place in which citizens find themselves. More often than not they have reflected and do reflect positively on this reality. If they are in relative concord, they celebrate the place. If they are in conflict, they wage it with a particular map under their feet or a distinctive story in their imaginations. They almost never withdraw from the scene or emigrate.

What It Means to Share a Space, a Place

Justice Frankfurter, addressing the issue of the common good, spoke of a "free society" but did so without noting where such a society was to be found. Of course, because he ruled on the grounds of the U.S. Constitution in a decision affecting American citizens, it is natural to equate such a society with a nation-state in general and with the

United States in particular. But entities larger than nations— churches, international organizations, movements, peoples—also bid for loyalty. And smaller ones—regions, states, tribal territories— do the same. So there are good reasons to pause and reflect on the nation-state as the space, the place, where a free society is to be nurtured.

Thus groups like Amnesty International, while keeping their eye on the United States, sound the alert when citizens anywhere are at ease in the face of violations of human rights. Similarly, those who promote symbols of the "human family" should be uneasy about focusing so much energy and loyalty on the nation. Those who adhere to world religions like Christianity, Judaism, and Islam enjoy extranational commitments to community and to transcendent realities that can conflict with the demands of particular nations.

There are other reasons for citizens to keep some distance from the practice of overinvesting in the nation-state as the locus of discourse and loyalty. The religions of nationalism, the totalist, coercive, efficient, and ambitious governmental movements, have attracted idolatry and produced terror unmatched in our century. Patriotism easily turns into chauvinism. Enforced orthodoxies and imposed rights run counter to the very notion of a free society. But the reasons for taking the risks with language in support of loyalty are also valid, say those who are at all attentive to nations and nationalism.

Why do they say so? First, they answer, nations *will* attract profound loyalties and fanaticisms, no matter what the sober advocates instill by way of reservation about chauvinism and idolatry. If the summoning of such attachments is completely in the hands of the unguardedly patriotic and jingoistic, citizens will have few options for expressing loyalty short of mere or utter self-worship.

Second, say the defenders: if one grants that nations as civil associations have to make room for even minimal positive functions and that they may or should exercise some of these functions themselves, they need to invoke common symbols.

Third, remembering what the physician Willard Gaylin called events that promote "proximal identification," we see the role of place as being naturally part of national experience. We have "our" plane crashes and hurricanes, "our" Olympic victories and celebrations, and others have "theirs." These events appear to evoke irrepressible responses originating deep in human nature. Even and maybe especially an ungenerous citizenry will relate to them without bringing perspective to the occasion and without needing encouragement.

Finally, at least for now: by reflecting on what a nation can aspire to in respect to symbols, sentiments, and stories, it will be possible to see more clearly where national functions and prospects stop and where the symbiotic subcommunities and groups start to exercise their appeal and make their demands.

How Nation-States Relate to Space and Place: The Definition of Ernest Gellner

At this turn, because I want to speak of the common good of a nation, I have to spend a moment making clear what is meant here by *nation, state,* and *nation-state.* Ernest Gellner wrote on nations and nationalism in ways that can inform our inquiry. Because he does not define *nation* as community but as association or society, he allows for the rich pluralism that one expects of a country like the United States.

He also relates the nation to the concept of culture. This relating will inevitably be done by anyone who has a concern for the "binding ties of cohesive sentiment," tradition, and civilization. The nation as a civil association lives by securing consent to its laws. But since this association depends upon and welcomes all the "agencies of the mind and spirit" to help generate cultures, it is impossible to complete a discussion of nation and nationalism without reference to culture.

Elsewhere Gellner has connected culture with the issue of its transmission through time:

> Historical transformations are transmitted by culture, which is a form of transmission which, unlike genetic transmission, *does* perpetuate acquired characteristics. In fact, culture *consists* of sets of acquired characteristics. A culture is a distinct way of doing things which characterizes a given community, and which is not dictated by the genetic make-up of its members . . . It seems that any culture on earth can be assimilated and internalized by an infant of any given "racial" group, just as any infant can acquire any language. Cultures are not genetically transmitted, even though cultures can and do use genetic traits as symbols and markers.

Cultures can loosely be defined as systems of concepts or ideas which guide thought and conduct . . . Cultures are socially transmitted, but the converse argument—societies are perpetuated by cultures— should not be accepted lightly. It is in fact contentious and deeply problematic.

Gellner introduces that last point to remind us that the line between idealists and materialists persists in societies like our own. The materialist says that perpetuation of a society "depends on more earthy factors, such as physical coercion or threats of hunger." Gellner asks, "Why assume that the question [of cultures] has the same answer in all places and at all times? Concepts do constitute a social constraint; but not all social constraints are conceptual."[1]

Governments do impose social constraints, sometimes even touching on religion, when they remove religion from the voluntary realm of ideas and creeds and faith and move it into the realm of imposed practices and rituals. Our question, posed in Frankfurter's terms, is how the "agencies of the mind and spirit," which are socially transmitted cultures, can relate to the larger civil association and produce the "binding ties of cohesive sentiment." How do they do this within a nation?

Gellner begins the definition of the nation-state that I shall borrow by citing the apparently cynical and certainly realistic observation of Max Weber that the nation-state is "that agency within society which possesses the monopoly of legitimate violence." Though not always the case, this "underlying principle, Gellner says, "does, however, seem valid *now,*" at least where the well-centralized Western state prevails. For defining or pointing to the nation, Gellner employs "two very makeshift, temporary definitions" that make a contribution:

1. Two men are of the same nation if and only if they share the same culture, where culture in turn means a system of ideas and signs and associations and ways of behaving and communicating.
2. Two men are of the same nation if and only if they *recognize* each other as belonging to the same nation. In other words, *nations maketh man;* nations are the artefacts of men's convictions and loyalties and solidarities. A mere category of persons (say, occupants of a given territory, or speakers of a given language, for example), becomes a nation if and when the members of the category firmly

recognize certain mutual rights and duties to each other in virtue of their shared membership of it. It is their recognition of each other as fellows of this kind which turns them into a nation, and not the other shared attributes, whatever they might be, which separate that category from non-members.

Gellner is aware of how complex a task it is to talk about culture. He chooses not to say what culture *is* as much as to note what it *does*. It is our business to observe how these two elements are at issue in the debates between totalists and tribalists. The former would impose and coerce a "system of ideas and signs and associations" at the expense of the tribes and interest groups. The tribes, in turn, say that the voluntary approaches are effective only within the tribe and not in the chaos of pluralism or when an elite dominates. Gellner recognizes this:

> Any definition of nations in terms of shared culture is . . . [a] net which brings in far too rich a catch. Human history is and continues to be well endowed with cultural differentiations, and these will not and cannot normally or generally converge either with the boundaries of political units . . . or with the boundaries of units blessed by the democratic sacraments of consent and will.[2]

Supporting the idea of the nation in respect to culture and cultural differentiations is very different from advocating the idea that nationalism can or should produce community. William Pfaff, an expert on international affairs, sees community produced on other, more intimate levels. But he also rightly accents nationalism's "links to the primordial human attachments to family, clan, and community." Further, the journalist Michael Ignatieff visited a cathedral in Ukraine as congregants sang their Alleluia and noted:

> Standing among men and women who do not hide intense, long-suppressed feelings, it becomes clear what nationalism really is: the dream that a whole nation could be like a congregation—singing the same hymns, listening to the same gospel, sharing the same emotions, linked not only to each other but to the dead buried beneath their feet.

Pfaff went on to quote Ernest Renan, who spoke (as does Gellner)

of "will" as an important element in the making of the nation. Thus a
nation is a "daily plebiscite," a "spiritual principle," a "moral consciousness." In defining a nation in 1882 Renan held that the "essence
of a nation is that its people have much in common and have forgotten much." This observation referred to the fact that "citizens must
deliberately put behind them events which have divided them." In
American life, we have seen this in Robert E. Lee's statement that the
defeated Confederacy was not "agreeing" but "acquiescing," which
was its own way of forgetting. Pfaff also cites Hugh Seton-Watson,
who after a lifetime of study was "driven to the conclusion that no
'scientific definition' of a nation" could be devised. Even so, the nation
exists:

> All that I can find to say is that a nation exists when a significant
> number of people in a community consider themselves to form a na-
> tion, or behave as if they formed one. It is not necessary that the whole
> of the population should so feel, or so behave, and it is not possible
> to lay down dogmatically a minimum proportion of a population which
> must be so affected. When a significant group holds this belief, it pos-
> sesses "national consciousness."[3]

The comment by Seton-Watson locates us where we want to be:
in the realm not of the genetic but of the cultural and especially the
voluntary and the affective with respect to the nation as a civil association. Here is the sphere of national consciousness but not of
nationalism or of nationalism *as religion*. There remains the task,
then, of beginning to point to some of these shared elements and
experiences. This is done in the face of totalists who want more loyalty expressed to their *unum,* the whole nation, as they set the terms
for it. Such a task, when effectively pursued, also counters tribalists.
They want all devotion to be directed to their group, their part of the
plures, in the form of subcommunities that provide particular identities.

What do people in a nation share? Gellner mentioned the obvious,
the theme with which we began talking about the common good.
People in a nation start by sharing a territory. Evocation of territory
brings with it shadows and specters of territorialism, of turf protection and acts of aggression by nations to gain more land at the expense of their neighbors. But a more benign side to territorial think-

ing also exists, one that American citizens share: a love for the place itself. This love would be dangerous, of course, if it were translated into idolatry of the locale, region, or place where the national gods visited, but such translation is by no means inevitable.

Some early Americans were convinced that their God had preserved their colonial place and protected it until they could arrive. God had chosen them specifically and exclusively. He had caused the Protestant Reformation, to prepare a ready people to people a readied land. Some Catholics on occasion have claimed to have experienced an apparition of the Virgin at some spring or on some hill in the United States. Native Americans usually revere their own sacred places, lakes, and mountains. Taken together, however, such historical claims and phenomena are quite rare. They make news when they issue in competing claims to ownership and reach the courts. They have not occurred frequently enough to lead one to qualify the generalization that Americans tend to regard their fifty-state entity with its many landscapes as being somehow sacrally endowed as a whole.

This sense is expressed in colloquial terms as "God's country." One can find such affirmations of American place in the texts left by immigrant Jews who slaved in dark, hot, upper-story sweatshops in New York. A North Dakota woman of whom I have heard kept a diary during the drought and depression of the 1930s. One day one drop of dew on one blade of grass inspired her to crouch on the ground and watch the morning sun be prismed through it. In her notebook she wrote: "Beautiful. This is God's country!" Zealous Chinese refugees in our time choose to be stuffed into boxes or tankers and smuggled at great expense into the American place. Contemporary immigrants display regard for the streets, shops, cities, and rural sites anywhere. They kiss the soil when their planes land, as longtime residents may not.

Visitors, whether they were the anonymous seamen who by their foreignness disturbed the settled colonial population whenever they came ashore or notables like Tocqueville, wondered at the land they saw, and said so. But visitors, explorers, and commentators have little investment in a place. The act of settling at a specific site makes all the difference. Mircea Eliade dealt chiefly with primitives, but his point is applicable to the theme of common ground elsewhere—not even metaphorically, but literally: "Settlement in a new, unknown, uncultivated country is equivalent to an act of Creation . . . the transformation of chaos into cosmos by the divine act of Creation. By cultivating the desert soil, they in fact repeated the act of the gods, who organized chaos by giving it forms and norms."[4]

The colonials who transformed the wilderness into the garden made it their settlement. Homesteaders engaged in their own acts of creation, even when they were huddled in sod houses. They may not have celebrated formal rituals about the soil or associated any sacral meaning with those towns that quickly became ghost towns. But most records of those who settled and stayed in the West show that they regarded what they were doing as an act of creation and invested their lives and hopes in that creation.

Vestiges of this sense remain even in some suburban settlements, where the first arrivals have to build the firehouses, schools, and churches. The sense of participating admittedly becomes vague in the modern urban high-rise or condominium. Still, citizens of all sorts have a way of transferring their sense of creation and of sacralization to the nation as a whole. By the millions they visit the national parks. God's country.

Totalists sacralize the whole nation according to their single interpretation and then demand assent to it. "Love it or leave it." Tribalists sacralize their group and its own place exclusively. And most Americans, though situated between these poles, rarely regard the national landscape and cityscape as patently profane. Prophets on occasion have to come along to denounce those who make too much of their natural setting. People are to revere their place with approaches that reflect penultimate, not ultimate, seriousness. The warnings are necessary in God's country. Surveying all, the onlooker facing the American scene asks, What is the place of place?

The common experience of Americans begins with theory (*theoria*, Greek for "behold"): citizens of all sorts possess a proprietary sense that can easily be explored and even exploited when they visit their overcrowded national parks. Environmental aesthetes scorn the commercialism, artificiality, and kitsch that go with the act of camping in those parks when campers use expensive recreational vehicles topped by satellite dishes and including all the comforts of home. Yet the enjoyers of folk, low, and popular culture at least are *there*. They

choose to view the environments they partly own as tourists for centuries have done, out of a variety of motives. They are placing themselves. Citizens may live in partly incommensurable universes of discourse, but in beholding the place where they settle or the landscape
they visit, they find some measures of commensurability and reasons
for staying on the scene. God's country.

Thereupon follows reflection: "Surely the Lord is in this place."
"Land where our fathers died." "This hallowed ground." "This land is
your land, this land is my land," sang Woody Guthrie. Wallace Stevens said, "we live not in a place but in a description of a place."[5]
Glacier National Park is described as "ours" and, so far as national
boundaries are concerned, is "ours." Waterton Lakes Park in Alberta
is separated from Glacier by no visible boundary, only the artificial
national line. It is at least as beautiful as Glacier. But it is "theirs," as
are Mont Blanc and Popocatepetl and Mount Fujiyama.

After reflection comes awe. "Take the shoes off your feet, for the
ground on which you are standing is holy ground." The graffiti-paint-
ing vandals violate holy landscapes. Wright Morris looked at drab
prairie landscapes and derelict deserted farm places and treated them
lovingly with camera and typewriter: "Was there, then, something
holy about these things? If not, why had I used the word? For holy
things, they were ugly enough."[6]

Yi-Fu Tuan, an observer of the meaning of place, deals with its
ambiguous relation to religion. "Religion could either bind a people
to a place or free them from it." Mobile Americans, largely an immigrant people, tend to be free from attachment to specific shrines,
but they are at least loosely bound to the whole environment—where
they meet one another. Mobility does change the relationship. Speaking of being bound to place, Yi-Fu Tuan continues in reference to
tribal pacts: "The neighboring state might be so near at hand that one
could hear the cocks crowing and dogs barking in it. But the people
would grow old and die without ever having been there."[7]

Many Americans, thanks to tourism and mobility, may homogenize
landscapes in their imaginations and then make all places appear to
be the same, in a "geography of nowhere." The prefabricated building,
unsited and situated anywhere, is expressive of this tendency. Mech-
anization works against the sense of immediate specific place. Marshall McLuhan said that "nothing can be further from the spirit of

the new technology than 'a place for everything and everything in its place.' "⁸ But the variety of sacred places within the American setting is at least a counterforce, beckoning for awareness of differences.

Walter Ong, S.J., once mentioned that America had no real shrines marking apparitions; the most popular images for Catholics here were the Holy Family, with Mary and Jesus on a donkey and Joseph walking, or St. Christopher, who blessed transportation and movement. But far from signaling the profanization of place, such saints helped travelers extend a sense of the sacral to any place.

I am not saying that only Americans possess these sensibilities and make use of them. Anything but that. Tribal or largely immobile people certainly have shown a stronger sense of place than do most other Americans. Belden Lane, in *Landscapes of the Sacred,* an exploration of geography and narrative about American spirituality, addresses this theme directly:

> A first question confronting the study of sacred place within American spiritual traditions is one that derives from the distinctive American penchant for mobility and placelessness. Can it actually be argued that this same passion for place, discerned in so many traditional cultures, is also to be found in *American* consciousness, known as Americans are for their relentless transience, their perennial "Song of the Open Road"? Americans may be fascinated by "space," but their attachment to particular "places" may often be negligible . . . The American people have, at best, been ambivalent in their attachment to place.⁹

Aware of this complication, Lane pressed on and produced a book rich in detail about how Americans, despite ambivalences, became attached to place. Similarly, I am stressing the sense of place precisely because one would expect to find it utterly diminished in this country. Instead one finds profound attachment to the environment as a whole. Every fifth American may move each year. No problem: the landscape is portable. The Yankee Taverne can be in Santa Fe and Casa Grande in New Hampshire. Yet, when serious, most citizens relate also to specific places. Freya Stark expresses the idea or feeling behind the attachment of many:

> In smaller, more familiar things, memory weaves her strongest enchantments, holding us at her mercy with some trifle, some echo, a

tone of voice, a scent of tar and seaweed on the quay. . . . This surely
is the meaning of home—a place where every day is multiplied by all
the days before it.[10]

So America becomes a home place, among underclasses who would
escape the urban ghetto—for other, better urban sites—and among
upper classes, only a few of whose members would emigrate to other
shores to renounce citizenship for tax purposes. The subgroups in,
for example, the Hispanic American group may have a variety of
home environments: Spanish Harlem in New York for Puerto Ricans,
Miami for Cubans, San Antonio for Mexicans. Yet they all would
reject the notion of returning to a place in a nation other than the
United States, a nation where poverty or politics made living uncongenial. They are all invested in the American place. Asian Americans,
be they Japanese or Korean, Malaysian or Cambodian, Punjabi or
Vietnamese, create subcultural colonies, but when the issue of citizenship comes up, they affirm the whole American place. When
means are available, they are ardent visitors to all kinds of American
sites. Do they all live in "incommensurable universes of discourse"?
Yi-Fu Tuan relates the sense of place to the nation-state:

> The sentiment that once tied people to their village, city, or region had
> to be transferred to the larger political unit. The nation-state, rather
> than any of its parts, was to achieve maximum visibility. How could
> this be done? One method was and is to make the state the object of
> a religious cult [as the French Legislative Assembly did in 1792]. In
> patriotic fervor men say, "We must protect our sacred soil." They are
> saying, in effect, that "the land which is our country must be protected
> as if all of it were like a church." The field and the cesspool upon the
> land are details, mundane and irrelevant. To make the idea of the sacred
> country seem real, sacred places that can be directly experienced are
> created.

In the United States, says Yi-Fu Tuan, these special places are not
cathedrals, but more likely civic buildings or sites like Independence
Hall or the Vietnam Memorial and other monuments in Washington.[11]

Agents of many ethnic groups in America may at first hearing speak
critically of any references to place. After all, they would say, someone

else got here first. That someone was usually of the dominant and oppressive population stock. The European American male, it is often said, had already desecrated the place before the later immigrants came. He had committed genocide against Native Americans or put them on reservations, enslaved the blacks, exploited the Chinese miners and railroad builders, and oppressed the workers. Did he not think of the land as his and minorities as people to be exploited?

Such articulations do not do full justice to the long history of ethnic minority affirmation, which should first be listened to. One becomes a participant in a place by experience and affectivity. A classic expression, replicable a thousand times, is that of the militant ex-slave David Walker, who opposed efforts by American philanthropists to free slaves and send them back to Africa: "America is more our country than it is the whites'—we have enriched it with our *blood and tears*." Richard Allen, founder of the African Methodist Episcopal church, was just as eloquent: "This land, which we have watered with our tears and our blood, is now our mother country, and we are well satisfied to stay where wisdom abounds and the gospel is free."[12]

Periodic efforts by blacks to persuade other African Americans to resettle in Africa have always been resounding failures: the freed slaves have owned this landscape and land as much as anyone. They also have no difficulty understanding why Native Americans retain a sense of their American place, just as heirs of continental European immigrants do. In the first generation many immigrants may have nostalgia for the old country, but just as many can be caught by photographers kissing the soil upon their return.

This historical sense of attachment to place as the first mark of a shared life continues into the present. The Mexican Americans who settle in southern California and New Mexico or Arizona do not even have to become familiar with alien place names, so many of these reflect their Mexican and Indian heritages from centuries ago. In many cities, ethnic groups share parks and there encounter each other, not always in hostile ways. One will come across a circle of lesbians committed to one another and dancing in an urban park. Nearby a gay pride parade is made up of people saying, in effect, "These streets are also ours." The battles over crèches and menorahs on courthouse lawns are less acts of Christian or Jewish devotion than efforts to say "We majorities (or we minorities) belong here."

Emphatically, the reference to place is not all aesthetic, gentle, or benign. Places present varieties of plots for the people in them. Americans have their Three-Mile Island, their Love Canal, their despoiled strip-mined plateaus alongside purple mountain majesties. They recognize demolished landmarks, and they have abandoned sick places. They have done nuclear bomb testing, and they have let the plains erode.

Many citizen groups have also known what E. V. Walter calls "ominous space."[13] The journals of fighters on both sides in the Civil War or the records of Native Americans and the U.S. military are full of references to threatening places. The ghetto is alien to the suburban white, while the African American poor may find suburban malls or leafy streets ominous. But such spaces do not detract from the drama of place; reflection on them thickens the plot that evokes myth. Much of the spell of life in the cave in *Huckleberry Finn* or on the run in the Underground Railroad in *Uncle Tom's Cabin* derives from just this ominous factor.

Attachment to the whole American place, the territory occupied by a nation-state with its cultures, connects immediately with the mythic language that citizens tend to prefer when dealing with nature and history in America. This may be another point of continuity with ancients. E. V. Walter in *Placeways* cited a student of astronomy and myth, Jerome Lettvin, to make the point about ambiguities in mythic encounters with place. The myth

> only adds to the richness and, if you wish, the memorability of the ideas. For myths are more memorable the more things one can map on them. And there is for me a great poetic quality in a language whereby the relations of animals to each other, people to each other, the heavens to the earth, the gods to humankind, can all be worded in about the same way, until finally, by a single set of sentences, I can remember all of the universes as if they were maps of one another.[14]

This is exactly right for the American situation of *e pluribus unum*: if myth and symbol were univocal and could thus be reduced to single meanings, the totalists could misuse them. If only one place and one myth were available, the tribalists would not need to stay around to inquire or converse. But Lettvin finds many myths, each with many meanings, to serve as a charter for pluralist understandings.

So we have begun on the ground, seeking common ground, and have gone to the physical basis for the spiritual basics, and this for good reasons. Americans in groups and subcommunities who currently have difficulty talking to one another or who disdain the act of doing so are at least condemned to share the same place of one nation-state with its many cultures. When citizens reduce everything to the rational dimensions of power relations, they may talk past one another or shout or not talk at all. But when they ponder their landscape, their environment, and are drawn to deal with it mythically, they become locked with one another.

Walter quotes Ernst Cassirer, the expert on myth, to help move to the prerational or "not only rational" mode in respect to the land. This prerational approach undergirds the well-worn examples of rational debate and political positioning over the one and the many. In the spirit of Paul Ricoeur, who said "the symbol gives rise to the thought," Cassirer said, "it is the *image* which opens up the true essentiality and makes it knowable." He adds: "For mythical thinking the relation between what a thing 'is' and the place in which it is situated is never purely external and accidental; the place is itself a part of the thing's being." Walter comments:

> The sense that a place is friendly or unfriendly is an extremely primitive quality of experience—more primitive, Cassirer shows, than the perception of color or form . . . The soul or spirit of a place, therefore, may be perceived as the quality of its expressive space, and the spirit of a place means an independent expressive energy that evokes feelings and representations.[15]

This attempt to connect the American nation-state with the groups that contend within it thus begins with an awareness of shared American place and space. This awareness could be misread as a suggestion that the environment, seen by the various *symbiotes* as revelatory and redemptive, works a magic. No, the myths connected with a place, be it a welcoming or an ominous space, like all myths, acquire power from the way they are interpreted by the people who live with them.

The Jewish workers in the sweatshops, the slaves who had watered America with their tears, the Native Americans who cherish a particular lake, the immigrants who kiss the soil are not attached to the physical molecules that make up these environments. The places evoke memories: stories of successes and betrayals, of happy connections and disappointments. The people in these environments experience loss of place when death or departure occurs. Memories are then altered, but the stories go on because place is constant. Saint Augustine felt thus about his place, Thagaste, after his childhood friend had died:

> My heart was now darkened by grief, and everywhere I looked I saw death. My native haunts became a scene of torture to me, and my own home a misery. Without him everything we had done together turned into excruciating ordeal. My eyes kept looking for him without finding him. I hated all the places where we used to meet, because they could no longer say to me, "Look, here he comes," as they once did.[16]

Intimate attachments such as those that come with friendship, however, belong to the zone of community, not association. To picture elements like friendship, sentiment, and affection on a scale larger than that provided by intimate subcommunities is more difficult. Citizens need to tell stories of the origins of their common life. In our culture these may be mythic accents of the documents that helped such national existence into being. This, as we shall see, they have done and can do again, though in ever reconceived ways.

CHAPTER TEN

The Constitutional Myth

Space and place may ground the stories of American nature, but the stories of American history center in events. They deal with struggles for the common good and with crises when such a good eludes them. As in the case of most societies, the accounts of their genesis demand retelling. The era of founders and foundings provides originating tales. The narratives of the American Revolution help serve for this. But in a peculiar way the achievement of a written document, the U.S. Constitution, and its subsequent development and use through more than two centuries of national life, has furnished more than a mere basis for legal life. It has taken on an additional role in the form of what I will call the constitutional myth. Here, as so often, the word *myth* has nothing to do with the issue of truth and untruth. It has to do instead with the fact that certain truths or debates about untruth take on a characteristic form, an almost unavoidable one, that transcends mere reporting and chronicling. As is the case with originating myths in other cultures, this myth or collection of myths helps supply elements of identity for the groups that have been assured their freedom in the Constitution, and offers elements of meaning for those who seek the common good.

Michael Oakeshott has argued that a civil association makes no other demand on citizens than the commitment to *lex*, or law, which provides the legal basis of society. James Madison urged additionally that the purpose of government is justice. The framers of the Constitution went further still in their Preamble, which stated the purposes of the fundamental law. The drafters wrote that through this Constitution the people were acting "to form a more perfect Union, establish Justice, insure domestic Tranquility, provide for the common defence, promote the general Welfare, and secure the Blessings of Liberty."

A Division of Labor

Americans have often shown an ability to differentiate between the creedal demands of their churches and the legal obligations their nation places on them as citizens. But the natural impulse to turn loyalty to the Constitution into something religious itself is strong. The document gets treated as scripture. Myths support it, and symbols surround it. Because the potential for the constitutional myth to attract too much devotion is as great as the danger that in some sectors it will be remembered too little, citizens busy themselves with drawing lines that reflect some division of labor in the use of the document and its story.

In respect to the limits of myth and the salutary division of labor, one thinks of a story told about the notably uncharismatic British prime minister Harold Macmillan. Once asked to be more charismatic for his nation's good, he responded that if the people wanted charisma they should go to their "bloody archbishop."

In respect to the Constitution, citizens often cross such a line. They will not read a document as being charismatic. But they may well regard it in such a way that it can provide a means for the symbiotic one and the many to link up around a sacred center. If the sacrality is underemphasized, the tradition can be trivialized and law disrespected. But if people want the law to serve for all sacred purposes, they might be better advised to seek their own "bloody archbishop" or shaman or guru for something deeper or more appropriate for personal needs.

To say that Americans have often turned their Constitution into something storied and mythic is not to suggest that troubadours should sing about it. It does happen that the narratives about what has been called the "miracle of Philadelphia" in 1787 do not amount to dull history. But one does not picture that they will heat up a crowd of teenagers around a campfire or inspire a singer in a downtown nightclub. The Story Lady at the local library would be hard pressed to get a hearing for the Philadelphia story. Even in law school courses on the Constitution's history, students may yawn. Clearly something else is meant when people say that the constitutional myth is vital in American life. Some observers say that it is a remarkable thing that the United States makes so much of a written constitution. But we have to reexplore what role it plays in the traditions of a nation, what part it can play in a renewed search for the common good.

Is This a "Nation with the Soul of a Church"?

Efforts to move beyond the Constitution's Preamble into more elaborate philosophical or creedal commitments have been frequent. Among the best known of these are tales and treatises that take off from a comment by a British visitor earlier in the twentieth century, G. K. Chesterton. "Somewhat irked and then amused by the questions he was asked [about the Declaration of Independence] when he applied for a passport to the United States," according to Sidney E. Mead, Chesterton went fishing for what "makes America peculiar."

The circumstance of Chesterton's report of being irked and amused has always puzzled me. He made everything of the Declaration of Independence of 1776, not the Constitution of 1787. Yet passport and customs officers, certainly in Great Britain, have no business asking their citizens questions about the Declaration. Devotion to its propositions belongs wholly to the persuasive and voluntary aspect of commitment even in America itself. The Constitution, being *lex*, is by nature coercive, imposed. Whatever the circumstance, however, Chesterton came up with this:

> America is the only nation in the world that is founded on a creed. That creed is set forth with dogmatic and even theological lucidity in the Declaration of Independence ... It enunciates that all men are equal in their claim to justice, and that governments exist to give them that justice, and that their authority is for that reason just. It certainly does condemn anarchism, and it does also by inference condemn atheism, since it clearly names the Creator as the ultimate authority from whom these equal rights are derived.[1]

Prove it, one is tempted to say. The Chesterton quotation raises many questions. If the "it" that is the creed on which America is founded does "by inference condemn atheism," does that make atheists second-class citizens, or even traitors? Certainly the author of what Chesterton called the American creed, Thomas Jefferson, did not think so. Just the opposite: whether the citizen believed in one or twenty or no gods was civilly and constitutionally irrelevant, wrote the drafter of the Declaration. The citizens who assent to the propositions in the Declaration—and one hopes that virtually all do, somehow—may agree with everything in the Chesterton paragraph. But they cannot render their agreements and opinions into anything implying legal sanctions.

The whole language of creed and much of the discourse about community make many nervous. If the United States and its Constitution truly exist to create a national community with boundaries and an ideology voiced through creeds, there will necessarily be some exclusion of those not part of it. Thus Garry Wills, when commenting on Abraham Lincoln's devotion to the Union, says "if there is an American *idea,* then one must subscribe to it in order to be an American." But, asks Wills, who spells out the idea, who interprets the creed, who enforces conformity to it? When such questions come up, Wills answers: "Unless we know what our fellows *think,* we do not know whether they are American at all, much less whether they are *truly* American."[2]

How can one know what all think? In a creedal church, believers at least hear and speak the creeds and confessions. Do the several lines of propositions contained in one paragraph of the Declaration of Independence serve as a creed? Can they be inclusive enough to involve the whole nation and its groups?

Whose Declaration, Whose Constitution?

Mention of groups recalls that element of national conversation that is most interesting to agents of identity politics. Their spokespersons tend to question, demythologize, and subvert the stories of the founding documents. None of those three efforts is necessarily *only* destructive. The potential for mischief on the part of those in power in any time or place or institution, including the people who run the national show or tell the story (or, some would say, who run the show because they *get* to tell the story), are enormous. Holding them to account is part of the job of prophets, critics, and opposition leaders.

So we do well to listen to the group and subcommunity leaders when they question certain myths and stories about the founding documents: whose Declaration, whose Constitution are these?

Today's Native Americans are all too aware, and they find it necessary to remind others of the fact, that they were not included in the founding documents. Even in 1868 when the Fourteenth Amendment assured rights to former slaves and Asians and anyone else born here, the Indians were still "alien though dependent powers." Not until 1924 were they included, and even then they were taken in only with significant provisos and limits. The Indians have the best case against Jefferson and the other drafters of the Declaration and Constitution. They perform a service whenever they irritate those who are complacent about the contexts of constitutionalism.

African Americans perform a similar service when they subvert the stories of equality in the accounts of American origins. After 1787 they were still to be governed by people who gave them no rights. As slaves, they could not be part of the civil association. The most revered founders, including Thomas Jefferson, Patrick Henry, and George Washington, well knew how contradictory were their own postures, but they did little about it. The Negroes, to the Constitutionalists, were not blacks or Africans or slaves; they were, in Article I, section 2, number 3, "three fifths of all other Persons."

The recent attacks on Jefferson himself, many of them savage, are at their root not always entirely misplaced. Jefferson knew and said that holding slaves was wrong for himself personally and for the nation, but can be faulted for failing to exercise imagination or find the will to do much about the evil. Yet many of the critiques today come from people whose only advantage over Jefferson is that they were born later and have the benefit of hindsight. These attackers are not likely to be moral superiors to the founders. People of the past need to be seen in the context of their own possibilities and awareness of their own flaws, rather than being reduced to a role in which they are nothing but oppressors and thus able to be dismissed despite their other achievements or ideals. Because of their flaws, shared with all humanity, their examples can on occasion inspire reflection on the partiality and brokenness of all figures and events in history. This reflection can evoke moral meditation on the cosmic flaws in history's agents, of whatever race, religion, gender, class—or time.

Jefferson lived in a day when most enlightened (and Christian) people had not yet fully awakened to the evil implications of slavery. Slavery had been taken for granted throughout ancient, biblical, Greco-Roman, medieval, and most other history in the corporate memory of the founders. Only in their time had visionaries begun to say that slavery had to end. The Northern abolitionists, themselves few in number and usually ambiguous and timid in outlook, may have begun to stir by 1787, but they had less at stake than did Southern plantation owners. The game of excluding those not of one's own group did not begin with identity politics near the end of our century. It was also played by landowners who were at the center of early national life. This fact complicates all discourse about creedalism, about faith and works, about the good old days in a national community.[3]

Although religions, well represented in interest groups today, were only a minor issue for constitutionalists, even they created problems. Most of these problems surfaced in state constitutions. Although the U.S. Constitution said nothing about the issue of religious freedom for all, only in two states did Jews have full citizen rights. Limiting the rights of Jews, Muslims, "infidels," and others was by no means as acute an issue as was that of excluding Indians and blacks, but it existed.

The problem for constitutional association as a legacy of the founders' era in contemporary instances is of a different, even opposite, character. It arises whenever assertive citizens try, as they did in the nineteenth and early twentieth centuries, to privilege the notion of a legally based Christian America. They want to amend the Constitution so that it does what the original drafters thought about but then resisted: giving favor in the *lex* to religion over nonreligion, and to one genus of religion over other genera.[4]

Constitution as Scripture, as Amendable, Interpretable Icon

The purpose of the Constitution is not to promote a creed or a consensus or anything else substantive. This is not to say that the Constitution does nothing beyond stipulating the framework of all the laws of the land. Many kinds of people in many kinds of groups, citizens who live some aspects of their lives in their presumed incommensurable universes of discourse, come to regard the Constitution and constitutional principles with a kind of sacral sense.

Preservationists in Washington work over the originals of the eighteenth-century documents, caring, molecule by molecule, about the ink and the paper. Yet making icons of the material documents does not mean that one has effectively grasped their spiritual substance. At the time of the bicentennial of the Constitution in 1987 and of the Bill of Rights in 1989, historians expressed concern. They could find few commercial tie-in possibilities during the observances. Without these, how could they gain publicity and hence generate public curiosity about the events? Many feared that the observances would pass by virtually unnoticed.

Instead, during the summer of 1987, daily television featured Colonel Oliver North defending himself against charges that he had been misusing the Constitution and violating the terms of the separation of powers in government. That same year the Supreme Court nominee Robert N. Bork was engaged in discussing his earlier legal philosophy before a senatorial committee. Televised hearings in both cases attracted large audiences and inspired heated disputes; the nation was engrossed.

Whether over the separation of powers in government or over judicial interpretation based on "the original intent" of the drafters, the hearings provoked no noticed element of the public to say, in effect, "tear up the Constitution and give us—" what? Anarchy? Another constitution? Monarchy? None of the above. Similarly, in the years of radical dissent from the political and cultural left in the 1960s, or in the civil rights debates just before them, almost no one showed up in the polls to say "we need a new constitution" or "we need no constitution."

Instead, from the beginning, Americans in significant numbers have mythologized, theologized, or idolized the Constitution, something that people in the various groups and subcommunities also tend to do. Milton M. Klein has collated some of the more extravagant expressions and to some extent has accounted for them, beginning with near-contemporary efforts to find American distinctives. To set the stage he quotes Kensuke Fukae, a naturalized Japanese American who had fought in the Japanese army during World War II: "Our loyalty was to our leaders—America's must be to the Constitution."

It is not likely that American soldiers interviewed in 1941–1945 would have put the difference between the nations and their military forces that way. But upon reflection back home, the serious ones among them could have found reasons to agree with Fukae. Klein also cites an earlier but fairly typical example of efforts to rank religion in a hierarchy of documents that began with the Mayflower Compact. In 1923 the Church of Christ, Scientist, from its Boston headquarters took out a full-page advertisement in the *New York Times* to proclaim its founder Mary Baker Eddy's word: "I believe strictly in the Monroe Doctrine, in our Constitution, and in the laws of God." Klein's comment: "Even to the founder of one of the country's organized religions, God placed only second to the Constitution."

Contemporaries of ours who would never be typed as chauvinist, people who have reason to speak for victims of American injustice, have found the Constitution valuable in their efforts to enlarge and ensure freedoms now. Thus Congresswoman Barbara Jordan, an African-American activist leader, in 1974 spoke extravagantly as she found the document of use during the Watergate crisis: "My faith in the Constitution is whole. It is complete. It is total. I am not going to sit here and be an idle spectator to the diminution, the subversion, the destruction of the Constitution."

Klein, who quotes these affirmations, balances them against the fact that Americans have not always acted in the spirit of the Constitution. While they celebrated the centennial of the Statue of Liberty, their polls showed great support for immigration restriction. Similarly, polls by the Hearst Corporation and studies by Diane Ravitch and Chester E. Finn in the bicentennial year 1987 revealed unsurprising ignorance of the contents of the Constitution and unwitting or uninformed disagreement with many of its key clauses.[5]

In 1989 People for the American Way took a survey that showed lack of interest among young people in voting, in service to the community, and in the reasons to support democracy. The report concluded that there was a particular lack of understanding of the ways individual and civil responsibility connected:

> Young people have learned only half of America's story. Consistent with the priority they place on personal happiness, young people reveal notions of America's unique character that emphasize freedom and

license almost to the complete exclusion of service or participation. Although they clearly appreciate the democratic freedoms that, in their view, make theirs the "best country in the world to live in," they fail to perceive a need to reciprocate by exercising the duties and responsibilities of good citizenship.[6]

Those who scorn the young for their ignorance and unconcern might profitably ask: Who taught them? Or who failed to teach them? Did the senior generations of the last several decades embody, exemplify, or elaborate on the connections between rights and responsibility? Despite the signs of ignorance and distortion, however, the very fact that vestigial senses of the constitutional tradition remain ought to provide some basis for rebuilding. What people think of a document matters more than does knowledge of every line of content, when a story supporting cohesive sentiment is at issue.

As with myth, so with symbol. Klein also connects the constitutional myth with symbolism, in the spirit of Justice Holmes's "we live by symbols" theme.

> Symbols supply an overarching sense of unity in societies that might otherwise be riddled with conflict. They evoke, as illusion or reality, the implicit principles by which a society lives; they are visible signs of an often invisible belief; they simplify and emotionalize loyalties; and they require no formal proof. What they stand for may be only partly true, or not true at all, but for those who accept them, symbols are as real and objectively verifiable as the Rock of Gibraltar. In politics, symbols serve to link the individual to the larger political order, to synchronize the diverse motivations of different individuals, and to make possible collective action.

Max Lerner, cited by Klein, argued that only a naive government would rely on rational appeals or brute coercion. A seasoned one will welcome symbols to evoke loyalty. People are "notably more sensitive to images than to ideas, more responsive to stereotypes than to logic, to the concrete symbol than to the abstraction." People "possess thoughts, but symbols possess" people, as we saw in the opening chapters. Few Americans revealed better knowledge of this than Abraham Lincoln, who on the fiftieth anniversary of the Constitution urged that it should be "preached from the pulpit, proclaimed in legislative halls, and enforced in courts of justice . . . In short, let it become the *political religion* of the nation; and let the old and the young, the grave and the gay, of all sexes and tongues, and colors and conditions, sacrifice increasingly upon its altars."

Lincoln's was a mild statement compared with the hyperbole—dangerous, we would have to call it—that early and often came to be associated with the cult of the Constitution. Thus some Jeffersonians spoke of Judge Alexander Addison of the Pennsylvania Court of Common Pleas as "the transmontane Goliath of federalism."[7] Addison gave them good reason for this appellation in a typical charge to a jury as early as 1791: "The laws and Constitution of our government ought to be regarded with reverence. Men must have an idol. And our political idol ought to be our Constitution and laws. They, like the ark of the covenant among the Jews, ought to be sacred from all profane touch."

The later crisis of constitutionalism that occurred when the South wanted to secede from the Union before the Civil War led many citizens in the North to reevaluate the role of the Constitution. So did the troubling interpretations of the period of Reconstruction after the Civil War. There were, as there should have been, critics, prophets, cynics, and questioners. But by the time of the centennial in 1887 the Constitution was back in its place in the ark, the symbol of the American covenant, more honored as symbol than for its content.

Through all the years there also developed a tradition voiced by civil rights advocates such as Barbara Jordan and Martin Luther King, who used its contents to help struggle for and ensure rights. Although the original Constitution had little to offer women, slaves, Native Americans, and many others, it is significant that every realization of rights by another group has been in an extension of constitutional logic. Nothing had to be taken out to make room for elaborations.

The Constitutional Role in Civil Religion

The role of the Constitution in the citizens' search for the common good can never be uncontroversial. Its sacral role is not unambiguous. In his essay "Religious Pluralism and Durkheim's Integration Thesis," Philip E. Hammond speaks of legal institutions as religion. American constitutionalism, in Hammond's eyes and arguments, has been the center and heart of its civil religion. The Supreme Court justices have been spoken of from time to time as "the nine high priests in their black robes."[8]

In recent times, however, citizens have once again become more divided, more guarded, more contentious, more cynical about their charter documents. Even so, the Constitution occupies a place unmatched by such documents in most republics. It is held in common, however differently interpreted it may be, in the various subgroups. Perhaps in the times of greatest contention it is constitutionalism with its aura, myths, and symbols that most promotes cohesive sentiment in this civil association. Schopenhauer's figurative porcupines knew that in the worst cold they most needed one another. In times of severe chill, citizens, though they have not huddled together at the risk of getting pricked, have on occasion shared measures of warmth.

Others in times of spiritual chill have picked up on Hammond's clue and have seen constitutionalism as a form of civil religion. To story, myth, and symbol, they add concern for the constitution's role in rites. The constitutional expert Sanford Levinson has focused on this interest. For example, revisiting Felix Frankfurter, he recalls how the justice himself had taken the oath of citizenship as an immigrant. For such an awestruck newcomer, the ceremony contributed to a sense of bonding: "American citizenship implies entering upon a fellowship which binds people together by devotion to certain feelings and ideas and ideals summarized as a requirement that they be attached to the principles of the Constitution."[9]

Many who buy into the constitutional myth insist on its community-building character. Levinson regards those who take the oath of citizenship or swear to support the Constitution to be joining the United States as a "distinct 'faith community.' The Constitution is its central sacred text." Immigrants especially have cherished the oath-taking ritual. But in our argument, the notion that one becomes a part of something as large and as close as a national *community* is an invitation to the frustration of expectations. A citizen may feel intensely loyal to the Constitution, but that does not commit her to all the intimate and profound connections we associate with community. And too much devotion may give rise to schism, idolatry, and heresy-hunting.

Not all have resisted the temptation to idolize the document that stated those principles and inspired some to experience community. Judge Alexander Addison had plenty of successors. In 1920 Edward Corwin could even write of "the Worship of the Constitution." Such worship has been observed for a long time. Corwin deduced that "the *legality* of the Constitution, its *supremacy,* and its claim to be worshipped, alike find common standing ground on the belief in a law superior to the will of human governors." Levinson also reports on a radio address by Louis Marshall in 1928 in which the lawyer called the Constitution "our holy of holies, an instrument of sacred import." As recently as 1981 Michael Kammen included references to the worshiplike regard many had for the Constitution in his book *A Machine That Would Go of Itself.*[10]

Fortunately Levinson is not so blinded that he sees the Constitution only as an agent of unity and integration. Noting the sectarian impulses of religionists, he also shows that the rival interpretations of the Constitution generated something like sects and sectlike fragments. The document and fights over it have often contributed to the threats of national disunity and disintegration. The passions roused by the hearings involving Oliver North and Robert Bork illustrate this potential. The consequent sect formation even follows predictable lines that parallel those in the world of religious institutions.

Levinson, for instance, discerns what he calls "Protestant" and "Catholic" strands in interpretation. Protestants have traditionally accented "scripture"; Catholics have done the same with "tradition." So it is with constitutional-centered devotion in which Levinson draws his distinctions.

The one school, that of the scripturalists, tries to be literal about the "original intent" of the people who wrote and ratified the Constitution. The other school, more dynamic, treats the document as part of a living tradition. While referring to these two schools Levinson introduces the subject of hermeneutics in the context of constitutionalism. This science of interpretation recognizes that all interpreters impart world views and preconceptions to their acts of interpreting. For example, the passions that various parties of citizens bring to debate over the political outlooks of new Supreme Court appointees suggests that they know there is no single, objective, universally acceptable meaning to the document. It is a scripture that generates myths and demands interpretation within reading communities.[11]

What good does it do to promote the common good if there is so much controversy over the interpretation of the document and its heritage? Some might argue that only if the Constitution united everyone into a national community would it be effective in this integrating role. My purpose in bringing up the subject is different, however. The Constitution is the basis for civil association, not national community. But today, when many charge that we citizens have nothing in common at all across the boundaries of our subcommunities and groups, nothing to talk about that transcends our separate loyalties, it is important to see that constitutionalism at least helps make it possible for the public to move beyond states of confusion to the point of disagreement. John Courtney Murray among others showed how important such a move was if there was to be argument, and how integral argument was to the health of the republic.

Community and the Division of Loyalties

Levinson, with his eye on the devotion to the Constitution, does acknowledge that "a 'community' truly open to all comers is almost a contradiction in terms." In particular he quotes Robert Post, who introduces this qualifier: "A community without boundaries is without shape or identity; if pursued with single-minded determination, tolerance is incompatible with the very possibility of a community."[12] Like all myths, then, constitutionalism is seen as dangerous, ambiguous, rich in potential for developing the common life and also, unavoidably, for fragmenting it.

One of the most important issues Levinson takes up concerns divided loyalties and multiple community memberships. These arise when *community* instead of *association* is the goal of national existence. Levinson quotes Michael Walzer to the effect that "a pluralist, at bottom, is a man with more than one commitment, who may at any time have to choose among his different obligations." If through the oaths one joins a community that has scriptures and creeds, this choice can be most difficult. If one has relativized and loosened the bond to the Constitution and the nation, it is less difficult for the religiously or philosophically committed to make choices about loyalties.

For example, loyalty to a spouse within the bounds of the "marital community" or to one's God in the "religious community" may sometimes put one at variance with the claims of the civil association. It may seem paradoxical that the state can call for, exact, and expect death as a price for the logic of citizenship, as in times of war, while an even more profound community may not (though it also may) ask for the same. Here we have to recall that the nation as a civil association is a purposive agency. If its purposes call for the defense of the citizens through military means, this goal may be pursued faithfully by someone who has relativized the call of the nation. One may indeed die for the relative and live for the absolute.[13]

The reason one would advisedly keep talk of constitutional creedalism and ideology to a minimum is that life within the legal order is inescapable, even in the case of radical dissenters. True, I do not need to swear loyalty to the Constitution unless I am a new immigrant or someone entering the military or taking public office. Most citizens can go through life never being asked whether they "believe" in the Constitution; yet they must live by its law. There is no place to go to escape governmental impositions of some sort. There are no legal "world citizens." Someone may be very grudging about participating in republican life and may consider government to be evil, even demonic, as Jehovah's Witnesses do. Yet they cannot escape living under constitutional government.

Custodians of no other framework can demand assent or punish disloyal acts by all citizens. No other document, including the Declaration of Independence, provides a charter that calls for and permits such demanding and punishing. The founders did not set up an Enlightenment theocracy, or on the part of the deists among them, what we might call a deocracy, or a Judeo-Christian or Christian commonwealth. They willed a civil association, and nothing more. But legally it is enough.

Walter Berns, a conservative commentator, is correct: if the founders had intended a Christian commonwealth, "it was remiss of them,—indeed, sinful of them—not to have said so and to have acted accordingly." The citizens of the United States may be "a religious people," as Justice William O. Douglas called them in 1952. But their religions are not at the base of the Constitution. Berns is right to remark that for the framers, the "state of nature" instead was at the base, and this state is "incompatible with Christian doctrine." The Constitution does not promote faith in God. But the question remained for its drafters: what, then, should they do with religion?

Berns sounds irritating to many of the religious, but he is again correct when he says that "the origin of free government in the modern sense coincides with, and can *only* coincide with, the solution of the religious problem, and the solution of the religious problem consists in the subordination of religion." The founders were proreligion but found no way to support religion constitutionally. In fact, hints Berns, the framers were being friendly to religion precisely by ruling it out of the coercive element in constitutionalism. They had read Montesquieu, who said that the way

> to attack religion is by favor, by the commodities of life, by the hope of wealth; not by what drives away, but by what makes one forget; not by what brings indignation but by what makes men lukewarm, when other passions act on our souls, and those which religion inspires are silent. *Règle générale:* with regard to religion, invitations are stronger than penalties.[14]

The notion that the Constitution subordinates religion may be offensive, in the perspective of faith and theology. God beyond the gods is certainly to be conceived as beyond the Constitution, never subordinated to it. It should be made clear that devotion to the themes of the subcommunities may from time to time call for citizens to engage in fundamental protest against the Constitution in the name of a "higher law." They may be committed to notions that their devotion to church and God transcend all earthly, including political, commitments. Berns in this context again tries to be offensively bold: as it works out, in constitutional liberalism, a citizen "renders unto Caesar whatever Caesar demands and to God whatever Caesar permits."[15]

The fact that legally the church is subordinated is clear from the fact that the churches go to the state for tax exemption; the state does not go to the churches to be exempted from ecclesiastical stewardship programs. Similarly, the churches look for laws to ensure the integrity of people who are conscientious objectors to military service; the state does not go to any church to ask for citizens' exemption from churchly demands. Churches have to follow zoning and fire and police restrictions. They have to obtain a state charter to be listed as nonprofit agencies for tax reasons.

All these instances display subordination of religion to constitutionalism. All of them suggest good reasons why the constitutional tradition should be kept free of doctrinal and ideological commitments. This means that the liberal constitutional tradition allows citizens to be religiously indifferent just as the state must be. It must tolerate any and all religious traditions and communities except in rare instances where, in Jefferson's terms, they may "break out into overt acts against peace and good order."[16]

A Godless Constitution, a Godly People

During the bicentennial celebration I was to lecture on religion and the Constitution at a state university in Utah, on a campus and in a community made up largely of Latter-day Saints. When I landed there, a host commented that I demonstrated great *chutzpah* or had been merely foolish for having announced this topic: "America: Godless Constitution, Godly People." The Mormons, I was informed, consider the Constitution to be divinely inspired; how could it then be godless? I was even made aware of how some strain to find God in the ink marks on the document. One critic pointed out that I had overlooked the fact that there was a reference to God at the end. The framers mentioned that they were writing in "the year of Our Lord 1787"!

My intent in Utah as here was to show that the silence of the Constitution on matters of godliness helped produce this curious and some would say ironic outcome: citizens tend to be more friendly to and involved with religion in the United States than are their European counterparts in the nations there. Where legal establishments of religion endure, as they have, however weakly and vestigially, in many European nations, there also survives some legally based baggage. This included imposition of the idea that religion has to be better than nonreligion and that some religions make better contributions than others, so they could have higher status. Therefore anticlericalism, criticism of religion, and indifference to it follow whenever someone dissents against a regime that establishes religion.

Needless to say, to make my intentions clear I instantly changed the first few paragraphs before I spoke that day in Utah. I found it necessary to explain the title. But I shall not forget the occasion, because I was so well reminded of the awe in which people hold the

Constitution. No wonder it acquires a sacred aura, even among those who scorn particular generations of administrators of justice in its aegis.

Here I do not wish to undersell the rationales that reinforce the Constitution's contribution to the "binding tie of cohesive sentiment." For a constitution to be effective, a people must first choose to be law-abiding. A small minority, of course, may be anarchists. Others who occupy republican space will be treasonous, conspiratorial, and antigovernment. But they are all actually under law, even when they choose to reject the minimal terms of civil association.

Much more than mere cowering compliance is needed and has consistently been produced by way of proconstitutional sentiment on the part of citizens. The founders and framers knew that there could never be enough police to enforce all laws; people could get away with much more law-breaking than they do. Worries about precisely this question persist into our own time. Creative jurists still issue warnings and impart advice about the problem. Among the most noted of these worriers was Judge Learned Hand, who wrote in 1960, just before the modern rights revolution began to be extended beyond African Americans:

> I often wonder whether we do not rest our hopes too much on constitutions, upon laws and upon courts. These are false hopes; believe me, these are false hopes. Liberty lies in the hearts of men and women; when it dies there, no constitution, no law, no court can save it; no constitution, no law, no court can even do much to help it. While it lies there it needs no constitution, no law, no court to save it.[17]

How can civil life and virtue be ensured? In the War of Independence the colonists had figuratively killed the king: they had destroyed the notion of the divine right of kings and the belief that divine law passed through the monarch to the people, who were then forced to consent and obey. Now it all depended on the people. "We the people of the United States . . ."

The liberal constitutional tradition said, in effect: "We will promote cohesive sentiment." The illiberal tradition says, in effect: "We cannot trust dispositions of people in a pluralist society. We must impose a common ideology and a single definition of citizenship."

Rewriting the Story of the Framers

Many who argue today for a Judeo-Christian constitutionalism like to charge that heirs of the liberal tradition overlook the godliness of the founders and framers of the "godless constitution." Of course these men were religious, though most of them would be seen as heretical from the viewpoint of most who would today impose religious interpretations. But the eighteenth-century debaters and drafters kept their religion out of their godless constituting document.

Further agreeing that a republic needs cohesion, some argue that the government must be a participant in providing it coercively. Schools, they say, must teach a particular ideology or religion as the truth about life; the religion of the majority, it is thought, serves best for this. Or, they say, legislation concerning the National Defense Education Act should stipulate that everything taught in the schools be compatible with and even issue from what is termed the "Judeo-Christian tradition." No matter that in European nations where such teaching goes on in public schools, the participation of citizens in religious life is drastically lower than in the United States. It is apparently important to the imposers both to declare who really belongs in the republic versus who must be at best tolerated *and* to provide the foundation for morals and values and law.

I find it important to insert an aside after averring that no religious tradition should be taught as the "truth about life" in the schools. I am in the company of those who argue with some vehemence that teaching religion, which here means teaching about religion, belongs in the schools. It is impossible to make sense of the Native-, African-, European-, Asian-, or Hispanic-American peoples and their traditions without engaging in profound exploration of their religious dimensions. It is similarly impossible to make sense of the speeches of Abraham Lincoln, the novels of Herman Melville or Flannery O'Connor, the poetry of Emily Dickinson or Robert Penn Warren without developing awareness of the biblical lore that they affirmed or twisted or rejected.

Similarly, one does students a disservice in preparing them to interpret the present-day scene while keeping them ignorant of religion. It is a major agent in the volunteer life that helps keep American life here and there compassionate and humane. How can one account for the volunteers without reference to what motivates them? It is similarly a major element in healing, caring for the ill, and promoting therapy. How to explain alternative medicine, or much medical practice, without having explored religious interpretations? Religion, in the hands of terrorists, militants, and revolutionary forces, is an agent of killing hundreds of thousands of people around the world every day. How can one make sense of such challenges to sense without promoting knowledge of the various religions of that world?

I have put all of this demurring in an aside because it is a topic that demands development in works beside this one. But in many contexts it becomes clear that religion, other than constitutionalism as religion, has to be part of American story, myth, and symbol.

Some of those contending for a religious interpretation of the Constitution have had to rewrite history. One hears endlessly from them that at a crucial moment in the Constitutional Convention at Philadelphia in 1787 Benjamin Franklin called for prayer by those assembled. The religious interpreters do not stay around long enough to note that the convention members did not then engage in corporate prayer. These promoters of Franklin as a priest of civil religion fail to consider that his call for prayer may well have been ironic. Certainly on other days Franklin could make fun of those who wanted God to intervene in human affairs. For instance, he twitted his brother John about the effect of prayer at the time of the New England effort to capture the French fortress at Louisbourg. Franklin calculated that 45 million prayers had been prayed for military success there in a five-month period. "If you do not succeed, I fear I shall have but an indifferent opinion of Presbyterian prayers in such cases, as long as I live." He urged that "in attacking strong towns I should have more dependence on *works,* than on *faith.*" Franklin apologized for not having cited Scripture on this point, "but," he said, "I cannot adorn the margin with quotations, having a bad memory, and no Concordance at hand."[18]

One would not expect formal theological commitment to the divine in a national constitution, least of all in a nation whose colonies could not agree within or among themselves on who God was and how God was to be worshiped. A constitution intends functions different from the imposition of theology. One does not expect to find discourses on Plato in a warranty that comes with a washer and dryer.

Unless its packager is of the New Age, one does not open a cereal box and expect to read in it stipulations by the Buddha about selling and eating the cereal. Why should a constitution discourse about religion instead of law?

The weight of tradition, of course, lay on the side of mentioning God and creed in a charter document. The Magna Carta and the Mayflower Compact, for instance, invoked divine authority. The American founders felt some pressure to stay in that tradition. They were conscious that the eyes of the world were on them. They feared anarchy and rebellion in the backwoods. They needed means of disciplining the unruly and contentious and knew that resort to divine appeals might frighten some into obedience. But they resisted resort to that tack.

Further, there were reasons of social class for the founders to try to exploit others by invoking God as the authority behind their own respectability. The propertied had more reason to claim God and to teach virtue based on their interpretation than did the nonpropertied who might be restless. The framers themselves were devoted to God, and, deists and theists alike, believed that God held humans responsible under human government. Still, despite all these reasons, they did not insert God or godliness into constitutionalism.

To say that the godless Constitution is connected with a godly people is not to make a qualitative judgment on American godliness. A nation with a tiny minority of disciplined and faithful believers in some religion or another may produce a higher quality of piety and good works than might an America in which the majority signs up with religious institutions and a huge number wants to be counted godly. Justice Douglas's statement that "we are a religious people" was an empirically supportable comment on the fact that the people when polled or through other expressions of sentiment showed decisively that they wanted to be regarded as responsive to religious appeals and symbols. But these are not found in the Constitution.

Why Americans Are Religious

Why, one asks, did the United States turn out the way it did religiously? Critics might say that its leaders promoted religion (though not through the Constitution) in order to retain dominance. Others see them as using religion to assuage the torments of conscience, to legitimate their enslavement of blacks, their treatment of Indians, and their exploitation of workers and the poor.

This is not the place to go into the details of that broadly Marxian style of criticism. But it is appropriate to say that though it may be a necessary explanation, it is certainly an insufficient one. For many today the inspiring saint behind American development would more likely be Adam Smith or anyone else who praised competition. America, when freed of establishment and religious privilege on legal grounds, became a spiritual free market in which pioneers and peasants, black slaves and industrial slaves, and people of all classes were appealed to by entrepreneurs who found new ways to package old religions or invent new ones. They recognized a level field as they made their divine appeals, and religious forces thus prospered and continue to prosper. Because this is not a book of evangelism (or anti-evangelism), let it be noted here simply that moving the substance of theology and the search for virtue from the compulsory "civil associational" zone to the voluntary "mediating community" level was indeed liberating for religion. Opponents of religion in civic life might do well to side with those who want to privilege it. They might thus effectively weaken it.

Still, if there is to be rule of law to which Americans give assent as they regard the charter documents sacrally, must there not be some foundational *consensus juris,* some basic agreement on which law is grounded? Such was the base that, centuries earlier, Cicero had argued was necessary for the development of good particular laws. Can one dismiss the whole notion of consensus as easily as did British political scientist Bernard Crick, who all but sneered at its advocates:

> *"Consensus"* is a favourite magic formula both of the simple and of the over-subtle . . . If its hard-core of meaning, derived from Cicero's *consensus juris* (which he thought a necessary condition of a Republic), is something like "agreement about fundamental values," then it fails on empirical grounds. Where is the *consensus* in Canada, for instance? Or anywhere, between Catholic, Protestant (High or Low), Muslim, Hindu, Jew, Sceptic, Agnostic, Freethinker, Atheist, and Erastian, who commonly share some common political allegiance—if they take their fundamentals seriously and take them to be directly applicable to politics? Either this *consensus* is *very* fundamental—"a man's a man for a'

that," or "a rose is a rose is a rose" [Crick footnote: "or G. Marx's existentialist *cri de coeur:* 'Take care of me. I am the only one I've got.' "], which probably *is* a necessary assumption of any civilized governmental order, indeed of any legal or political judgment; or else it is simply, in our sense, narrowly political . . .

Those who say we desperately lack a *consensus* of values, and have such a thing to offer (usually a "fighting faith for democracy," or else monotheism), are in fact simply trying to sell us a particular brand of politics while pretending they are not, as it were, in trade themselves.[19]

Against every move to promote coercion and the privileging of consensus is the tradition of framers like James Madison. As Paul Weber has made clear, the Madisonians were opposed to both religious establishment and religious privileging.[20] They took such a stand, as we have seen, for clear reasons. They wanted the Constitution to make clear that no one's religion dared serve as a disability amid individual or communal contention or in policymaking in the public realm. Hence the religion clauses concerning establishment and the free exercise of religion.

Madison and the other framers did not solve substantive problems. They left efforts to do so to the "factions" or to the "associations" that Tocqueville later discovered and admired in the United States. The question in modern times has become this: are people ready to turn to family, neighborhood, church, school, club, friendship circles, and, on a larger scale, to media, academe, and the like to thresh out questions of what constitutes virtue, values, morals, and the good life in the republic? I argue that if one remains a constitutionalist who is against coercion in matters of philosophy and religion, then one is advised to promote the "binding tie of cohesive sentiment" in voluntary and persuasive ways for the sake of the very reasons spelled out in the godless Constitution's Preamble.

Voluntary Support for Constitutionalism

The Constitution and devotion to it become part of the common good because of voluntary support for it. This support occurs through voluntary associations and subcommunities. Thus against Rousseauean concepts of a top-down civil religion, Benjamin Franklin called for a "publick religion." It would draw upon the overlapping consensus and moral visions of the separate religions and would be "useful." Franklin did less well on the subject of ethnic groups who spoke languages other than English, but his identification of the need for religious support of the commonweal, despite one's particularities and based entirely on a voluntary basis, provided an example for other types of contributions to the common good.

Two hundred years later, pervasive gloom about these prospects results from several factors. First, memory fades, and with the passing of time one may forget eighteenth-century ideas that were associated with the Constitution. There can also be radical transformations in ethos, and these can corrupt the originating ideas. Whereas liberty was necessary back then so that people would be free to be responsible as citizens, two centuries later the claim is often heard that freedom means only "to do your own thing as long as it hurts no one else."

A second reason for uncertainty today has to do with the disappearance of articulated support for the Enlightenment philosophy of reason and nature and law which helped leaders move beyond the boundaries of colony, ethnicity, and religion. Pluralism and chaos are a third factor. When subcommunities not only are indifferent to the common good but even oppose expressions of it, insisting that only members of their community can pursue the interests of human beings in it, they move into their separate and "incommensurable universes of discourse."

All those worries are justified. But to pay attention to them is not a resort to coercion by those who wish to form a basis for consensus. Citizens are called instead to strengthen the subcommunities and then set up the circumstances in which conversation about and activity toward the common good are pursued. Under this policy, for example, Jews or Christians, following the norms of their religion, should be freer to contribute to this goal. They should be more able to share elements of their universes of discourse than would be those coerced toward consensus.

The Landscape Left by Constitutionalism

Constitutionalism, then, belongs to the spiritual landscape of America despite all the changes in the recent past. I have often had occasion to quote Ernest Gellner on the way such landscapes get formed. What he says applies to the framers of the Constitution over two centuries ago and the scene ever since:

> The ideology with which a society has passed the hump of transition [to its approved social contract] is likely to remain its nominal doctrine, thereafter: indeed it is likely to become, locally, the symbol of that overcoming of the painful hump, of the achieved satisfactory order which is now the true "social contract." . . . The effective content may be eroded, becoming ever more selective, symbolic, "spiritual," etc. As time recedes [such a system of thought] still carries with it a heavy moraine . . .
>
> A thoroughgoing intellectual reform, which would eliminate the "moraine," is ever inconvenient, and generally far more so than the awkwardness of retaining this or that currently embarrassing piece of intellectual moraine . . . The inconvenience of thorough revisionism [is] that the levels of sophistication move at unequal speeds, the flow of the glacier is not the same in all its parts, and an adjustment suitable for one part will place a strain on another.[21]

No one has been more emphatic than Gellner about the "thoroughgoing intellectual reform" forced on the former Soviet Union when communism "imploded," leaving great discontent and confusion behind it. But the United States does not appear to be quite so ready to see its ethos, ideas, practices, and institutions similarly implode. Concern for the common good is part of an effort to see that it does not. Those who would promote the "binding tie of cohesive sentiment" are as dedicated as are the supporters of civil religion or Judeo-Christianism. But they do not need to see the philosophy spelled out in legal documents.

Benjamin Franklin, as noted, thought that public religion would be useful and that it should be supported voluntarily, as it would be in the Pennsylvania Academy he was helping found. But neither he nor any of the other founders locked any version of public religion into the Constitution and the obligatory, lex-based part of national life. As recently as 1931, a Supreme Court decision could still make passing reference to the United States as a "Christian nation." But neither the Court nor anyone else could provide documentary legal backing for such an observation, any more than the Court in 1952 could provide legal backing for its claims that this was a "religious people."

Article VI of the Constitution served to keep religious questions at a distance by proscribing religious tests for people seeking or holding office. The First Amendment keeps the Court at a distance by prohibiting Congress from making a law respecting the establishment of religion or limiting the free exercise of religion. That is it. There is no base for finding in the Constitution a validation of religions, ethnic groups, lifestyles, classes, interests, or ideologies.

The purposive elements of the Constitution were sketched in the Preamble, but the substantiation of these was located in the voluntary sector, where assent and dissent, argument and conversation, rhetoric and organization were called upon. The totalists chafe because none of this locating is compulsory. The tribalists argue that even persuasive attempts to address the republic as a whole reflect efforts to gain dominance and give privilege to the long-dominant groups at the expense of those long oppressed. But for most citizens the Constitution provides the base for argument, not disintegration.

Does the Constitution Imply a Civil Religion?

There is one leftover piece of business on the question of the Constitution and religion. Walter Berns argued that the Constitution was made possible because of the natural rights philosophy that the founders regarded religiously. Is there therefore an implicit civil religion, a public religion, that comes with the Constitution and that belongs to the coercive life of the nation? When some advocates in each generation have attempted to devise or recognize such a religion, they have been frustrated and have had to make their way in the voluntary and persuasive sector. To say that such a religious philosophy made possible the Constitution and that it throws light on constitutionalism no more implies an establishment of a civil religion than to say that Calvinist views informed the Constitution and that therefore the nation should privilege Calvinism.

So far I have argued that the godlessness and religionlessness (in the usual senses of that term) of the Constitution have helped ensure that free Americans individually or in groups could attempt to contribute to the development of morals, values, virtues, and responses to law. At the same time I have stressed that such attempts belong to the voluntary endeavors of citizens who are free to persuade others. Throughout, my assumption is that more reasons to pursue the common life abound in a situation of freedom than in one where a specific approach is taken and its methods involve some kind of coercion. But what is said in the persuasive realm where subgroups thrive and provide voices and energies?

Here I argue that Americans, while disagreeing with one another and in part sharing incommensurable universes of discourse, can and do pursue the common good through the ideas sketched in the second paragraph of the Declaration of Independence. It was the Declaration and what it represented that divided the people of whom John Jay had spoken as "the same" from the Tories who had to leave the colonies when war came. Otherwise the two peoples were the same: they were both English and spoke English; both sets were Protestant, and they shared similar customs. But the Declaration led one set to become a nation; in Madison's words, "to form one society."[22]

An Empty Shrine, a Rich Story

John Courtney Murray had at least this part of the whole controversy right when he quoted Thomas Jefferson's lines in the Declaration and made them his book title: *We Hold These Truths*. If we do want to use Chesterton's terms, the constitutional tradition provides for the nation with the body of a state and the Declaration a nation with the soul of a church. But whether there should be any creedal propositions implied in the whole of national life is itself at issue.

Daniel J. Boorstin at mid-century argued in *The Genius of American Politics*, a book written when the idea of national consensus was in its prime, that Americans could come together precisely because there was no scroll of doctrines, there were no icons in the shrine. He recalls the absence of images in ancient Judaism and portrays America similarly. His depiction is still applicable:

> When we penetrate the Holy of Holies of our national faith, we must not expect the glittering jewels and filigreed relics of a pagan temple. The story is told that when the Temple of Solomon in Jerusalem fell in 63 B.C. and Pompey invaded the Holy of Holies, he found to his

astonishment that it was empty. This was, of course, a symbol of the absence of idolatry, which was the essential truth of Judaism. Perhaps the same surprise awaits the student of American culture, if he finally manages to penetrate the arcanum of our belief. And for a similar reason.

Far from being disappointed, we should be inspired that in an era of idolatry, when so many nations have filled their sanctuaries with ideological idols, we have had the courage to refuse to do so.[23]

Boorstin may be right. I believe he is right, insofar as the shrine keepers had the instruments of law behind them. That is, it was their decision to keep any shrine as ideologically bare as possible. But throughout American history many citizens have used the powers of persuasion to fill their arcanum with images that would provide substance and purpose. They have normally tended to do this by drawing on the language of particular "unlicensed" philosophies and religions. On that field and in that game, any number can play, and many have, drawing on the particularisms of their subgroups and communities.

By far the largest evocation has been by some Protestants who have wanted to see the United States as a biblical republic. *Judeo-Christian*, a term invented in this century, fit well for their purposes. Jews and Christians have had reasons to want to get together on many causes. The Hebrew Scriptures set forth more elements of government than did the New Testament, as American Christians through three and a half centuries have known. Many Jews and many Christians have regarded the United States as a "scripted" nation, some if not all of whose major doings were occurring under a provident God. But the Bible has made its way in the voluntary, not the coercive sphere. There are, of course, no special legal limits to its use in the voluntary sector.

The Bible is popularly privileged because no other book has come close to influencing so many citizens in their moral life. That there is a Creator, that America was covenanted, that it had a mission and a destiny, that moral responsibility was expected of citizens, and that a just God wanted justice were taken for granted from the earliest days right down through Martin Luther King, Jr., and many citizens since.

The founders did not draw on the Bible explicitly when drafting the original documents. This is not to say that they did not know the Bible. They did. James Madison at age sixteen had to be able to translate any passage from the New Testament Greek into Latin to matriculate at Princeton. In the White House, Thomas Jefferson excised the miracles and pasted together the surviving teachings of Jesus in the Gospels in English, French, Latin, and Greek. One tabulation found the Bible to be by far the most cited of books by founders and framers. It far outshone Enlightenment, Whig, common law, classical, or other references in "public political literature written between 1760 and 1805." Of course, many of these documents were sermons. But even allowing for this provenance the figures are impressive.[24]

The authors knew they could not privilege the Bible or build the legal republic on it. The full impact of the Bible came from those who believed it to be a supernatural revelation. But the founders themselves had highly varying views of the Bible. Few of them could have held membership in a "born again" evangelical church today, given their deist commitments.

Yet the Bible has enormous influence in the hands of those who would shape public morality, interpret American destiny, and minister to individual citizens. When suggestions that the Bible should be privileged come up, problems arise with it. Some believers ask: would not such civil use of the Bible distort its character, since obviously the Bible does not anticipate anything like the American republic? Who would arbitrate when significant numbers of the people of God have disagreed over details and even over the essence of biblical faith? Would it be legitimate to impose their book, their faith in a supernatural revelation, on people of no book or of other books?

Because all those questions could be raised about the biblical approach to constitutional life, other approaches came to be offered, some of these even from within Christianity. Thus John Courtney Murray spoke up persuasively for Catholics after mid-century in his book *We Hold These Truths*. He was invoking Thomas Jefferson and the Declaration to say that America's charter was often misconstrued because most major interpreters had been Protestants. Murray did argue for the "American consensus" in an essay titled *"E pluribus unum."* This phrase, said Murray, meant "one society subsisting amid multiple pluralisms," and the first principle of this consensus was the "sovereignty of God over nations as well as over individual men."

The Jesuit knew that such a principle could not be imposed on all citizens, there being a "share of agnostics and unbelievers," but it could still inform the majority. Next, for Murray, was the tradition of natural law, which Catholics shared with Enlightenment founders more than Protestants could. To this Murray added the theme of the "consent of the governed," which was Oakeshott's main theme for a civil association.

> The unity asserted in the American device, "E pluribus unum" . . . is a unity of a limited order. It does not go beyond the exigencies of civil conversation . . . This civil unity therefore must not hinder the various religious communities in American society in the maintenance of their own distinct identities. Similarly, the public consensus, on which civil unity is ultimately based, must permit to the differing communities the full integrity of their own religious convictions.

Pages later: "It is not the function of government to resolve the dispute between conflicting truths, all of which claim the final validity of transcendence." Father Murray knew how hard it was to make the case for a particular reading of the consensus or the American proposition and have it be accepted. He spent more energy on the problem of the *plures* than of the *unum*. We have already read his argument that citizens must "go up higher" into some theoretical realm of generality to decide important issues in the commonwealth—but he knew that such "higher" common ground was difficult to find. Still he did not despair of the urgent search for the disagreements out of which argument could rise. Murray quoted Thomas Gilby, O.P.: "Civilization is formed by men locked together in argument. From this dialogue the community becomes a political community." But Murray knew how difficult this had become, and he had to ask: "How much pluralism and what kinds of pluralism can a pluralist society stand? And conversely, how much unity and what kind of unity does a pluralist society need in order to be a society at all, effectively organized for responsible action in history, and yet a 'free' society?"

Murray, speaking a quarter century ago precisely to the point of this book, saw reasons to shift the argument from the grounds of reason, eighteenth-century style, to affectivity, or emotional response, in the twentieth-century mode.

> Perhaps the ultimate tendency of the pluralisms created by the era of modernity is felt . . . rather in the realm of affectivity than in the realm

of reason as such. The fact today is not simply that we hold different views but that we have become different types of men, with different styles of interior life. We are therefore uneasy in one another's presence. We are not, in fact, present to one another at all; we are absent from one another. That is, I am not transparent to the other, nor he to me; our mutual experience is that of an opaqueness. And this reciprocal opaqueness is the root of an hostility that is overcome only with an effort, if at all.[25]

Such lines showed uncanny prescience about the American scene decades hence. They lacked only the notion that the "I" in each case belongs to identity groups that reinforce the opaquenesses. One of his interpreters reminds us, "Murray never did pay much constructive attention to racially, ethnically, and nationally based pluralism."[26]

Murray belonged to his age, a time of reductionist pluralism, not expansionist multitudinism. He thought that while there might be three hundred religious bodies in America, there were only three generic "styles" of religious belief. They were Protestant, Catholic, and Jewish, each having its own epistemology, and were not reducible to one another. It would be hard to find any serious thinker today who would find much homogeneity within each of the three styles or would find it possible to bring the smorgasbord of religious options down to three. Muslim, Asian, New Age, and many other basic styles have become evident.

If Murray's lines about opaqueness were prescient, his next were even more so. He gathered up the testimony of half a dozen witnesses in the spirit of Protestant philosopher W. Ernest Hocking, who had defined the day's problem as being the "passage beyond modernity." So Murray wrote: "The problem of pluralism has begun to appear in a new light. Perhaps the basic reason for this is the fact that we are entering a new era. Whether it will be a better or even a good era is another question that still remains open. In any case, we have reached the end of the era that gave itself the qualification 'modern.' "[27]

Postmodernity had arrived, and the "realms of affectivity" seemed even more "incommensurable" than did the "realms of reason." Although one may regret the eclipse of Enlightenment-style reason—there are other styles now, including critical Enlightenment thought—there are now opportunities within the realm of affectivity, as we shall later try to demonstrate. The fact that such a devotee of

reason as Father Murray would speak so warmly of affectivity, however, might well alert us to reexplore it in relation to arguments about
the charter documents.

Reason and Experience as Guides

Many commentators have pointed out that the framers of the Constitution made as much of experience as they did of the reasoned
philosophy of the Enlightenment. For example, Forrest McDonald in
a book originally called *E Pluribus Unum,* on the history of the rati-
fication of the Constitution, deals with both tendencies in the parties
that made up the group of founders. He has this to say about the
embrace of reason and rationalism by republicans, notably in Virginia:

> Such cultivated country gentlemen were familiar with all the branches
> of useful arts and sciences, and many that were not so useful. Because
> it was necessary to the conduct of their semifeudal domains, they ac-
> cumulated a wide variety of practical knowledge. Because there was
> not much else to do, they read a great deal: they read Thucydides,
> Virgil, and Cato in Greek and Latin, and Coke and Blackstone, Mon-
> tesquieu and Harrington, Locke and Hume in English; and not only
> could they cite this incongruous conglomerate of authorities to justify
> any action, they believed them as well. More mundanely, because they
> often found it difficult to feed their multitudes of slaves, they embraced
> humanitarianism; because they were over their heads in debts to mer-
> chants who faithfully swindled them, they cursed the city and com-
> mercial life; and because it offered a way out of their material plight,
> they adopted, with passionate faith, rationalism and doctrinaire repub-
> lican idealism. Particularly suited to Virginia's needs was that part of
> the gospel of rationalism that preached the desirability of a clean break
> with the past.

Elsewhere McDonald linked the Virginians with the other "hard-
shelled republicans," this time of Eastern provenance. "In public life,
they heartily embraced the rationalist tradition, which meant that
their thinking was systematic and encumbered by a minimum of
superstition and sentimentality, and that they believed in the natural
rights of man and the possibility of a clean, rational break with the
past."

210 • THE ONE AND THE MANY

But then McDonald looked at the nationalists, people like Benjamin Franklin, John Dickinson, Robert Morris, James Wilson, the Livingstons, and a South Carolina faction that included John Rutledge and Christopher Gadsden. "Most were likely to be robust and lusty, and all . . . enjoyed a good drink and a not-so-good woman. Most of them were also incurable romantics":

> Indeed, though they were intelligent enough not to broadcast it, few of them believed in the rights of man at all, nor even in the rationalism that underlay them. They could think as systematically as any rationalist, but their systems were based in history, not in logic; accordingly, they believed that men have rights, but only such as have, over the years, been won and incorporated into tradition. As to the Age of Reason, Hamilton could offhandedly dismiss the whole idea: "A great source of error," he wrote, "is the judging of events by abstract calculations, which though geometrically true are false as they relate to the concerns of beings governed more by passion and prejudice than by an enlightened sense of their interests." And Dickinson could echo, "Experience must be our only guide. Reason may mislead us."[28]

What can go overlooked in the talk about pluralism is the fact that so many disparate groups found in the spirit of constitutionalism and in the soul of the Declaration of Independence enough grounds for common life that they could disagree with one another and thus argue. True, there are incommensurable dimensions in the experiences, histories, and languages of the various groups, but they do share some elements of common universes of meaning, and can act on them. The partly commensurable is often celebrated by many.

At times along the way in this chapter we have made so much of contradictions and complications in respect to the founding documents that the idea of using them as an aspect of the search for the common good may seem to have died the death of a thousand qualifications. We have posed them against the background of community versus association; creed versus statement; exclusion versus inclusion; communities of interpretation versus other such communities; those who pursue original intent versus those who wish for fluid interpretation; the perspectives of those not included—blacks, Native Americans, and others—versus those of the heirs of insiders.

What is left? But this is precisely the point: these documents prompt argument, debate, and controversy. The arguments are not so often over the Monroe Doctrine, the Emancipation Proclamation, or anything else. These do not constitute America as a nation, a people in civil association. The answers to the questions about who we are begin to emerge only in the course of the ensuing conversations. Without possessing or being possessed by motifs from these documents in their original and current contexts and through the course of time between the beginnings of the nation and now, we would live in incommensurable universes of discourse whence we might not even know how to seek commensurable ones. We could not have any kind of discourse at all. But as things are, those who would be reflective and responsible can tell stories and thus address the common good. They will have shared an affective life and risked sentiment. They will also have contributed to a climate in which arguments, originating in the several groups, may again be intense without causing trauma. They will be ready to experience and exemplify sentiment and affection.

CHAPTER ELEVEN

Cohesive Sentiment

To speak of sentiment and affections as promoters of the common good, and to do so at the turn of this cynical and bloody century, in a polarized and conflictual society, involves risks to the reputation of the speaker. Sentiment, as those suspicious of it are quick to point out, easily descends into sentimentality. Sentimentality is a weak expression in an age when suspicion and hatred between individuals, groups, and the larger society tend to rule. Affection, meanwhile, easily gets equated with the mush of Valentine's Day cards. The word evokes hearts and flowers. Such affection, when advertised as virtuous for a citizenry, deserves to be laughed at as foolish. Those who deal realistically with militant and exclusive groups know that their members are not naturally minded or strategically interested in showing affection toward other groups.

Sentiment by itself, however, always involves the mental life. It does not connote mindless mawkishness. And affection in the longer past involved both the head and the heart. It had to do chiefly with affectivity, with the sensibilities of those who had experienced events and expressed emotions together.

Intimate communities and communions, because of the closeness and commitment that they express, depend upon love. Citizens, however, cannot express sentimental attachment or personal affection for all fellow citizens in societies conceived as civil associations. They certainly will not credibly display love, because of the impersonality of the bonds of association and the heterogeneity of those who are encompassed by them.

Schopenhauer's porcupines, unable to do without one another for practical purposes such as staying warm, also had to find a "certain distance" from one another to avoid getting pricked. The philosopher, observing them, noted that the act of their finding the value of proper distance mixed with appropriate nearness did not lead the beasts to imagine the result of their discovery "to be an independent source of happiness, like finding a friend." Yet he did say that at the certain distance they "could both delight in one another's individuality and enjoy one another's company."

The notion that in a republic great numbers of citizens can "enjoy one another's company" ought to be easy to grasp. Yet one introduces it warily, fearing a sneering response. It is in the interest of interest-group leaders to rage against other groups or, even more, against people they conceive of as dominant, even oppressive elements in societies.

To see, for example, the fury of the newest convergence in identity politics, the "angry white male voters," squaring off against their nemesis, the "militant feminists," is to be made aware of volcanic forces from which one would judiciously keep a more than moderate distance. Let someone from a gay and lesbian organization encounter a senator who votes against funding AIDS research while assigning blame to AIDS victims for their disease. Then let him snipe back. Here is another scene that those who have a distaste for verbal firestorms or metaphoric blood will want to shun. How could these two ever come to a "certain distance" in which one could use words like *delight* and *enjoyment*?

Realistically, one may have to give up hope for attracting certain people to the conversation. Articulators of us-against-them or us-against-all-of-you may resist invitations and opportunities at all prices and on any terms. Some people, such as many of the sexually abused, may carry such deep psychic traumas into later life that they understandably cannot let themselves be open and vulnerable to others. Those who bring obsessive commitments to particular ideologies possess a heavy lifelong investment in seeing these reinforced. For them, this means also forming clienteles and constituencies for the sake of company. They seek only their own interpretive community with which to connect in order to have their perceptions and resolves reinforced.

Some religious groups find it convenient to demonize others. They have been trained to depict any positive motion toward themselves as being conspiratorial, even satanic. They keep their distance from occasions that would bring their enemies in range. Civil associative society therefore has to include room for parties that bristle, for figurative porcupines who would fling their quills at anyone near them.

Most citizens do not have investments as heavy as do these leaders of groups in expressing resentment or seeking revenge. Overwhelming majorities of citizens express tolerance for the neighbors who are not like them, even if this tolerance is often superficial and untested. Is there not some significance in the very idea that they read the American situation as one in which positive instead of negative attitudes to others are expected and cherished? If that is the case, consider it empirical evidence for the fact that many would enjoy and delight in the company of those who are at a certain distance.

The Limits to Sentiment, Affection, and the Search for Justice

Human nature being what it is, both in civil association and in intimate community, one can gather evidence for what has been called the only empirically verifiable Christian doctrine, original sin. When four expressway lanes are narrowed to two, and some motorists, despite the placement of signs calling them to merge early along their way, shoot along a shoulder to cut into jammed lanes at the last moment, all rules of civility are broken. Crowds trample innocents at entrances to rock concerts. In some cities people take macho delight in advertising themselves as being unfriendly on subways and elevators—they want to project a perverse image that warns away the country folk or tender sorts. The record of violence and crime, the dark shadows on empty streets, the need for security systems, the full prisons—all illustrate the limits of positive human concern.

These images, however, tell only half the story. People are constantly transgressing boundaries of their own subgroups. Intermarriage rates these years are high. Images from one culture penetrate other cultures in television sitcoms. At an athletic event, parade, music festival, celebration, food fair, or amusement park, people of various races and classes intermingle. The camaraderie in the sports bar on the night one's team moves into first place may well be ad hoc, superficial, momentary, and easily dispelled when the comrades disperse in the wee hours. But this spirit could not be present at all if there were no ways for people to delight in one another across the bounds set by ethnic or interest-group leadership and rhetoricians.

To such evidence one could add countless other signs, not least among them the systems of citizen volunteering, something unheard of and unmatched in many homogeneous societies. People volunteer in patterns that often reveal true generosity and hospitality to those who are unlike the volunteers. This has to count for something. What are we to make of such boundary-crossing activities, so frustrating to those who profit from interethnic, cross-class malice? What name shall we give it?

Defining Affection

Philosophers and theologians like to devote attention to the grand words that are expressive of the most profound actions and emotions: *eros, agape,* and *caritas,* three terms for love, will do on the positive side. Anger, hate, and violence are at the outer limits of the negative expression. Only occasionally do the classic thinkers deal with middle range elements like friendliness or benevolence. The middle range word that applies best to the enjoyment of civil association, I would argue, is *affection.*

Barriers appear the moment it is cited. Yet if one listens and speaks carefully, it becomes clear why the term is in place. "I would like to make some gesture that shows affection" carries a weight very different from "I love you," which allows for no distance or graceful retreat. Affection is more reserved, tentative. We sometimes sign letters "Affectionately" when we don't want the full import of "Love." Affection also permits other and stronger emotions to accompany and overwhelm it when appropriate.

What is it that a person would connote by resurrecting the concept of affection? One begins with recall of the narrative self in Alasdair MacIntyre: in our actions and practice, as well as in our fictions, we "storytelling animals" ask, "of what story or stories do I find myself a part?" We enter human society needing to learn what characters and roles are, "in order to be able to understand how others respond to us and how our responses to them are apt to be construed." We ask in various settings: Do I keep my guard up? Am I to be suspicious? Are all people wolves to each other all the time? To speak of common affection is to refer to the fact that you and I, your group and mine, have had moments of delight and enjoyment when we needed each other. Such a word has a history of connotations, so if we wish to resurrect and apply it, we need to handle it with care.

This unsentimental treatment of sentiment and this unaffected regard for affection include the suggestion that the sense of sharing affective life, having experiences and recognizing common emotional responses to them, does not mean loving or liking everyone with whom one is involved. In fact, affective life often grows in the company of strangers, among people for whom there was little prior history of a sort that would predispose them to be affectionate. One thinks of soldiers who share a beleaguered position or those who huddle in common shelter in a storm.

In a comment on the functions of social conflict, Georg Simmel came to the conclusion that in conflict "it is *expedient* to hate the adversary with whom one fights (for any reason), just as it is expedient to love a person whom one is tied to."[1] *Love* is a stronger word than we seek here; but the case is the same for affection, which can be an enduring by-product of situations resulting from shared affective life.

During floods along the Mississippi River in the summer of 1993, I am told that the all-white population of one small southern Illinois town was impressed by the flood-fighting endeavors of often-dangerous state prisoners, most of them African Americans from large cities. They had been released from jail so that they could help fill and pile up sandbags and produce other defenses against the flood in that town. Of course, at the end of each day they were returned to prison, where they remained at the end of the first period of flooding.

When some days later new flooding occurred, the citizens had two choices: to put their own young people, home from college, to work or to engage the prisoners. They chose the prisoners, having by then been impressed by them and having bonded with them. Meanwhile the prisoners, most of them from Chicago's ghetto, mentioned that never in their lives had they even visited a small town, been among white people, lived where people knew and trusted one another or where there were lawns and yards. Townspeople, in their turn, had a new experience, and both sets of people were stirred by their common response. No one expects utopian endings to follow such occasions. Lessening of suspicion by one party and the rehabilitation of the other cannot occur on such sudden and simple terms as these. But all parties had lived out a parable of life in civil association.

The *Oxford English Dictionary* traces *affection* to the Latin *affectionem,* "disposition, inclination, fondness." Immediately the notion of middle distance is established. To be disposed to someone is not to give one's self over utterly to him or her: we save such giving over for circumstances of friendship or love. "Inclination" implies a tilt but not a full commitment. We save commitment for marriage or church. "Fondness" is a pleasant leaning, not a plunge: we save the plunge for more profound contacts.

"Generally and literally," we learn from the dictionary, affection is "the action of affecting, acting upon, or influencing," or, when viewed passively, "the fact of being affected." I show affect or act upon or influence you when you and I keep up each other's cheer through the night when your busload of senior citizens and my busload of high school basketball players are jointly stranded at a rest stop in a blizzard. Now we turn to affection "of the mind": "an affecting or moving of the mind in any way; a mental state brought about by any influence." You bring about a different mental state in me if your church group volunteers to provide an apartment complex for the homeless, and I belong to that usually voiceless interest group. Believe me, we will find a voice now.

Affection further connotes a "state of the mind towards a thing; disposition towards, bent, inclination." In civil association I can be affective toward certain trophies, monuments, and souvenirs, without making idols of them and without loving them. Affection is "good disposition towards, goodwill, kind feeling, love, fondness, loving attachment." (Admittedly, "love" does sneak in here.)[2]

The History of Affection and Sentiment

In American history, the word *affection* has a long record. Thus New England's most noted theologian and revival preacher of colonial times (and probably unmatched since), Jonathan Edwards, elevated "affections" to central status, even including the concept in one of his book titles, *A Treatise Concerning Religious Affections*. His usage was theocentric: humans were to direct their emotions, their affective and responsive capabilities to God, in a way that both paralleled and transcended reason.[3]

In the philosophic ancestry of Edwards, affection related as much to inanimate things as to persons or to God. This notion derived from the logic of Renaissance philosopher Petrus Ramus. It held sway in the generations before Edwards matured. Thus Samuel Johnson, a tutor at Yale by Edwards's time wrote in his *Synopsis of Natural Philosophy:* "Relativity is an affection of nature in accordance with which nature is fit to be relative or to have relations. And all creatures are without exception related." Such relation certainly is appropriate as a middle-distance concept. In England, William Ames, who was being commended to Yale students when Edwards was there, spoke in Ramist terms of "technometry." In it, as Stephen H. Daniel summarizes, "the intelligible order that pervades all reality is contained in the arguments (or things) that comprise the world." Thus:

> Reason, relation, and the mutual affection of things shine forth around the type from all sides and from its every part, so that by this means the things themselves are conveyed to our understanding, which does not perceive otherwise than under reason and some affections. Hence the principles of discoursing.

Edwards was ready to carry this notion of "affection of things" so far that he reached into astrology, alchemy, medicine, and magic to study the affects and their effects. Stars and planets, for instance, "may act upon sublunary things, as plants, animals, bodies of men, and, indirectly, upon their souls too, by that infinitely subtle matter diffused all round them."[4] But Edwards came especially alive to affection in the personal realm and defined what he meant carefully and extensively. For an example of his compressed and abstract but helpful thinking:

> In some sense, the affection of the soul differs nothing at all from the will and inclination, and the will never is in any exercise any further than it is affected; it is not moved out of a state of perfect indifference, any otherwise than as it is affected one way or the other, and adds

nothing any further. But yet there are many actings of the will and inclination, that are not so commonly called affections: in everything we do, wherein we act voluntarily, there is an exercise of the will and inclination, 'tis our inclination that governs us in our actions: but all the actings of the inclination and will, in our common actions of life, are not ordinarily called affections. Yet, what are commonly called affections are not essentially different from them, but only in the degree and manner of exercise. In every act of the will whatsoever, the soul either likes or dislikes, is either inclined or disinclined to what is in view.[5]

That such a view of affection, applied to God and things alike, has a bearing on the other persons in civil association is obvious. But the heirs of Edwards later broke apart the synthesis he had wanted to sustain. Most of them felt they had to choose between the reason of the Enlightenment and the affections of Edwardsean piety, not remarking how their mentor and master had stayed alert to reason and not learning from him.[6]

Similarly, in respect to the Enlightenment tradition, Thomas Jefferson (better than the many other possible representatives) made much of affection, both in the realm of civil association and in personal relations. Garry Wills has resurrected this motif in the writings of the enlightened president, who has usually been shelved on the "reason" side of equations by people who dichotomize. They are wrong, or at least not entirely right.

In fact, in his first draft of the Declaration of Independence Jefferson summarized his attack on King George III with this line in which he speaks for the colonists: "These facts have given the last stab to agonizing affection." Wills calls the Declaration a scientific, moral, and finally "sentimental" paper in the sense that Felix Frankfurter and the argument of this book use the word. Thereupon Wills takes his readers back into the world of the eighteenth century and of a favorite novelist of Jefferson, Laurence Sterne, who wrote of a "sentimental journey." People, says Wills, agreeing with Sterne, "should not only *exercise* their sensibility before grand or affecting sights, but *display* that sensibility in their record of the journey." Jefferson carried this kind of Sternean grasp into all his writings about nature, awe, and the sublime. Some of this tendency was evident in that first draft of his most important document.

Less momentous but not less revelatory was another document. Jefferson wrote a celebrated letter to Maria Cosway, a married British woman to whom the widower from Virginia was attracted during a Paris assignment in 1786. The letter took the form of a dialogue between the Head and the Heart. Jefferson was therein reflecting the influence of Sterne. In an attempt at a *tour de force* reading, Wills says (and to my satisfaction shows) that "Jefferson considered 'sentiment' the superior faculty in man . . . Jefferson was a 'sentimentalist' in Sterne's meaning of the term." Thus "the development of French '*sensibilité*' roughly paralleled (and cross-pollinated) Scottish thought on the moral sense," a form of thought and sense that Jefferson favored. The philosophers in the 1765 *Encyclopédie* "reflect an overwhelming consensus among the philosophes that '*sensibilité*' was the highest moral guide for man."[7]

Here is the philosopher of Reason reflecting heartfully, "affectionately," "sentimentally," on the Revolution itself in the very letter to Cosway:

> If our country, when pressed with wrongs at the point of the bayonet, had been governed by it's heads instead of it's hearts, where would we have been now? hanging on a gallows as high as Haman's. You began to calculate and to compare wealth and numbers: we threw up a few pulsations of our warmest blood: we supplied enthusiasm against wealth and numbers: we put our existence to the hazard, when the hazard seemed against us, and we saved our country: justifying at the same time the ways of Providence, whose precept is to do always what is right, and leave the issue to him.[8]

Now we are more ready than before for the lines from the Declaration itself. Jefferson accused the monarch: "These facts have given the last stab to agonizing affection." The committee that cut this climax of the document from it before adoption must have given a stab to Jefferson's own agonizing affection. Examining the earliest drafts, Wills found that Jefferson disapproved of the committee's reference to "unjust" British. He wanted to substitute "unfeeling." And it had said: "This is too much to be borne even by relations," a strange term to use for a country and its colonies.

Wills offers this jab: "Those who think of Jefferson and his time as hard bargainers into the individualistic contract of John Locke should be simply impatient with all this talk of 'affection,' the feelings of 'brethren,' and 'former love.' What kind of revolution begins with the recollections of a jilted lover?" This one, Wills answers, the American War of Independence. Jefferson in his Declaration of Causes in 1775 had earlier said that at times American colonists submitted to assumptions of power by the parliament; these were "finally acquiesced in thro' warmth of affection."[9]

Wills, mindful of the influence of Frances Hutcheson on Jefferson, shows how the Scottish Enlightenment thinker used the word *affection* in terms relevant to our discussion: "Whatever place we have lived in for any considerable time, there we have most distinctly remarked the various affections of human nature. We have known many lovely characters; we remember the associations, friendships, families, natural affections, and other humane sentiments." Wills describes Hutcheson here as always "thinking of the affections in terms of gravitational force." And Thomas Paine, not far from Jefferson's side, was interpreting events thus in *Common Sense:*

> To talk of friendship with those in whom our reason forbids us to have faith and our affections, wounded through a thousand pores, instruct us to detest, is madness and folly. Every day wears out the little remains of kindred between us and them; and can there be any reason to hope that, as the relationship expires, the affection will increase . . . ?

Given such language by his mentors and contemporaries, and given the care with which Jefferson put the language about "affections" into his draft, there is little wonder, says Wills, that Jefferson all his life preferred the climactic words of his version to the committee's version, which excised them.[10]

Affection and Kinship

To leap from eighteenth-century figures like Johnson, Ames, and Edwards or Sterne, Hutcheson, Paine, and Jefferson to the end of the twentieth century and then seek to rescue a term and a concept from the past may seem an antiquarian and archaic attempt at restoration. It might be embarrassing for a politician to speak of having an affection for the people—though we have heard presidents doing so—or people having an affection for a politician—though I recall many speaking thus of "the Happy Warrior" Hubert Humphrey or of President Eisenhower. "I Like Ike," not "I ♥ Ike," was a proper use of the term. Very large elements of the population showed affection for Franklin Delano Roosevelt and Ronald Reagan, both of whom used language that elicited such a response.

There are credible cognates to *affection*. Paine put us on to one when he spoke of affection and of the former relation of colonists to Great Britain as "kindred." I once mentioned to Bill Moyers my envy of his communicative skills. I was sure that he could find a way to communicate the idea of affection, in the eighteenth-century sense, to his television publics in the late twentieth. Had he any ideas on how to do this without suggesting Valentine's Day? Yes, said the Texan to this Yankee. Where he came from, they had words that got at the notion: *kin* and *kinfolk* and *kinship* and *kindred*.

I looked up the word *kin:* beyond blood-related family, it connotes from Old English days "people, nation, tribe." *Kindred* builds on it and suggests "allied in nature, character, or properties; possessing similar qualities or features." At first hearing I thought these would not do for civil associational life: kin, relatives, people with whom one shares blood descent from a common ancestor do not stand at a "moderate distance" but are close, intimate, part of community, demanding and meriting love and not affection.

Moyers, however, reminded me that kin also included all those in-laws and divorced or separated hangers-on; all the foster and stray children; all those who arrive for beer at the party where someone says, "Y'all come!" In short: a family reunion. I was reminded that the last thing you expect at a family reunion is that everyone loves everyone. Indeed, affection in civil associations can be a creative counterbalance to the intense loves and hates inspired within the most intimate family circle, the smallest office or club, or the most intense identity-politics group.

Bronislaw Malinowski observed what is obvious in the plot of too many family dramas: "aggression like charity begins at home." There can be the "flaring up of anger over immediate issues, where divergent interests occur or . . . are imagined to occur." Again, many of us recognize this in our personal experience: "Indeed, the smaller the group engaged in co-operation, united by some common interests, and living day by day with one another, the easier it is for them to be mutually irritated and to flare up in anger."[11] They are not given the luxury of moderate distance available in and integral to public life. Often we are accidentally given glimpses of the inner life of leadership among interest groups. We find that while they employ a rhetoric of hostility against outsiders or the establishment, they reserve their worst furies for the behind-the-scenes infighting that goes on "all in the family," as it were.

Back now to the family reunion. Family participants ordinarily come to the gatherings, no matter what the risks. Some do it out of self-defense, to avoid being talked about behind their backs. More do so because they share a common story. The newest comers, in-laws, like converts to churches or immigrants to nations, often catch on most quickly and note nuances unheard by those who have been long related.

One observes the sequence of the typical reunion day. However cordial the blessing of the food at the picnic, in the course of the hours these relatives under this tree start complaining about who got grandma's amethyst. Those under that other tree gossip about who is disgracing whom. Before long others rue the notion of being in any way related, or having come together at all. But none would want to miss next year's reunion.

The further we explore the ritual and reality of family reunions, the more evident it becomes that *kin* and *affection* are in their own way kindred words. The notion of the "binding tie of cohesive sentiment" that Frankfurter promoted is not just transmitted through the Head and Reason, or through law and proposition and constitution. It becomes equally evident that reflecting on and propagating kinship may be a way of restimulating the national conversation that would be disrupted by interest groups, ignored or disdained by those perceived to be in power, or looked to without hope by those at the margins.

Gwen Kennedy Neville has studied family reunions in the American South. Her description of what goes on in their rituals replicates descriptions of American rites when civil associates gather for national holiday celebrations:

Every reunion will include certain features that are obligatory, without which it would not be a reunion. In analyzing the Passover Seder, Meyerhoff calls these obligatory features "fixed elements." In the reunion these include the gathering of descendants of a common ancestor; the shared meal, preferably on outdoor tables adjoining a family home, a church, or a campground; . . . the kin visiting, greeting, and storytelling; and the recurrent time and traditional place. Other features may appear and disappear—the business meeting, the ceremony of introductions, the previous night's cookout, the visit to the graveyard, pictures, history books, and newspapers referring to ancestors or kinfolks.

And the meal, yes, the meal. Neville cites Gillian Feeley-Harnick on "commensality," which can be understood "in terms of interrelated cultural systems and associated behavior." For "in establishing who eats what with whom, commensality is one of the most powerful ways of defining and differentiating social groups."[12]

Perhaps Justice Frankfurter could have advanced national cohesiveness less by coercing Jehovah's Witness children to salute the flag than by attending a Labor Day weekend ballgame. There he would have joined in the commensality provided across the boundaries of identity groupings by wolfing down hamburgers in the company of others and thus promoting common affection. The interest here is not in anyone's being social activities director for civil associations. At this level our concern has to do with what stories citizens tell about their lives within and across the boundaries of their subgroups and how they conceive of themselves corporately in light of these.

The whole idea of seeing the interest groups and those devoted to identity-politics as *symbiotes* is intended not to suppress differences but to enhance them. Ironically, these groups are at present too much like one another, not different enough.

If groups exist only to protest against their victimhood and to keep naming the oppressor while blaming the dominant elites, those who hear them will ordinarily find them to be replicas of one another. Only superficial details differ. But if they tell their story and accent what gave integrity to their group life in the first place, they will not so readily conform to one another's plot lines. They will be harder to forget, impossible to dismiss. They will be more likely to make their case, to win attention and even sympathy.

If groups exist only to assert power, to ensure that they will get what they feel they are entitled to, those who hear them will again find them replicating one another. A presiding bishop of a denomination who feels besieged by caucuses, an academic dean beleaguered in the face of groups that demand special curricular programs, a humanities council busy trying to please all the citizen interests will find a certain sameness among them all. Whether the protesters are united by their race, sex, class, ethnicity, religion, nationality, language, or culture, the language of dissent or demand will be predictable, as will be most responses.

If the groups exist to represent their story in its true distinctiveness and amplitude, the predictability will disappear. So will patterned responses. In their place there will be some chance that hearing and understanding can begin to occur. Where a group has suffered, its special story needs to be told and will be. Where a group has endured and produced achievements, these will awaken respect and wonder. Where a group shows concern for the common good and shows interest in other stories, it will be doing what symbiotes are supposed to do: live off others and give life to others.

In the heat of the conflict that marks the end of this century, one expects little of this to happen in the immediate future. The trauma in the body politic, the civil network, the social organism, continues. But in the meantime, and for the sake of a longer future, every story well told, well heard, and creatively enacted will contribute to the common good and make possible the deepening of values, virtues, and conversation. At the outset I described this book as an effort to contribute to the restoration of the body politic, or, with the many groups in view, the bodies politic. We have been speaking throughout of the "re-storying" of the republic and its associations. The advice for every citizen who wishes to participate in American life and its necessary arguments: start associating, telling, hearing, and keep talking.

Notes

1. Restoring the Body Politic

1. Gerda Lerner, "The Necessity of History and the Professional Historian," in *The Vital Past: Writings on the Uses of History*, ed. Stephen Vaughn (Athens: University of Georgia Press, 1985), 104–116, esp. 106, 108, 111, 114–115.

2. Alasdair MacIntyre, "The Virtues, the Unity of a Human Life, and the Concept of a Tradition," in *Why Narrative? Readings in Narrative Theology*, ed. Stanley Hauerwas and L. Gregory Jones (Grand Rapids, Mich.: Wm. B. Eerdmans, 1989), 89–112, esp. 101–102.

3. "The Hunger for Wholeness: The Trials of Modernity" is the title of chapter 4 in Peter Gay's *Weimar Culture: The Outsider as Insider* (New York: Harper and Row, 1968), 70–101.

4. Walter Ong, S.J., *American Catholic Crossroads: Religious-Secular Encounters in the Modern World* (New York: Macmillan, 1959), 64.

5. Eugen Rosenstock-Huessy, *I Am an Impure Thinker* (Norwich, Vt.: Argo Books, 1970), 121–122, 135.

6. Harold R. Isaacs, *Idols of the Tribe: Group Identity and Political Change* (New York: Harper and Row, 1975), 1, 2, 3, 24.

7. Niccolò Machiavelli is cited in an epigraph in Dominick LaCapra, *History and Criticism* (Ithaca, N.Y.: Cornell University Press, 1985), 15.

8. Eugene Goodheart, *Culture and the Radical Conscience* (Cambridge: Harvard University Press, 1973), 8–10, 15.

2. Possessing Our Common Stories

1. Malcolm McConnell, *Challenger: A Major Malfunction* (Garden City, N.Y.: Doubleday, 1987), 92–93. These comments and much of the narrative that follows are based on McConnell's account.

2. Ibid., 93–94.

3. Ibid., 102.

4. R. T. Hohler, *"I Touch the Future . . .": The Story of Christa McAuliffe* (New York: Random House, 1986), 46, 15.

5. McConnell, *Challenger*, 104. For the casting of the crew, see chap. 6, "The Politics of Space Flight," 91–104, esp. 93–94, 104.

6. For dialogue between crew members and ground control, see McConnell, *Challenger*, 242–245.

7. Reinhold Niebuhr, *The Irony of American History* (New York: Scribner's Sons, 1952), 63.

8. McConnell, *Challenger,* 8.

9. Sally Rimer, "After the Shock, a Need to Share Grief and Loss," *New York Times* (hereafter *NYT*), 29 January 1986, A1.

10. Crystal Nix, "New York Honors the Challenger's 7," *NYT,* 3 February 1986, A14.

11. Bernard Weintraub, "Reagan to Lead Memorial in Houston," *NYT,* 30 January 1986, A17.

12. Robert Suro, " 'Deep Sorrow in My Soul,' Pope Says"; Serge Schmemann, "Gorbachev Expresses His Condolences"; and Judith Miller, "A Message from Qaddafi," all from *NYT,* 30 January 1986, A16.

13. Bernard Weintraub, "Reagan Pays Tribute to 'Our 7 Challenger Heroes,' " *NYT,* 1 February 1986, A1. A full transcript of Reagan's eulogy is on A11.

14. Robert Reinhold, "The Mourning Families Return Home," *NYT,* 30 January 1986, A1.

15. Robin Toner, "Space Museum Becomes a Memorial," *NYT,* 30 January 1986, A18.

16. William E. Schmidt, "Dream Lives for Pilgrims at Canaveral," *NYT,* 7 February 1986, A1.

17. "Reflecting on Loss: Welling of Tears, a Desire to Press On," *NYT,* 29 January 1986, A8.

18. Daniel Goleman, "Anger, Confusion, and Fear in the Nation's Grief," *NYT,* 1 February 1986, A11.

19. Weintraub, "Reagan Pays Tribute," A1.

20. "Reflecting on Loss," A8.

21. Thomas J. Knutson, "Service for Shuttle Pilot," *NYT,* 3 February 1986, A14.

22. Thomas J. Knutson, "400 Honor Dr. McNair," *NYT,* 3 February 1986, A14.

23. "Reflecting on Loss," A8.

24. Matthew L. Wald, "500 Attend Mass for Space Teacher," *NYT,* 4 February 1986; Wald, "In Concord, McAuliffe's Neighbors Mourn Loss of 'Shining Example,' " *NYT,* 30 January 1986, A17.

25. Pauline Yoshihashi, "Ellison Onizuka," *NYT,* 11 February 1986, A1. I was instructed in the connotations of "talk-story" by Grant S. C. Lee of the Hawaii Conference of the United Church of Christ, who wrote a Doctor of Ministry dissertation at San Francisco Theological Seminary on the subject in 1988: "Talk-Story: A New Approach to Evangelism in Hawaii."

26. Howard S. Schwartz, *Narcissistic Process and Corporate Decay: The Theory of the Organizational Ideal* (New York: New York University Press, 1990), 108; Clifford Geertz, *The Interpretation of Cultures* (New York: Basic Books, 1973), 443.

27. Schwartz, *Narcissistic Process,* 108, condensing a theme of J. J. Trento, *Prescription for Disaster: From the Glory of Apollo to the Betrayal of the Shuttle* (New York: Crown, 1987).

28. Schwartz, *Narcissistic Process,* 108–109, 114–116.

3. One People, One Story

1. Alexander Hamilton, John Jay, and James Madison, *The Federalist,* no. 2 (Washington, D.C.: Robert B. Luce, 1976), 9.

2. Thomas Jefferson, *Notes on the State of Virginia*, in *Jefferson: Writings*, ed. Merrill Peterson (New York: Library of America, 1984), 210–211.

3. Quoted by two racist authors, Madison Grant and Charles Stewart Davison, *The Alien in Our Midst* (New York: Galton, 1930), 215.

4. Quoted in David Freeman Hawke, *Franklin* (New York: Harper and Row, 1976), 95.

5. Edward Shils, *The Constitution of Society* (Chicago: University of Chicago Press, 1982), 4, 58–59.

6. Quoted by Charles Leslie Glenn, Jr., *The Myth of the Common School* (Amherst: University of Massachusetts Press, 1987), 163.

7. Ibid., 165–166. Here Glenn quotes the *Ninth Annual Report of the Secretary of the Board* (Boston: Dutton and Wentworth, 1847), 66–69, and the *Eleventh Annual Report of the Secretary of the Board* (Boston: Dutton and Wentworth, 1848), 31, 90–91.

8. William Kailer Dunn, *What Happened to Religious Education? The Decline of Religious Teaching in the Public Elementary School, 1776–1861* (Baltimore: Johns Hopkins University Press, 1958), 77, 289.

9. Glenn, *Myth,* 178.

10. Ibid., 288.

11. Ruth Miller Elson, *Guardians of Tradition: American Schoolbooks of the Nineteenth Century* (Lincoln: University of Nebraska Press, 1964).

12. Ibid., vii.

13. Quoted in ibid., 1–2. To minimize the scholarly apparatus in this book, I shall not provide the titles or publishing data for the books Elson cites. I encourage readers with interest in this field to consult Elson's bibliographies and notes.

14. Ibid., 7.

15. Quoted in ibid., 314, 282.

16. Quoted in ibid., 309.

17. Ibid., 83.

18. Quoted in ibid., 105, 168.

19. Quoted in ibid., 168, 169, 182. For criticism of the South, see 174.

20. Quoted in ibid., 124, 125, 127.

21. Quoted in ibid., 67, 69.

22. Quoted in ibid., 79, 81.

23. Quoted in ibid., 87.

24. Quoted in ibid.

25. Isaiah Berlin, *Four Essays on Liberty* (New York: Oxford University Press, 1969), 167.

4. Forcing One Story on the Many

1. *Minersville School District v. Gobitis,* 310 U.S. 586 (1940), at 596.

2. *West Virginia State Board of Education v. Barnette,* 319 U.S. 624 (1943), at 641, 642.

3. H. N. Hirsch, *The Enigma of Felix Frankfurter* (New York: Basic, 1981), 148, 151; he draws on correspondence in the Frankfurter and other archives. Hirsch remains a valuable commentator on these issues, though some critics have found his psychoanalytic approach to his subject a bit overdone.

4. *West Virginia State Board of Education v. Barnette,* 319 U.S. 624 (1943), at 662.

5. Hirsch, *The Enigma of Felix Frankfurter,* 237–238, quoting correspondence.

6. Michael Oakeshott, *Morality and Politics in Modern Europe: The Harvard Lectures,* ed. Shirley Robin Letwin (New Haven, Conn.: Yale University Press, 1993), 89, 90. He gave these lectures in 1958.

7. George P. Fletcher, *Loyalty: An Essay on the Morality of Relationships* (New York: Oxford University Press, 1993), 91–93, 111–112.

8. This sequence is drawn from chapter 9 in Jeffrey Stout, *Ethics after Babel: The Languages of Morals and Their Discontents* (Boston: Beacon Press, 1988), 191–219 and esp. 191–192, 200, 205, 209–214, 216–217, 218. See also Alasdair MacIntyre, *After Virtue,* 2d ed. (Notre Dame, Ind.: University of Notre Dame Press, 1984), 263, 5, 6, 54, 405; and Alasdair MacIntyre, *Short History of Ethics* (New York: Macmillan, 1966), 266. The phrase *overlapping consensus* is borrowed from John Rawls, *A Theory of Justice* (Cambridge: Harvard University Press, 1971), 387–388.

9. MacIntyre, *After Virtue,* 1st ed. (Notre Dame, Ind.: University of Notre Dame Press, 1981), 201, 220, 203.

10. Stephen Mulhall and Adam Swift, *Liberals and Communitarians* (Oxford: Blackwell, 1992), 90, quoted in John Horton and Susan Mendus, "Alasdair MacIntyre: *After Virtue* and After" in *After MacIntyre: Critical Perspectives on the Work of Alasdair MacIntyre,* ed. Horton and Mendus (Notre Dame, Ind.: University of Notre Dame Press, 1994), 11; Horton and Mendus also comment on the passages on narrative just cited, 8–10.

5. Plural Possessors, Single Intentions

1. Horace Kallen began to formulate a theory of cultural pluralism as early as 1915; the term began to become familiar when he published a collection of essays in 1924; not until 1956 did it appear in a book title, *Cultural Pluralism and the American Idea* (Philadelphia: University of Pennsylvania Press, 1956).

2. "Pluralism—National Menace," *Christian Century* 68 (13 June 1951), 701–703.

3. Will Herberg, *Protestant, Catholic, Jew: An Essay in American Religious Sociology* (Garden City, N.Y.: Doubleday, 1955).

4. Gerhard Lenski, *The Religious Factor: A Sociological Study of Religion's Impact on Politics, Economics, and Family Life* (Garden City, N.Y.: Doubleday, 1961).

5. Bernard Sternsher, *Consensus, Conflict, and American Historians* (Bloomington: Indiana University Press, 1975).

6. Ibid., 227.

7. Ibid., 124.

8. See Martin E. Marty, *A Nation of Behavers* (Chicago: University of Chicago Press, 1976), 164–168.

9. Ernest Gellner, *Contemporary Thought and Politics* (London: Routledge and Kegan Paul, 1974), 180.

10. John Courtney Murray, S.J., *We Hold These Truths: Catholic Reflections on the American Proposition* (Kansas City, Mo.: Sheed and Ward, 1960), 23.

11. Lewis Coser, *The Functions of Social Conflict* (New York: Free Press, 1956). On p. 49 Coser notes that often "conflict arises exclusively from aggressive impulses which seek expression no matter what the object," making more important the existence rather than the nature of the target. He aptly quotes John Dewey: "Men do not shoot because targets exist, but they set up targets in order that throwing and

shooting may be more effective and significant." See also Eric Hoffer, *The True Believer: Thoughts on the Nature of Mass Movements* (New York: Harper and Bros., 1951), 89–90, who asserts that "mass movements can rise and spread without belief in a God, but never without belief in a devil. Usually the strength of a mass movement is proportionate to the vividness and tangibility of its devil."

12. Paul Ramsey, "How Shall We Sing the Lord's Song in a Pluralistic Land?" *Journal of Public Law* (1964): 353–400.

13. Lloyd A. Brown, *The Story of Maps* (Boston: Little, Brown, 1949), 86.

14. Murray, *We Hold These Truths*, 15–16.

15. Alasdair MacIntyre, *After Virtue* (Notre Dame, Ind.: University of Notre Dame Press, 1981).

16. Robert Booth Fowler, *Unconventional Partners: Religion and Liberal Culture in the United States* (Grand Rapids, Mich.: Wm. B. Eerdmans, 1989), 4–5.

17. Nicholas Rescher, *Pluralism: Against the Demand for Consensus* (Oxford: Clarendon Press, 1993), 5, 80, 90, 93.

18. Ibid., 98, 103.

19. Ibid., 113, 114, 121.

20. Ibid., 156–157, 163, 164.

21. Ibid., 165, 167, 199.

6. The Exclusivists' Stories

1. Nancy Fraser, "Toward a Discourse Ethic of Solidarity," *Praxis International* 5 (1986): 428; quoted in J. Donald Moon, *Constructing Community: Moral Pluralism and Tragic Conflicts* (Princeton, N.J.: Princeton University Press, 1993), 181.

2. Iris Young, *Justice and the Politics of Difference* (Princeton, N.J.: Princeton University Press, 1990), 164; Young, "Polity and Group Difference: A Critique of the Ideal of Universal Citizenship," *Ethics* 99: 261–266; both quoted in Moon, *Constructing Community*, 182–186.

3. Moon, *Constructing Community*, 181–189, discusses problems with Fraser's and Young's positions and, by indirection, those of other advocates of special rights treatment for the collectives from the viewpoint of political liberalism of a special sort.

4. I intend to do this elsewhere, as part of the plot of volume 4 of my *Modern American Religion*. The first volumes are *The Irony of It All*, vol. 1, *1893–1919*; *The Noise of Conflict*, vol. 2, *1919–1941*; and *Under God, Indivisible*, vol. 3, *1941–1960* (Chicago: University of Chicago Press, 1986, 1991, 1996).

5. James Baldwin, *The Fire Next Time* (1963; reprint, New York: Vintage International, 1993), 94 (quotation from later edition).

6. Neil J. Smelser, *Theory of Collective Behavior* (New York: Free Press, 1962), 12–18, at 16.

7. Ibid., 17.

8. David A. Hollinger, *Postethnic America: Beyond Multiculturalism* (New York: Basic Books, 1995).

9. David Carrasco introduces the literature on the subject and summarizes the research in "Human Sacrifices: Aztec Rites," in *The Encyclopedia of Religion*, ed. Mircea Eliade (New York: Macmillan), 6:518–523. An attempt to set the practice into a context appears in a popular work, Deborah Manley, *The Guinness Book of Records, 1492: The World Five Hundred Years Ago* (New York: Facts on File, 1992), 166, which

reports that "according to various sources, between 20,000 and 84,400 captives were supposed to have been sacrificed in 1487 at the dedication ceremony of the great dual Aztec temple of Tenochtitlan."

10. Benjamin Barber, *Jihad vs. McWorld* (New York: Times Books/Random House, 1995).

11. Anthony C. Yu, ed. and trans., *The Journey to the West,* 4 vols. (Chicago: University of Chicago Press, 1977–1983).

12. Ellen T. Charry, "Literature as Scripture: Privileged Reading in Current Religious Reflection," *Soundings* 74, nos. 1–2 (Spring/Summer 1991): 64–65.

13. Ibid., 68, citing David Bleich, "Epistemological Assumptions in the Study of Response," in *Reader-Response Criticism: From Formalism to Post-Structuralism,* ed. Jane P. Tompkins (Baltimore: Johns Hopkins University Press, 1980), 151.

14. Here Charry (p. 69) refers to Stanley Fish, "Interpreting the Variorum," in Tompkins, *Reader-Response Criticism,* 174, and again to Bleich, "Epistemological Assumptions."

15. Charry, "Literature as Scripture," 70–71.

16. Ibid., 73–75.

17. Ibid., 78–79; see Carol Christ, *Diving Deep and Surfacing* (Boston: Beacon, 1979).

18. Charry, "Literature as Scripture," 82; see Delores S. Williams, "Black Women's Literature and the Task of Feminist Theology," in *Immaculate and Powerful: The Female in Sacred Imagery and Social Reality,* ed. Clarissa W. Atkinson, Constance H. Buchanan, and Margaret R. Miles (Boston: Beacon, 1985), 88–110.

19. Charry, "Literature as Scripture," 86–87.

20. Ibid., 91. See James Evans, *Spiritual Empowerment in Afro-American Literature* (Lewiston, N.Y.: Edwin Mellen Press, 1987).

21. See Charry, "Literature as Scripture," 94–95. I have converted some of Charry's propositions into questions without, I hope, doing violence to them, in the interest of suggesting that the conversation must go on.

22. Ibid., 96–97.

7. Association over Community

1. Michael Oakeshott, "Talking Politics," in Oakeshott, *Rationalism in Politics and Other Essays* (Indianapolis: Liberty Fund, 1991), 460–461. For the original parable, see Arthur Schopenhauer, *Parerga and Paralipomena: Short Philosophical Essays,* vol. 2, trans. E. F. J. Payne (Oxford: Clarendon Press, 1974), 651–652.

2. George Will, *Statecraft as Soulcraft: What Government Does* (New York: Simon and Schuster, 1983).

3. Michael Oakeshott, *On Human Conduct* (Oxford: Clarendon Press, 1975), quoted in Josiah Lee Auspitz, "Michael Oakeshott, 1901–1990," *American Scholar* 60, no. 3 (Summer 1991): 365–366.

4. Michael Oakeshott, "The Rule of Law," in his *On History and Other Essays* (Oxford: Blackwell, 1983), 137.

5. Michael Oakeshott, *On Human Conduct* (Oxford: Clarendon Press, 1975), 265–266.

6. *The Politica of Johannes Althusius* (abridged from *Politica Methodice Digest, atque Exemplis Sacris et Profanis Illustrata,* 3d ed.), ed. and trans. Frederick S. Carney (Indianapolis: Liberty Fund, 1995), 17, 28, 39, 207–208.

7. Robert Nisbet, *The Social Philosophers: Community and Conflict in Western Thought* (New York: Thomas Y. Crowell, 1973), 7, 149, 387, esp. 388, 399.

8. David A. Hollinger, *Postethnic America: Beyond Multiculturalism* (New York: Basic Books, 1995), 24, 23. Readers should consult this book for extensions of the argument condensed here and for further elaboration of the ethnic species of the group genera. See also Will Herberg, *Protestant-Catholic-Jew: An Essay in American Religious Sociology* (Garden City, N.Y.: Doubleday, 1955).

9. Aristotle, *Politics,* trans. Benjamin Jowett (Oxford: Clarendon Press, 1923), chap. 2, sec. 5, 13–15, and 2, 2–3. In the sequence of quotations that follows, from Aristotle through Althusius, I have been dependent on selections and comment in Nisbet's *The Social Philosophers: Community and Conflict in Western Thought* (see note 7). I have consulted it often for well over twenty years, appreciating particularly chapter 6, "The Plural Community," 385–444. I would like to acknowledge the influence here and commend his writing to others. Of course, as a student of American history, I have done independent work on Madison, Tocqueville, and Frankfurter (only Tocqueville is mentioned in Nisbet) and, as a friend of Frederick S. Carney since graduate school days, have also sustained an independent interest in Althusius. See also Edmund Burke, *Reflections on the Revolution in France* (1790; New York: Penguin Books, 1986), 243–244.

10. Burke, *Reflections on the Revolution in France,* 243–244.

11. James Madison, in *The Federalist,* by Alexander Hamilton, John Jay, and James Madison (Washington, D.C.: Robert B. Luce, 1976), 340.

12. William B. Allen, "Justice and the General Good: *Federalist 51,*" in *Saving the Revolution: The Federalist Papers and the American Founding,* ed. Charles R. Kesler (New York: Free Press, 1987), 131–149.

13. Ibid., 131, 132, and 135, quoting chiefly *Federalist No. 51* but, in the final instance, "Notes for the National Gazette Essays," written between December 1791 and March 1792.

14. James Madison, *The Papers of James Madison,* ed. William T. Hutchinson et al., 17 vols. (Chicago and Charlottesville: University of Chicago Press and University of Virginia Press, 1962–), 14:163–164; quoted in Richard K. Matthews, *If Men Were Angels: James Madison and the the Heartless Empire of Reason* (Lawrence: University Press of Kansas, 1995), 168.

15. James Madison, in *The Federalist,* nos. 10, 54. Interests and factions are discussed throughout no. 10, 53–62.

16. Ibid., 56, 54.

17. For these citations and for comment on the passions/interest dichotomy, see Matthews, *If Men Were Angels,* 71–82.

18. Mary Ann Glendon, *Rights Talk: The Impoverishment of Political Discourse* (New York: Free Press, 1991), 115–116.

19. Alexis de Tocqueville, *Democracy in America,* trans. Phillips Bradley, 2 vols. (New York: Alfred A. Knopf, 1945), 2:302, 1:194–195, 2:115.

20. Glenn Tinder, *Community: Reflections on a Tragic Ideal* (Baton Rouge: Louisiana State University Press, 1980), 2–4.

21. Robert Nisbet, *The Making of Modern Society* (New York: New York University Press, 1986), 24–25.

22. Ibid., 26–29.

23. Alexis de Tocqueville, *The Old Regime and the French Revolution,* trans. Stuart Gilbert (Garden City, N.Y.: Doubleday Anchor, 1955), 137.

8. Argument, Conversation, and Story

1. Max Lerner, "Court and Constitution as Symbols," *Yale Law Journal* 46 (1937): 1293.

2. Dan Jacobson, *The Story of the Stories: The Chosen People and Its God* (New York: Harper and Row, 1982), 1–2, 9–10, 206–207, 126–127.

3. T. W. Adorno, "Thesen über Tradition," in Adorno, *Ohne Leitbild* (Frankfurt, 1967), 34–35; quoted by Johann Baptist Metz, "A Short Apology for Narrative," in Johann Baptist Metz and Jean-Pierre Jossua, *The Crisis of Religious Language* (New York: Herder and Herder, 1973), 95.

4. Martin Buber, *Werke* (Munich, 1963), 3:71; quoted by Metz and Jossua, *Crisis of Religious Language,* 86–87.

5. Johannes Althusius, *Politica,* ed. and trans. Frederick S. Carney (1964; Indianapolis: Liberty Fund, 1995), 17–19, 28–29, 33–34.

6. Ernest Gellner, *Conditions of Liberty: Civil Society and Its Rivals* (New York: Penguin, 1994), 97, 100.

7. Sidney E. Mead, *The Nation with the Soul of a Church* (New York: Harper and Row, 1975), 125.

8. Robert N. Bellah, "Religious Evolution," *American Sociological Review* 29 (June 1964): 371.

9. Alfred Schutz, *On Phenomenology and Social Relations: Selected Writings,* ed. Helmut R. Wagner (Chicago: University of Chicago Press, 1970), 255, 252. See also William James, *The Principles of Psychology,* vol. 1 (Cambridge: Harvard University Press, 1981), 380–382, 402, 386.

10. Schutz, *On Phenomenology,* 112–114. For further elaborations, see Martin E. Marty, "Committing the Study of Religion in Public," *Journal of the American Academy of Religion* 57 (Spring 1989): 1–22; Martin E. Marty, "Religion: A Private Affair, in Public Affairs," *Religion and American Culture* 3 (Summer 1993): 115–127.

11. For comment on the modes of experience, see Robert Grant, *Thinkers of Our Time: Oakeshott* (London: Claridge Press, 1990), 37–49, 65; also Michael Oakeshott, *Experience and Its Modes* (1933; Cambridge: Cambridge University Press, 1990), 69–81.

12. Oakeshott, *Experience,* 324.

13. Paul Valéry, "The Politics of the Mind," in *History and Politics,* trans. Denise Folliot and Jackson Mathews (New York: Pantheon, 1962), 92, 93.

14. David Tracy, *Plurality and Ambiguity: Hermeneutics, Religion, Hope* (San Francisco: Harper and Row, 1987), 18–19; Bernard Lonergan, *Method in Theology* (New York: Seabury, 1972), 231.

15. Michael Oakeshott, "The Voice of Poetry in the Conversation of Mankind," in Oakeshott, *Rationalism in Politics and Other Essays* (Indianapolis: Liberty Fund, 1991), 490.

16. Ronald Takaki, *A Different Mirror: A History of Multicultural America* (Boston: Little, Brown, 1993), 3–5, 15.

17. Ibid., 428.

18. Leszek Kolakowski, *The Presence of Myth,* trans. Adam Czerniawski (Chicago: University of Chicago Press, 1989), 69–71, 74, 80–82.

19. George P. Fletcher, *Loyalty: An Essay on the Morality of Relationships* (New York: Oxford University Press, 1993), 155–156.

9. Storied Places, Where Healing Can Begin

1. Ernest Gellner, *Plough, Sword, and Book: The Structure of Human History* (Chicago: University of Chicago Press, 1988), 14–15.

2. Ernest Gellner, *Nations and Nationalism* (Ithaca, N.Y.: Cornell University Press, 1983), 3, 7, 54.

3. Ignatieff et al. quoted in William Pfaff, *The Wrath of Nations: Civilization and the Furies of Nationalism* (New York: Simon and Schuster Touchstone, 1993), 57–58.

4. Mircea Eliade, *Cosmos and History: The Myth of the Eternal Return* (New York: Harper Torchbooks, 1959), 10.

5. Holly Stevens, ed., *Letters of Wallace Stevens* (New York: Knopf, 1966), 464.

6. Wright Morris, *The Home Place* (New York: Charles Scribner's Sons, 1948), 138–139; quoted in Yi-Fu Tuan, *Space and Place: The Perspective of Experience* (Minneapolis: University of Minnesota Press, 1977), 144.

7. Yi-Fu Tuan, *Space and Place: The Perspective of Experience* (Minneapolis: University of Minnesota Press, 1977), 152, 160.

8. Quoted in the epigraph to Joshua Meyerowitz, *No Sense of Place: The Impact of Electronic Media on Social Behavior* (New York: Oxford University Press, 1985).

9. Belden C. Lane, *Landscapes of the Sacred: Geography and Narrative in American Spirituality* (Mahwah, N.J.: Paulist Press, 1988), 185.

10. Freya Stark, *Perseus in the Wind* (London: John Murray, 1948), 55; quoted in Yi-Fu Tuan, *Space and Place,* 144.

11. Yi-Fu Tuan, *Space and Place,* 177.

12. Quoted in Martin E. Marty, *Pilgrims in Their Own Land: 500 Years of Religion in America* (Boston: Little, Brown, 1984), 240–241.

13. E. V. Walter, "Ominous Space," chap. 9 in *Placeways: A Theory of the Human Environment* (Chapel Hill: University of North Carolina Press, 1988), 159–175.

14. Ibid., 167. Walter cites Jerome Y. Lettvin, "The Gorgon's Eye," in Lettvin, *Astronomy of the Ancients,* ed. K. Brecher and M. Freitag (Cambridge: MIT Press, 1979), 135.

15. Walter, *Placeways,* 142, also quoting Ernst Cassirer, *Philosophy of Symbolic Forms,* 3 vols., trans. Ralph Manheim (New Haven, Conn.: Yale University Press, 1955–1957), 3: 63, 2: 92.

16. Yi-Fu Tuan, *Space and Place,* 140, sets these words of Augustine (from *Confessions,* book 4.4.9) in context.

10. The Constitutional Myth

1. Chesterton is quoted from *The Man Who Was Chesterton,* ed. Raymond T. Bond (Garden City, N.Y.: Doubleday Image Books, 1960), 125–126, by Sidney E. Mead in *The Nation with the Soul of a Church* (New York: Harper and Row, 1975), 20.

2. Garry Wills, *Inventing America: Jefferson's Declaration of Independence* (New York: Doubleday, 1978), xxii.

3. This account draws on "Constituting the People of the United States," chap. 1

in Walter Berns, *Taking the Constitution Seriously* (New York: Simon and Schuster, 1987); on American Indians, see 34–40; on blacks, see 40–58.

4. Ibid., 59–61.

5. Milton M. Klein, "Mythologizing the U.S. Constitution," *Soundings* 78 (Spring 1995): 169–188, esp. 169–173, 178. Klein quoted Fukae from the *New York Times,* 7 December 1985; Christian Science, from the *New York Times,* 2 December 1923; Barbara Jordan and Shelby Hearon, *Barbara Jordan: A Self-Portrait* (Garden City, N.Y.: Doubleday, 1979), 187, quoting a statement of 25 July 1974; *The American Public's Knowledge of the U.S. Constitution: A National Survey* (New York: Hearst Corporation, 1987); Diane Ravitch and Chester E. Finn, *What Do Our 17-Year-Olds Know?* (New York: Harper and Row, 1987), 57.

6. People for the American Way, *Democracy's Next Generation* (Washington, D.C.: People for the American Way, 1989), 27, quoted by Mary Ann Glendon, *Rights Talk,* 128.

7. Klein, in "Mythologizing the U.S. Constitution," quoted Max Lerner, "Court and Constitution as Symbols," *Yale Law Journal* 61 (1927): 1293; Lincoln's Lyceum Address at Springfield, Ill., 27 January 1838, is in *The Collected Works of Abraham Lincoln,* ed. Roy P. Basler, 9 vols. (New Brunswick, N.J.: Rutgers University Press, 1953–1955), I:112; the judge is quoted in Frank I. Schecher, "The Early History of the Tradition of the Constitution," *American Political Science Review* 1 (1915): 733.

8. Philip E. Hammond, "Legal Institutions as Religion," a subsection of his "Religious Pluralism and Durkheim's Integration Thesis," in *Changing Perspectives in the Scientific Study of Religion,* ed. Allan W. Eister (New York: John Wiley and Sons, 1974), 127–135.

9. Sanford Levinson, *Constitutional Faith* (Princeton, N.J.: Princeton University Press, 1988), 3, quoting Joseph Lash, ed., *From the Diaries of Felix Frankfurter* (New York: W. W. Norton, 1975), 211–223.

10. Levinson, *Constitutional Faith,* 14, quotes Edward Corwin, "The Worship of the Constitution," *Constitutional Review* 4 (January 1920): 3; for Marshall, he quotes Michael Kammen, *A Machine That Would Go of Itself: The Constitution in American Culture* (New York: Knopf, 1986), 235, but the Marshall reference, not given there, remains fugitive.

11. Levinson, *Constitutional Faith,* 51, but see the whole chapter on "The 'Constitution' in American Civil Religion," 9–53.

12. Ibid., 96–98; on the contradiction in terms, see Peter Schuck and Rogers Smith, *Citizenship without Consent: Illegal Aliens in the American Polity* (New Haven, Conn.: Yale University Press, 1985), and Robert Post, "The Social Foundations of Defamation Law: Reputation and the Constitution," *California Law Review* 74 (1986): 736–737.

13. Levinson, *Constitutional Faith,* 114; see Michael Walzer, "Political Alienation and Military Service," in his *Obligations* (Cambridge: Harvard University Press, 1970), 205.

14. Walter Berns, *The First Amendment and the Future of American Democracy* (New York: Basic Books, 1976), 11, 16, 26, and 27, where he cites Thomas I. Angle, *Montesquieu's Philosophy of Liberalism* (Chicago: University of Chicago. Press, 1973), 256–257.

15. Berns, *First Amendment,* 44.

16. Quoted in ibid., 40.

17. Learned Hand, "The Spirit of Liberty," in *The Spirit of Liberty,* ed. Irving Dilliard

(New York: Alfred A. Knopf, 1960), 189–190; quoted in Mary Ann Glendon, *Rights Talk,* 143. It was Glendon who made a note of the date of this essay just before the rights movement spread.

18. Quoted in Ralph L. Ketcham, *Benjamin Franklin* (New York: Washington Square Press, 1966), 175.

19. Bernard Crick, *In Defence of Politics* (Baltimore: Penguin, 1964), 176–177.

20. Paul Weber, "James Madison and Religious Equality: The Perfect Separation," *Review of Politics* 44 (April 1982): 163.

21. Ernest Gellner, *Thought and Change* (Chicago: University of Chicago Press, 1964), 123.

22. Berns, *Taking the Constitution Seriously,* 25, calls attention to this "constituting" aspect of the Declaration.

23. Daniel J. Boorstin, *The Genius of American Politics* (Chicago: University of Chicago Press, 1953), 170.

24. Donald S. Lutz, *The Origins of American Constitutionalism* (Baton Rouge: Louisiana State University Press, 1988), 140–142.

25. John Courtney Murray, S.J., *We Hold These Truths: Catholic Reflections on the American Proposition* (New York: Sheed and Ward, 1960), 28–30, 33, 45, 74, 15–16, 6, 132, 130.

26. J. Leon Hooper, S.J., *The Ethics of Discourse: The Social Philosophy of John Courtney Murray* (Washington, D.C.: Georgetown University Press, 1986), 220.

27. Murray, *We Hold These Truths,* 130.

28. Forrest McDonald, *The Formation of the American Republic, 1776–1790* (Baltimore: Penguin Books, 1965), 72, 3, 2, 5.

11. Cohesive Sentiment

1. Georg Simmel, *Conflict,* trans. Kurt H. Wolff (Glencoe, Ill.: Free Press, 1955), 34.

2. For comment on the ways *affectivity* and *cognition* relate in the work of Jean Piaget, Lawrence Kohlberg, Bernard Lonergan, S.J., and James Fowler, see the references to them and elaborations of their work in Walter Conn, *Christian Conversion: A Developmental Interpretation of Autonomy and Surrender* (Mahwah, N.J.: Paulist Press, 1986), especially in chap. 4, "Conversion: Moral, Cognitive, Affective," 105–157.

3. See Richard B. Steele, *"Gracious Affection" and "True Virtue" According to Jonathan Edwards and John Wesley* (Metuchen, N.J.: Scarecrow Press, 1994), and Stephen H. Daniel, *The Philosophy of Jonathan Edwards: A Study in Divine Semiotics* (Bloomington: Indiana University Press, 1994).

4. Daniel, *The Philosophy of Jonathan Edwards,* 72–74, provides extensive documentation surrounding these three quotations.

5. Jonathan Edwards, *Religious Affections,* ed. John Smith (New Haven, Conn.: Yale University Press, 1959), 97.

6. To see how one strand of clergy, called "catholick" by one historian, persisted in relating reason to affections—but here only as focused on God—see John Corrigan, "Catholic Congregational Clergy and Public Piety," in *Church History* 60 (June 1991): 210–222.

7. Garry Wills, *Inventing America: Jefferson's Declaration of Independence* (Garden City, N.Y.: Doubleday, 1978), 260, 279–280.

8. Cited in ibid., 281–282.

9. Ibid., 312–313. Note, by the way, Jefferson's use of the term *acquiesce;* it parallels and anticipates the use of the term by Robert E. Lee and developed in recent philosophy by Nicholas Rescher; it was commended above in Chapter 5, at n. 20.

10. Hutcheson and Paine, cited in Wills, *Inventing America,* 314–315.

11. Bronislaw Malinowski, "An Anthropological Analysis of War," in Malinowski, *Magic, Science, and Religion* (Glencoe, Ill.: Free Press, 1948), p. 285.

12. Gwen Kennedy Neville, *Kinship and Pilgrimage: Rituals of Reunion in American Protestant Culture* (New York: Oxford University Press, 1987), 56, 71–72. She cites Barbara Meyerhoff from a lecture at Southwestern University in 1983 and Gillian Feeley-Harnick, *The Lord's Table: Eucharist and Passover in Early Christianity* (Philadelphia: University of Pennsylvania Press, 1981), 11.

Index